GERMAN ARMY
ORDER OF BATTLE
October 1942

Lancer Militaria

Originally published by the Military Intelligence Service, 1942

Printed in the United States of America

ISBN 0-935856-08-0

Lancer Militaria
P.O. Box 886
Mt. Ida, Arkansas 71957
USA

TABLE OF CONTENTS

FOREWORD:

1. Order of Battle information is vital to the Military Intelligence Service. This information received from many agencies scattered all over the world is carefully pieced together in the Order of Battle Section, Military Intelligence Service, in order to present to the combat commands of the United Nations the best possible estimates of the enemy situation. The decisions which involve the lives of thousands of American soldiers are based at least partially on Order of Battle intelligence.

2. Order of Battle information is classified under two headings:

"Order of Battle - Strength"
"Order of Battle - Location"

3. "Order of Battle - Strength" is a careful tabulation of all of the units in the Axis Armies, and of those organizations of the other services, the Navy, and the Air Force, which operate with the field armies. An analysis of this information reveals:

Organization of enemy units
Composition of enemy units
Detailed identification of enemy units
Principles of employment (composition of special task forces)
Total strength of Axis armies
Strength of various arms of Axis armies
Changes in tactical or strategical procedure as evidenced by changes in organization.

4. This intelligence officers handbook, "The Order of Battle of the German Army", is published from the "Order of Battle - Strength" records. This text enables the unit intelligence officers in combat to identify the enemy forces with whom they are engaged. Also included is all of the known information on organization, history, the names and qualifications of the commanders and staff officers, the composition, the insignia, and the combat characteristics of the enemy units.

5. "Order of Battle - Location" gives the disposition of German units, and includes all information as to actual unit locations, movements, concentration areas, and changes in organization, equipment, and armament. A study of the dispositions, the terrain, and fortification activity, combined with a knowledge of enemy tactical and strategical procedure, will enable intelligence officers to assign priorities to enemy capabilities.

6. The mission of the Order of Battle is:

a. To provide a sound basis on which military decisions may be made;
b. To make available to intelligence officers in the field all information that will assist them to perform their duties efficiently.

7. The following constitute Order of Battle information:

    a. Identifications of enemy units;

    b. Names and qualifications of enemy commanders and staff officers - promotion lists published in papers are a good source;

    c. Dispositions (locations of enemy units);

    d. Movements;

    e. Concentration areas;

    f. Types of units: the location of Panzer or tank units, mountain units, artillery concentrations, and other arms of offense is especially important.

    g. Insignia: This includes personal insignia, unit insignia, decorations, and the like. Sketches showing dimensions and colors are very helpful.

    h. Military symbols and abbreviations: These are necessary in order that captured maps and documents may be translated.

    i. Captured maps, documents and other written material.

    j. Maps of all kinds, especially new ones.

    k. Lines of communications (changes in railways, canal systems, etc.)

    l. All information on mobilization: Case history of individuals, especially when they are typical, is of great assistance. Observe the promotion rates for senior commanders for indications of an expansion.

    m. Armament: Watch for new weapons, or modifications of standard weapons.

    n. Organization of enemy units (especially for particular operations).

    o. Casualties.

    p. Auxiliary units (labor units, truck-driver or labor-service formations, etc., which operate under military jurisdiction).

    q. Terrain.

    r. Climate and weather.

    s. Uniforms (particularly changes).

    t. Types of personnel (with particular attention to specialists).

    u. Special kinds of training.

    v. Changes in equipment: For example, a new canister for gas masks.

    w. Boundaries of zones of action, or sectors.

    x. Interest of Axis sources in special maps or special kinds of maps (indications of such interest are likely to occur in neutral countries).

    y. Any special Axis staff activity.

8. The information outlined in paragraph 7 applies to air and naval units as well as to land organizations, especially those units which operate with the field armies.

9. Order of Battle information should be transmitted to the Military Intelligence Service as quickly as possible. If it arrives too late, it belongs to still another classification, "Order of Battle - Historical".

10. Information pertaining to troop dispositions, identifications, movements, or anything which points toward a radical change in enemy procedure should invariably be cabled. Detailed information of all kinds, such as names of staff

officers, new insignia, description of fortifications, and lists of military abbreviations and map symbols, should be sent by air mail. If sufficiently important, a summary of detailed information should be cabled at the time of mailing.

11. Where the means are available, the location of enemy units should be posted by means of pins on mounted maps. This procedure assists greatly in evaluating Order of Battle reports at the information-collecting agency.

12. Well kept records of the data submitted by the various sources of information will enable the intelligence agencies to evaluate the reliability of the sources. This is important because some of the Axis powers intentionally plant false information (sometimes mixed with known reliable information) for our intelligence agencies to report.

13. The minute details are important. Some of these may have considerable significance when compared with information from other sources.

14. Officers and agencies should evaluate the Order of Battle information they receive and indicate their opinion of its reliability. The Order of Battle Section may not have any other means of evaluating the report.

15. Where practical, the source of the Order of Battle information should be indicated. If it is not desirable to mention names or sources in cables or reports, a list of code names to represent them can be transmitted to the Military Intelligence Service by secret letter.

16. As far as possible, exploit sources which are not available or known to representatives and agencies of the other United Nations.

17. Personalities are important. For example, the appearance at Gibraltar of Oberst (Colonel) Mikosch, the German Commander who captured Fort Eben Emael and who later broke the Maginot Line near Saarbrücken, may be extremely significant.

18. All Order of Battle information is normally classified confidential, unless for some special reason a particular message or report should be classified secret.

19. Intelligence officers expecting to be in combat with German forces should have the following texts in their possession:

The Order of Battle of the German Army
TM 30-450 Handbook of German Military Forces (a revised issue will be ready for distribution about January 1, 1943).
TM 30-255 Military Dictionary (English-German; German-English)

Intelligence officers should be certain that they have a complete set of German military symbols and military abbreviations in their possession in order that they can read and interpret the meaning of captured maps, tables of organization, orders and other dispatches. Intelligence personnel should be able to read the German script.

20. All Order of Battle information on the German armed forces will be included in this text. The original issue is the basis for other information which will be distributed in the form of revision sheets as it becomes available. This volume is so bound as to facilitate placing in a loose-leaf binder.

21. The subject matter of this text has been initially divided into seven parts. Part A is devoted to a brief discussion of the main features of the German High Command, with particular reference to the High Command of the Army. Part B deals with the basic structure by which the German Army is maintained in the field, and Part C contains classified lists of its component organizations, adding details of their commanders (where known) and histories. Part D consists of lists of miscellaneous units of the GHQ pool, given as far as possible according to the German classification of arms of the service, with an alphabetical index of the types of unit in the form in which they are likely to be found in documents. Part E gives lists, arranged alphabetically within ranks, of senior officers of the German Army and also of the German Air Force (since the titles of the latter are indistinguishable, except in the case of full generals, from those of army officers). Part F gives a brief account of the SS, Police and other semi-military organizations, insofar as they may be found operating with the German forces in the field. Part G, to be issued later, will be a detailed list of all German units which have been identified to date. It will include all of the information which was originally issued in the book "Order of Battle of the German Army" (pink book) now obsolete.

22. Parts A to F of this text include the material for a detailed study of the German military system and the units which comprise it. Part G is a ready reference list of all of the German units which have been identified and will be of more immediate use for the identification of German units in combat.

23. Errors, corrections, or any suggestions for the improvement of this text should be sent directly to the Evaluation and Dissemination Branch, Military Intelligence Service, War Department, Washington, D. C. Constructive comment will be greatly appreciated.

PART A--THE GERMAN HIGH COMMAND

CONTENTS

PART A

I. INTRODUCTION.

1. In Germany the Army is both by tradition and of necessity the predominant service. But under the Nazi regime the need for the closest cooperation between all three services has been met by the creation of a Defense Ministry (Oberkommando der Wehrmacht, abbreviated O.K.W.—see Section II below), which controls all matters of inter-service policy and directs the conduct of the war, leaving to the service ministries the detailed working out of purely military, naval or air force matters.

2. Under this system, Army, Navy and Air Force are regarded as branches of a single service, the Armed Forces (die Wehrmacht). For operations, units of one often come under the immediate command control of another. Similarly, senior officers may be transferred in the same or equivalent rank from one service to another. For an explanation of the system of command and the use of the task force, see the Order of Battle of the German Army.

3. In effect, therefore, the German High Command is divided into four parts, as follows: -

      Defense Ministry (Oberkommando der Wehrmacht, O.K.W.)
      War Department (Oberkommando des Heeres, O.K.H.)
      Navy Department (Oberkommando der Kriegsmarine, O.K.M.)
      Air Department (Oberkommando der Luftwaffe, O.K.L.)*

As regards the general direction of the war, the O.K.W. is supreme, while the O.K.H. is responsible for all purely military matters.

4. In war time, each department is divided into two echelons. An advanced echelon (consisting of C in C, the Chief of General Staff, and the bulk of the General Staff) moves out to its war station, the location of which depends on the theatre of operations selected for main attention; while the rear echelon remains in Berlin.

5. The object of the department divisions is to leave the C in C and his staff as free as possible from the administrative matters which necessarily obtrude themselves in the ministry in Berlin. Such matters are entrusted to a senior officer, directly responsible to the C in C (see Section IV), while the advanced echelon is able to concentrate on the control of the forces in the field. The advanced echelon of the War Department will be referred to as Army GHQ and the rear echelon as War Department in the present work.

---

*The full title for the High Command of the G A F is Reichsluftfahrt-ministerium and Oberbefehlshaber der Luftwaffe, abbreviated R.L.M.u.Ob.d.L.

II. THE DEFENSE MINISTRY

1. HITLER himself is Minister of Defense and Commander-in-Chief of Germany's Armed Forces. His deputy, in both capacities, is Field Marshal Wilhelm KEITEL, who as such is decribed as Chef des Oberkommandos der Wehrmacht— in effect, Deputy C in C.

2. The General Staff of the Defense Ministry is known as the Wehrmacht-fuhrungsstab, abbreviated W.F.St. (Armed Forces Operations Staff). The Chief of this staff, General Alfred JODL, is believed to be HITLER'S principal adviser on strategy and planning.

3. KEITEL is HITLER'S chief guide on all inter-service matters, profession-al head of the whole Defense Ministry (including departments concerned with the coordination of production, supply and manpower) and controller of the three fighting services (for his authority over the army, see Section III below),. JODL, , as his Chief of Staff, has the dual function of immediate control of the W.F.St. and general supervision of the whole of the Defense Ministry.

4. Under JODL, the W.F.St. is divided into sections entrusted with particular functions. The most important of these sections is the Joint Planning Staff, under Lt Gen WARLIMONT, which is responsible for all strategical, executive and future operations planning—functions which are excluded from the scope of the three service ministries.

5. The war station of the O.K.W. is known as the Führerhauptquartier (i.e., HITLER's GHQ). During the Polish campaign it was situated between Berlin and the Polish frontier, moving to the Rhineland for the campaign of 1940 and to East Prussia for the early stages of the attack on the U.S.S.R.

6. The O.K.W. selects the commanders for all operations, and decides what forces are to be allocated to them. It may give an officer of one service general authority over all three services within a particular area. In such cases Wehrmachts- will form part of his title (e.g., The GAF General CHRISTIANSEN is Wehrmachtsbefehlshaber or Armed Forces Commander in Holland. In a lower echelon, a Wehrmachtsnachrichtenkommandantur is a signal command the personnel of which is provided by more than one of the three services).

7. One section of the O.K.W. is solely concerned with inter-service com-munications. It provides a special network of land cables and maintains special channels for radio communications between HITLER's GHQ and the Hq of army groups and armies, and the principal Hq of the German Navy and GAF. For this purpose it has at least two army signal regiments, which carry the distinguishing title of Führungs-Nachrichten-Regiment (see Part D). Other army or GAF signal units may come under its control.

8. The personnel of the W.F.St. and of the O.K.W. generally is drawn from all three services, but the army has the largest representation.

III. ARMY GHQ

1. Army GHQ, to which the advanced echelon under von BRAUCHITSCH (then C in C) moved from Berlin on mobilization in 1939, was originally distinct both in name and in place from HITLER's GHQ. In consequence, however, of the supersession of von BRAUCHITSCH by HITLER himself in December, 1941, the two headquarters have now (it seems) been combined.

2. Field Marshal KEITEL is now Deputy C in C of the O.K.H. as well as of the O.K.W. In this capacity he has as Chief of Staff Col Gen Franz HALDER, who is regarded as an exceptionally able and self-effacing officer (for that reason he seldom appears in the news), and the main organizer of the German Army.

3. Under HALDER, the advanced echelon is divided into two parts, which correspond to the intelligence and operations and administration and supply groups on the staffs of German units. The intelligence and operations part (O.K.H. Genstb.d.H. — High Command of the Army, Army General Staff) is sub-divided into departments under Deputy Chiefs of General Staff (Oberquartiermeister, abbreviated OQu). OQu I is Director of Operations and OQu IV Director of Intelligence. OQu II (Training), OQu III (Organization) and OQu V (Historical), it is believed, remain with the rear echelon (see Section IV).

4. The head of the administration and supply group is known as the Generalquartiermeister (abbreviated Gen Qu). His function is to control, under the general direction of the C in C and C of S, all questions affecting the administration and supply of the armies in the field (but not in Germany itself, which comes immediately under the War Department).

5. Until recently General PAULUS (now commanding the Sixth Army) was OQu I. It is not yet known who has succeeded him as Director of Operations. The Director of Intelligence is Maj Gen MATZKY, formerly German Military Attache in Tokyo, who succeeded Lt. Gen v. TIPPELSKIRCH as OQu IV in the spring of 1941. The Generalquartiermeister General Eugen MÜLLER, a former OQu III and Commandant of the Staff College, has held the post of GenQu since the beginning of the war.

6. Army GHQ is responsible for the operations of all army forces in the field, under the direction of the O.K.W. It exercises that control through army group Hq or army Hq, not only by the normal chain of command but also through the General Staff Corps.

7. The German General Staff is at the same time a corps, to which officers may be permanently transferred from their original arm of the service, and a staff (at GHQ, with an echelon at the War Department in Berlin) the personnel of which is drawn from that corps. In consequence, the Chief of the General Staff, though immediately in charge of the staff, is also head of the whole corps, and all General Staff Officers are responsible to him wherever they may be serving.

8. The number of GSOs is strictly limited (for a list of those known, see Part E). The rule holds good that a GSO has authority over all other officers holding appointments on the same staff, even though some of them may be senior to him in rank. For example, in each of the two sections of Military Intelligence, prior to the outbreak of war, the Head of Section was a Major, General Staff, and the officers subordinate to him included colonels on active duty.

9. The small number of GSOs at unit Hq may be shown best by some concrete instances. In November. 1941, there were only five GSOs at Hq of the Panzer Army of Africa (C of S, G-2, G-3, "Chief Quartermaster" and "First Quarter-master"). The subordinate African Panzer Corps included two only (Chief of Staff and G-3, and there were five GSOs between the three German divisions.

10. Not only do GSOs look to the C of GS as the head of their corps, but they have the right, and in certain conditions the duty, to report directly to him. In particular, the chief of staff of an army corps or any higher unit is in duty bound to report to the C of GS in writing, any major difference of opinion between him-self and his commander. In such a case, the commander takes responsibility for the course of action decided upon, and the chief of staff complies to the best of his ability, but his opinion is on record.

11. It follows that the C of GS at Army GHQ, is kept in very close touch with the course of the war. But if he thinks it necessary he may go further, and send a GSO as special liaison officer to army group or army Hq, with the duty of send-ing daily direct reports on the course of events (if necessary, from personal observation, if sufficient information is not available at unit Hq) either by courier or by telegraph.

12. It is a commonplace that German commanders and chiefs of staff are expected to use their initiative. Individual responsibility for action is the Ger-man precept which officers of all ranks are required to observe. But Army GHQ is enabled, through the system outlined above to keep in the closest touch with the course of operations, and so to direct their subsequent course with full knowledge of the situation.

IV. THE WAR DEPARTMENT

1. On mobilization, when the advanced echelon of the War Ministry moved out to its war station at Army GHQ, the rear echelon, including all War Depart-ment branches and the whole basic structure (described in Part B) was placed under the command of a senior general, with the title Chef der Heeresrüstung und Befehlshaber des Ersatzheeres, commonly abbreviated to Ch H Rü u. B d E. The importance which the Germans assign to this office, and the system which it involves, may be measured by the fact that its holder, General Fritz FROMM, was promoted Col Gen and decorated with the Knight's Cross of the Iron Cross on the conclusion of the campaign in the West in 1940.

2. Under Col Gen FROMM are the Directors of Training and Organization (OQu II and OQu III), with the portion of the General Staff which remains behind in Berlin, and the main War Department branches.

3. The most important of these is the Allgemeines Heeresamt, abbreviated AHA (General Army Office), which controls all aspects of training, draft of personnel and supply within what may for convenience be termed the Home Command, both through specialist groups and through the inspectors of the different arms of the service similar to our former chiefs of branches. The present head of the AHA is General Friedrich OLBRICHT.

4. All matters concerned with the production of armaments and equipment are handled by the Heeres-Waffenamt, abbreviated WaA- (Army Ordnance Office), at present under General Emil LEEB (a younger brother of Field Marshal Ritter v. LEEB). The Heeresverwaltungsamt, abbreviated VA (Army Administration Office), under Lt Gen OSTERKAMP, is mainly concerned with those aspects of military administration which are assigned to officials (Beamten) — pay, rations, postal services, etc.

5. The Heeres-Personalamt, abbreviated HPA (Army Personnel Office) is set apart from the other sections and comes immediately under C in C, Army. Its head is General KEITEL, younger brother of the Field Marshal. This branch is responsible for the proper listing and promotion of all officers, and for the appointment of all except GSO s (who are appointed by the Central Department of the General Staff—Genstb.d.H./GZ), though appointments of officers to various specialist arms are made on the nomination of the heads of those arms.

6. As will be seen in Part B, the work of the War Department is considerably lightened by a large degree of decentralization to the military district Hq. Policy is laid down, and plans are drawn up, in Berlin, but much of the detailed work is left to the district Hq.

7. As Chef der Heeresrüstung (Head of Army Equipment), Col Gen FROMM is responsible for the provision and design of equipment of all kinds, both for the armies in the field and for all troops stationed within the area of the Home Command. As Befehlshaber des Ersatzheeres (Commander of the Training Army), he is responsible for the training system described in Part B, and in addition he command s such organizations or units of the field army as may be sent to Germany to rest or be reorganized.

8. He is also partially responsible for certain areas of occupied territory, in which training divisions and replacement training units are stationed (e.g., Denmark, Holland, Belgium and eastern France). The custom which has developed of forming new divisions in France has involved a further expansion of his sphere; but the military commanders in those countries are not subordinate to him.

PART B--THE BASIC STRUCTURE

CONTENTS

PART B

I. INTRODUCTION

Note.—The following military terms are adopted for the description in this part of the text:

Wehrkreis	Military district
Wehrersatzinspektion	Area (subdivision of Wehrkreis)
Wehrbezirk	Sub-Area (part of Wehrersatzinspektion)
Ersatz Division Nr. —	Replacement Training Division No —
Ersatz Regiment	Replacement Training Regiment
Ersatz (unit)	Replacement Training Detachment

1. The Germans try to relieve commanders in the field of as much purely administrative work as possible, and to provide as regular a flow as possible of trained recruits and of supplies to the field army. The method which they have adopted is the separation of the field army from the "Home Command" (to coin a convenient short title), and entrusting the whole charge of training, draft of personnel, supply and equipment to that command.

2. The German system is described in outline in the following paragraphs with special reference to the provision of recruits for the field army. Such parts of the organization as do not relate to that function are not referred to, but it should be noted that the provision of equipment (for example) is organized on similar lines.

II THE MILITARY DISTRICT ORGANIZATION

1. Germany is subdivided into seventeen military districts (there were only fifteen at the outbreak of the war), which in peace time contained the Hq and subordinate formations of the active Infantry Corps carrying the same Roman numerals (e.g., II Infantry Corps has its peace-time Hq at Stettin, in the II Military District). The military district is a territorial administrative command similar to our former corps areas. Many of its functions are identical to those of the corps areas. For a map of the Military Districts see Order of Battle of the German Army.

2. Before the war, there were also four Motorized Corps—XIV, XV, XVI and XIX—(in effect, staffs to control the organization and training of armored and motorized organizations) which had no corresponding military districts, but were served (as regards personnel and supplies) by the districts in which corps Hq or subordinate units had their peace stations.

3. In peace time, the commander of the Infantry Corps was also commander of the Military District; but because he was destined to take his corps into the field, his chief concern was to develop and maintain the fighting efficiency of the troops under his command. All administrative matters, therefore, were

assigned to the charge of a Second-in-Command or Deputy Military District Commander (General z.b.V.)—normally a general officer whose health or age rendered him unsuited for further active service in the field, while his seniority and experience qualified him for a post of great responsibility.

4. On mobilization, the commander of the Infantry Corps departed with his corps to join the field army, and thereupon the Second-in-Command assumed direct command of the military district. His staff was composed of reserve officers who lived near the Military District headquarters and who understudied their opposite numbers in peace time. These reserve officers worked out the details of the mobilization plans and have carried them into execution. The provision of trained draftees to all units of the field army mobilized in that district is one of the special concerns of the Deputy Military District Commander.

5. These units include the active units of the peace-time army which moved out with the active Infantry Corps and, in addition, all units formed on or after mobilization in the military district in question. To illustrate this point, a military district which contained the peace stations of three divisions under one corps staff might mobilize as many as four corps staffs and twelve or fourteen divisions for the field army.

6. It may be noted that at present the average age of the Deputy Military District commanders is about 64, while that of the known commanders of army corps in the field army is 54.

III WAR DEPARTMENT CONTROL

1. The War Department in Berlin retains close control over the whole system, but as much detail work as possible is decentralized. In general, policy is decided in Berlin, and the military districts are allowed a large measure of freedom to work out the plan decided upon.

2. All questions of supply, draft of personnel and training are directed by the "Head of Army Supply and Commander of the Training Army," who is in effect both:

    a. head of the rear echelon of the High Command of the Army (the advanced echelon being at Army GHQ), controlling all War Department sections on behalf of the C in C,

    b. specially concerned with the provision of drafts and equipment for the field army.

3. Under him, training and draft of personnel (including any reorganization of units temporarily withdrawn for that purpose from the field army) are looked after by the General Army Office of the War Department which issues such instructions as are necessary to the military districts.

1   4. The directives issued by the General Army Office insure uniformity of
results. An additional assurance is provided by special staffs, under that branch,
which keep close watch on any special program (such as the conversion of infantry to motorized or armored divisions), as well as by the Inspectors of the
different arms (similar to former chiefs of branches), who supervise the training of units of those arms throughout Germany.

IV CONTROL OF MANPOWER

1. Within the military district, the supervision of manpower (from civil life
into the armed forces, within the armed forces and back to civil life) is entrusted to Inspectors of Recruiting, each controlling an Area. For military districts
the population of which is relatively small, one Area suffices, but others are
sub-divided into two, three or (in two cases) four areas. The Inspector is a
Major General or Lieutenant General, similar in his qualifications to the Deputy
Military District Commander. He has the status and disciplinary authority of
a divisional commander*.

2. Each Area is subdivided into Sub-Areas, which cover the area of a greater
or lesser number of urban or rural local authorities, and are commanded by
Lieut Colonels or Colonels, selected from the same class of officers whose
suitability for active service in the field has ceased. They have the status of
regiment commander.

3. As regards manpower, the duty of the Areas and Sub-Areas is to provide
recruits to the replacement training units on such scale as may be called for
by Berlin, and to select suitable officers and trained personnel to fill vacancies
in the War Establishments of all units mobilized by the Military District concerned—in each case acting on instructions received from the Military District
Hq.

4. An example will illustrate this point. When the 33d Infantry Division was
being transformed into the 15th Panzer Division in the XII Military District
during the autumn of 1940, its horses and the personnel which cared for them
became superfluous, while the complete mechanization of the units selected for conversion involved the need for   many NCOs with motor transport experience.
Berlin laid down the use to be made of the bulk of the personnel and horses freed
by the conversion (in this case the majority of the NCOs and men concerned were
incorporation in the newly formed 129th Infantry Division); but the XII Military
District disposed of the balance among its own units.

---

* He is not necessarily a soldier. Some appointments of this type are given
to senior officers of the German Navy and GAF the manpower for which is provided by the same organization.

V CONTROL OF TRAINING

5. Within the Military District, the training of recruits is entrusted to a parallel system in the Areas and Sub-Areas. The training system involves Replacement Training Divisions (normally two to each Military District)and Replacement Training Regiments(a varying number under each Replacement Training Division). The Germans place great emphasis on combined training. The various replacement training battalions are tentatively organized into regiments and divisions for this purpose. These units, called Replacement Training Regiments and Replacement Training Divisions, also have administrative functions.

6. The commanders and subordinate officers are largely drawn from the category of officers passed over for further service in the field, but there are a number of experienced officers drawn from the field army who in due course may return to it again.

7. Each Replacement Training Regiment supervises such replacement training units as are assigned to it (there is no constant number of such units), and provides drafts— as directed by the Military District through the Replacement Training Division—for one or two specific divisions of the field army. The subordinate replacement training units are affiliated to specific units of those field army divisions.

8. It should be noted, however, that this system (like most German systems) is not a rigid one, and affiliations may be changed if necessary. Thus the III and XII Military Districts specialize in training troops for service in Libya, and a unit originally mobilized in one of the other Military Districts will have its affiliation transferred to a replacement training unit in the III or XII on its departure to Libya.

9. Replacement training units are provided on a scale described in some detail in Section VII.

VI SUMMARY

1. It will be seen, therefore, that the German system involves decentralization to Military Districts of a maximum of administrative detail. Units of the field army are administered by the appropriate Military Districts and not by the War Department directly.

2. The provision of personnel and the training of recruits, are arranged by the Military Districts through Replacement Training Divisions and Replacement Training Regiments, which have the sole function of supervising replacement training units assigned to their charge.

3. Following is a diagram of the organization of a Military District.

11

VII DRAFT OF PERSONNEL

1. The provision of trained drafts for divisions of the field army (in this context known as Felddivisionen) is organized through a system of special training staffs and units: -

> Ersatz-Division Nummer . . (e.g., Div. Nr. 182): Replacement training division—a staff responsible for the supervision of training within part of a military district (Wehrkreis).

> Infanterie-Ersatz-Regiment, abbreviated Inf.Ers. Rgt. or J.E.R. Infantry training regiment—a staff responsible for the administration of the replacement training battalions and companies which provide drafts for one or two specific divisions of the field army.

> Artillerie-Ersatz-Regiment, abbreviated Art. Ers. Rgt. or A.E.R. Artillery training regiment—a staff responsible for the administration of artillery and artillery observation replacement training units within part of a military district.

> Ersatz-Einheiten: Replacement training units (see the following paragraphs).

> Marschbataillon z.b.V., abbreviated Marsch-Btl.z.b.V.: Personnel replacement transfer battalion—a nucleus of officers and enlisted men provided by the training division, to conduct trained replacements from the military district to the theater of war.

> Feldersatzbataillon, abbreviated Feld-Ers.Btl. First line or forward reinforcement battalion—normally stationed in the rear areas which receives personnel replacements from the Marschbataillon and gives them further training until they are required by the division on the establishment of which the Feldersatzbataillon is shown.*

> Feldersatz-Division: Field reinforcement division—a staff responsible for the administration of forward reinforcement battalions in the rear areas of a front on which extensive operations are in progress.†

2. Notes on the main features of the system are given in the following paragraphs. American terms are used as far as possible, on the basis of the military terms used above.

---

* If casualties are heavy, there is no period of waiting, and the Feldersatzbataillon too becomes a personnel replacement transfer battalion.
† Felders. Divs. A-E have been identified in Russia.

VIII REPLACEMENT TRAINING UNITS: THE ORIGINAL ALLOTMENT

1. Every unit of the field army received replacement personnel as necessary from a replacement training unit stationed in the military district in which it was originally formed. The replacement training unit carried the same number as the field army unit to which it supplied personnel. In general, the replacement training unit was one degree smaller than the affiliated unit in the field army (for each regiment a replacement training battalion or equivalent unit, and for each non-regimental battalion or equivalent unit a training company). But there were two replacement training battalions for each regiment of the active (i.e. peace-time standing) army, and a training battalion in place of a company for each peace-time non-regimental battalion. This allotment of replacement training units may be made clearer by some concrete examples:-

Field army units:	Replacement training units:	
	Of standing army field army units	Of newly formed field army units
26th Inf Regt	I/and II/26th Inf Repl Tng Bns	
497th Inf Regt		497th Inf Repl Tng Bn
19th Arty Regt	I/and II/19th Arty Repl Tng Bns	
214th Arty Regt		214th Arty Repl Tng Bn
14th AT Bn	14th AT Repl Tng Bn	
157th Engr Bn		157th Engr Repl Tng Co

2. Specialist sub-units (such as infantry gun cos, infantry AT Cos, mounted infantry platoons, etc.) were supplied with personnel on the basis of one replacement training sub unit per division, carrying the division number, and serving the corresponding sub-units in each of its regiments. For example, in the case of the 22d Inf Div the 22d Inf AT Repl Tng Co provided personnel for the 14th (AT) Cos of the 16th, 47th and 65th Inf Regts.

3. All replacement training units serving the division infantry regiments were controlled by an infantry training regiment which carried the same number as the division. Thus the 22d Inf Training Regt at Oldenburg controlled all replacement training units of the 22d Inf Div. Artillery training regiments were provided on a lower scale, one for each division of the peacetime army. Thus, the 22d Arty Replacement Training Regt controlled the training of personnel for both the 22d and 269th Inf Divs.

4. In general, at this stage, a replacement training unit of the same number served each unit of the field army, and the identification of either justified the assumption that the other existed. Similarly, an infantry replacement training regiment and an infantry division of the same number could be mutually inferred*

---

* There were one or two exceptions, e.g. the 157th Inf Replacement Training Regt served the 57th Inf Div.

IX SUBSEQUENT DEVELOPMENTS

1. The above system has undergone substantial modifications, especially after completion of the initial expansion program (August 1939—January 1940), when the proportion of replacement training to field army units was reduced. Some of the original replacement training units were transferred to the field army, receiving new numbers (161st–164th, 167th-170th, 181st, 183d, 196th-198th and probably 199th Inf Divs were formed from such units). In consequence, there are now many infantry regiments without similarly numbered replacement training battalions, and one infantry training regiment will usually supply personnel to two divisions of the field army.

2. Again, in some cases infantry regiments of the field army have been disbanded, or converted to motorized infantry, but their original replacement training battalions still exist under numbers which now have no field army counterpart. A new series of infantry replacement training regiments has recenlty been identified, carrying numbers in the series 601 and upwards and so corresponding to no divisions of the field army.

3. The result of these changes has been to complicate the detailed study of the replacement supply structure, but the following notes give a general outline of the system now in force.

X THE PRESENT ALLOTMENT

1. Panzer divisions.—Personnel for the motorized infantry brigade of the Panzer division are controlled by a motorized infantry replacement training regiment (Schützen-Ersatz-Regiment, S.E.R.) Those for the remaining division units are directly under training division or artillery training regiment. There is one motorized infantry replacement training battalion for each pair of regiments, one motorcycle replacement battalion for each pair of Panzer divisions, and there are also specialist replacement training companies under the replacement training regiment. Thus, the 5th and 11th Panzer Divisions of Wehrkreis VIII have the following replacement training structure under the 85th mtz Inf Replacement Training Regt:

> 13th Mtz Inf Repl Tng Bn (serving 13th and 14th Mtz Inf Regts
>   of the 5th Pz Div),
> 110th Mtz Inf Repl Tng Bn (for 110th and 111th Mtz Inf Regts
>   of 11th Pz Div),
> 55th Mtrcl Repl Tng Bn (for 55th and 61st Mtrcl Bns),
> 85th Sig Repl Tng Co and
> 85th Gun Repl Tng Co (for the specialist sub-units of 5th and 11th Mtz
>   Inf Brig).

2. *Infantry divisions,— One infantry replacement training regiment may serve one or two field army divisions. The three infantry regiments of a division are usually served by two replacement training battalions. Similarly, a replacement training unit is likely, in most cases, to provide personnel for two units of the field army instead of only one as in accordance with the original system.

3. In general, it is inteneded that replacement training units should be permanently affiliated to specific field army units (for example, a proportion of the officers of the replacement training unit will have seen service at the front with the field army unit, and convalescent soldiers are attached to a Convalescent Co —Genesenden-Kompanie— of the replacement training unit before returning to t he field). In times of stress, however, the system becomes less rigid.

4. If very heavy casualties are sustained by organizations in the field, the Replacement Training Command is called on for larger drafts than can be pro v ided without improvization. In such cases, all the available men from each Wehrkreis are formed into personnel replacement transfer battalions, which receive either very high numbers (e.g., 2021) or double numbers (e.g., XIII/12— the twelfth battalion of a series provided by Wehrkreis XIII), and the men may be transferred from these battalions to whatever unit needs them most, even though its proper replacement training units are stationed in a different military district in Germany.

XI REPLACEMENT TRAINING UNITS IN OCCUPIED TERRITORY

1. In certain cases, the Germans have been able to effect a considerable economy in manpower by moving the replacement training units from one or more military districts into occupied territory, where they can combine training of recruits with assisting in maintaining internal security.

2. 1939-1940.— After the close of the Polish campaign, all replacement training units from Wehrkreise V,VI and XII were transferred to the Protectorate and to Poland (where the two new military districts XX and XXI had been formed).

3. 1940-1941.— After the Battle of France, the above units returned to their original districts, and replacement training units from Wehrkreis I (East Prussia) moved into the Protectorate. About the same time, many of the replacement training units from Wehrkreis X were transferred to Denmark, where Repl Tng Div No 160 (one of the two training divisions of Wehrkreis X) replaced a division of the field army.

4. 1941-42.— Once the attack on the U.S.S.R. had begun, the East Prussian replacement training units were brought back to Wehrkreis I from the Protect-

---

* The replacement training structure for motorized, light and mountain divisions is similar to that of infantry divisions, with suitable modifications of detail.

orate, where their place has been taken by units from the adjoining military districts(IV, XIII and XVII). At the same time, most of the replacement training units from Silesia (Wehrkreis VIII) were transferred to Alsace-Lorraine, where they come under the administration of Wehrkreise V and XII. During recent months, replacement training units under the control of these two military districts have been moved still further west into France proper, so that a corresponding reduction in the field army forces in Eastern France has been effected.

5. In cases where the replacement training units are absent from their home district, the recruits from that district report, not at the unit replacement training center but at a central Wehrkreis-Ersatz-Depot, from which they are conducted in groups to their replacement training commander.

6. Trained recruits arriving in small groups from the Home Command are sent to a Frontsammelstelle (Front Assembly Point), which distributes them to the units where they are required.

XII MILITARY DISTRICTS (Wehrkreise)

The following section outlines the essential facts concerning the military districts of Germany, i.e., the commander, units mobilized, geographical structure and basic training organization. American terms are employed for convenience throughout, except in the case of area and sub-area Hq, where place names are given in their German form as they will most commonly be encountered in German documents. Where a more familiar form exists this follows in parentheses and underscored.

1. Wehrkreis I (Hq:Königsberg)

East Prussia: Extended early in 1939 to include Memel and, after the Polish campaign, a portion of Poland.
Commander: General Peter WEYER (63)
C of S:
Corps mobilized: I and XXVI Inf
Divisions mobilized: 24th Pz (former 1st Cav); 1st, 11th, 61st, 161st, 206th, 217th, 228th, 291st, 340th and 714th Inf
Area Hq: Königsberg: Lt Gen RÜHLE v. LILIENSTERN (62)
  Sub-areas: Königsberg (Ostpr.) I-II, Tilsit, Gumbinnen, Treuburg, Barstenstein (Ostpr.), Braunsberg (Ostpr.)
Area Hq: Allenstein:
  Sub-areas: Alenstein, Ortelsburg, Lötzen, Zichenau (Plock)
*Replacement Training divisions: No 141: Königsberg
                                  No 151: Allenstein

Replacement Training regiments:
  Infantry: 1st: Insterburg   217th: Allenstein
            11th: Allenstein   228th: Lörzen
            61st: Königsberg
           206th: Gumbinnen
  Artillery: 1st: Insterburg
             11th: Allenstein
Training areas: Arys: Maj Gen SAUVANT (51)
                  Stablack:
Division staffs: 401 z.b.V.: Königsberg

2. Wehrkreis II (Hq:Stettin)

Mecklenburg and Pomerania
Commander: General Max FÖHRENBACH (70)
C of S: Maj Gen STEUDNER (62) (?)
Corps mobilized: II Inf, XXXVI (Corps Comd), LVII Pz

---

*From mid-1940 to mid-1941 most of the replacement training units from this military district were stationed in the Protectorate; during that period Div. No. 141 was at Prag and Div. No. 151 at Budweis.

Divisions mobilized: 12th Pz (former 2d Mtz); 12th, 32d, 75th, 122d, 162d, 258th, 292d, 302d, and 702d Inf; 207th "Sicherungs" (former Inf)
Area Hq: Köslin: Lt Gen MOYSES (59)
  Sub-areas: Stolp, Köslin, Kolberg, Neustettin, Deutsch Krone, Woldenburg (Neum.)
Area Hq: Stettin: Maj Gen v. AMMON (60)
  Sub-areas: Stettin I-II, Swinemünde, Stargard (Pom.), Greifswald, Stralsund
Area Hq: Schwerin:
  Sub-areas: Schwerin (Meckl.), Rostock, Parchim, Neustrelitz
Replacement Training division: No. 152: Stettin
                               No. 192: Rostock
Replacement Training regiments:
  Mtz infantry: 2d Mtz: Stettin
  Infantry: 12th: Schwerin   258th: Rostock
            32d : Kolberg
            75th: Stettin
            207th: Deutsch Krone
  Artillery: 2d Mot.: Stettin
             12th: Schwerin
             32d: Kolberg
Training areas: Altwarp:
                Gross-Born: Maj Gen THOFERN ( )
                Hammerstein:
                Wüstrow:
Division staffs: 272d "Inf": Neustrelitz
                 402 z.b.V.: Stettin

   3. Wehrkreis III (Hq: Berlin)

Altmark, Neumark and Brandenburg
Commander: General Frhr. v. DALWIGK zu LICHTENFELS (66)
C of S: Maj Gen HAUPT (60) (?)
Corps mobilized: III Pz XXVIII Inf, XXXIV (Corps Comd), LII Inf and Africa Pz
Divisions mobilized: 3d, 8th (former 3d L) and 21st (former 5th L Mtz) Pz;
  3d Mtz (former Inf); 90th L ; 23d, 68th, 76th, 93d, 111th, 123d, 163d, 208th, 218th,
  257th, 293d, 333d and 719th Inf
Area Hq : Berlin: Lt Gen BOCK v. WÜLFINGEN (60)
  Sub-areas: Berlin I-X
Area Hq.: Frankfurt/Oder: Lt Gen SATOW (55)
  Sub-areas: Frankfurt (Oder), Küstrin, Landsberg (Warthe),
    Crossen (Oder), Lübben (Spreewald), Cottbus
Area Hq.: Potsdam: Lt Gen Frhr. v. WILMOWSKY (61)
  Sub-areas: Potsdam I-II, Neuruppin, Eberswalde, Bernau b. Berlin (Berlin),
    Perleberg
Replacement Training divisions: No 143: Frankfurt/Oder
                                No 153: Potsdam
Replacement Training regiments:
  Mtz Infantry: 83d Mtz: Eberswalde
  Infantry: 3d Mtz: Frankfurt/Oder   208th: Cottbus

23d: Potsdam
68th: Guben
76th: Berlin
Artillery: 3d Mtz: Frankfurt/Oder
23d: Potsdam
Training areas: Döberitz:
                 Jüterbog: Col v. MALLINCKRODT (50)
                 Wandern: Maj Gen OELSNER (53)
                 Zossen: Maj Gen KOREUBER (52)
Division staffs: 403 z.b.V.: Berlin

218th: Spandau
257th: Landsberg/
            Warthe

4. Wekrkreis IV (Hq: Dresden)

Saxony and part of Thüringen: extended in 1939 to include the Northern frontier
  districts of Böhmen
Commander: General Erich WÖLLWARTH (70)
C of S:
Corps mobilized: IV, XXIX and XXXXIV Inf
Divisions mobilized: 14th (former 4th Inf) and 18th Pz; 14th Mtz (former Inf);
  24th, 56th, 87th, 94th, 134th, 164th, 223d, 255th, 256th, 294th, 304th and 704th
  Inf; 209th Inf (since disbanded)
Area Hq : Leipzig:
Sub-areas: Leipzig I-III, Naumburg (Saale), Halle (Saale), Altenburg, Eisleben,
  Bitterfeld, Wittenberg, Grimma, Döbeln
Area Hq: Dresden: Lt Gen PRAETORIUS (60)
  Sub-areas: Dresden I-III, Pirna, Bautzen, Zittau, Kamenz, Meissen, Grossen-
  hain, Leitmeritz, Böhmisch-Leipa, Riechenberg
Area Hq : Chemnitz: Lt Gen HENGEN (55)
  Sub-areas: Chemnitz I-II, Freiberg, Annaberg, Zwickau, Auerbach, Plauen,
  Glauchau, Teplitz-Schönau
Replacement Training divisions: No. 154: Dresden
Replacement Training regiments:
  Mtz infantry: 4th Mtz: Dresden.
  Infantry: 14th Mtz: Leipzig
           24th: Chemnitz
           56th: Dresden
           209th:

           223d: Dresden
           255th: Löbau
           256th: Meissen ?
           603d: Dresden

  Artillery:
Training areas: Königsbrück:
               Zeithain:
Division staffs: 404 z.b.V.: Dresden

5. Wehrkreis V (Hq: Stuttgart)
Württemberg and part of Baden; extended after the Battle of France to include
  the incorporated departments of Alsace.
Commander: General Erwin OSSWALD (60)
C of S:
Corps mobilized: V, XXV and L Inf
Divisions mobilized: 10th Pz, 25th Mtz (former Inf); 5th (former Inf) and

101st L ; 4th Mtn ; 35th, 78th, 125th, 198th, 205th, 215th, 260th, 305th, 335th and 715th Inf

Area Hq : Ulm:
  Sub-areas: Ulm, Tübingen, Ehingen, Ravensburg, Sigmaringen, Rottweil, Donau-
  eschingen, Konstanz, Freiburg (Breisgau), Lörrach

Area Hq : Stuttgart: Lt Gen TSCHERNING (60)
  Sub-areas: Gmund, Hall, Heilbronn, Esslingen (Neckar), Ludwigsburg, Stuttgart
  I-II, Horb (Neckar), Calw, Karlsruhe, Pforzheim, Rastatt, Offenburg

Area Hq : Strassburg:
  Sub-areas: (The organization of sub-areas in incorporated Alsace is not yet
  known.)

*Replacement Training divisions: No 155: Ulm
                                 No 165: Stuttgart?: Lt Gen HÜTTMANN (63)
                                 (?)
                                 No. 158 (from Wkr. VIII): Strassburg:
                                 Maj Gen SCHMIDT-KOLBOW (62)

Replacement Training regiments:
  Mtz Infantry: 86th Mtz : Stuttgart
  Infantry: 5th: Konstanz   205th: Ulm
            25th Mtz: Ludwigsburg   215th: Heilbronn
            35th: Karlsruhe   260th: Luneville
            78th: Ulm
  Artillery: 5th: Ulm
             25th Mtz: Stuttgart
             35th: Karlsruhe
  Infantry: 8th: Colmar   221st: Strassburg
            62d: Colmar
            213th: Mülhausen/Els
  Artillery: 8th: Strassburg
  Training areas: Heuberg: Col. BESCH ( )
                  Münsingen:
  Division staffs: 405 z.b.V.: Stuttgart

  6. Wehrkreis VI (Hq: Münster)
Westphalia and the Rhineland; extended after the Battle of France to include the
  Eupen-Malmedy district of Belgium; some replacement training units from this
  military district are at present stationed in Holland and East Belgium.

Commander: General GLOKKE (58)
C of S:
Corps mobilized: VI and XXIII Inf, XXIII (Corps Comd),LVI Pz
Divisions mobilized: 6th (former 1st L) and 16th (former 16th Inf) Pz ; 16th Mtz;
  6th, 26th, 69th, 86th, 106th, 126th, 196th, 199th, 211th, 227th, 253d, 254th, 306th,
  336th and 716th Inf

Area Hq : Münster: Lt Gen v. dem KNESEBECK (65)
  Sub-areas: Münster (Westf.), Coesfeld, Paderborn, Bielefeld, Herford, Minden,

---

*From late 1939 to mid-1940 most of the replacement training units from this
military district were stationed in the Protectorate; during that period Div. No.
155 was at Prag and Div. No. 165 at Olmütz.

Detmold, Lingen, Osnabruck, Recklinghausen, Gelsenkirchen
Area Hq : Dortmund:
Sub-areas: Arnsberg, Soest, Dortmund I-II, Iserlohn, Bochum, Herne, Hagen
Area Hq.: Düsseldorf:
Sub-areas: Düsseldorf, Neuss, Krefeld, München-Gladbach, Wuppertal, Mett-
mann, Solingen, Essen I-II, Duisburg, More, Oberhausen, Wesel
Area Hq.: Köln : Lt Gen Frhr. ROEDER v. DIERSBURG (57)
Sub-areas: Köln I-III, Bonn, Siegburg, Aachen, Julich, Düren, Monschau
*Replacement Training divisions: No 156: Köln: Maj Gen NOACK (60)
No 166: Bielefeld
*Replacement Training regiments:
Mtz infantry: 57th Mtz.: Wuppertal
Infantry: 6th: Bielefeld   211th: Köln
16th: Rheine   227th: (Düsseldorf)†
26th: (Köln)*   253d: Aachen
69th: Soest   254th: (Dortmund)†
Artillery: 6th: Münster
16th Mtz:
26th: Köln
Training areas: Deilinghofen:
Elsenborn: Lt Gen LEYTHAUSER (58)
Meppen:
Sennelager:
Wahn: Col BENCZEK ( )
Division staffs: 276th "Inf."?:
406th z.b.V.: Münster

7. Wehrkreis VII (Hq: München)

Southern Bayern.
Commander: General Edmund WACHENFELD (64)
C of S:
Corps mobilized: VII and XXVII Inf
Divisions mobilized: 17th Pz (former 27th Inf); 97th L; 1st Mtn; 7th, 57th, 88th,
167th, 212th, 268th, 337th and 707th Inf
Area Hq.: München: Lt Gen van GINKEL (60)
Sub-areas: München I-IV, Rosenheim, Traunstein, Weilheim, Augsburg, Kemp-
ten (Allgau), Landshut, Pfarrkirchen, Ingolstadt
Replacement Training divisions: No. 147: Augsburg: Lt Gen HELD (61) (?)
No. 157: München

---

*From late 1939 to late 1940, most of the replacement training units from this
military district were stationed in Wehrkreis XX; during that period Div. No. 156
was at Thorn and Div. No. 166 at Danzig.
†Those regiments in parentheses and marked with an asterisk are at present
stationed in occupied Dutch or Belgian territory.

Replacement Training regiments:
  Mtz infantry: 27th Mtz: Augsburg
  Infantry: 7th: München
          157th: Bad Reichenhall   268th: München
          212th: München
  Mountain rifle: 100th: Garmisch.
  Artillery: 7th: München
          27th Mtz: Augsburg
          79 Mtn:
Training areas: Hohenfels:
                Mittenwald:
Division staffs: 277th "Inf": Augsburg ?--
             407 z.b.V.: München.

    8. Wehrkreis VIII (Hq: Breslau)

Silesia; extended in 1938 to include the Sudeten districts of Böhmen; in summer
1939 to include part of Mahren and in autumn 1939 to include part of SW Poland.
Commander: General Hans HALM (63)
C of S:
Corps mobilized: VIII Inf XXXV (Corps Comd) XXXVIII Inf?
Divisions mobilized: 5th and 11th Pz; 18th Mtz (former Inf); 8th and 28th L
  (former Inf); 62d, 81st, 102d, 168th, 239th, 252d, 298th, 332d and 708th Inf;
  213th and 221st "Sicherungs" (former Inf)
Area Hq : Breslau: Lt Gen v. SCHAUROTH (57)
  Sub-areas: Breslau I-III, Oels, Brieg, Glatz, Waldenburg (Schles.), Schweid-
    nitz, Mährisch-Schönberg, Zwittau, Troppau, Freudenthal, Wohlau
Area Hq : Liegnitz:
  Sub-areas:· Liegnitz, Glogau, Sagan, Görlitz, Bunzlau, Hirschberg (Riesengeb.),
    Trautenau
Area Hq : Kattowtiz: Lt Gen CARP (56)
  Sub-areas: Kattowitz, Königshütte (Oberschles.), Lublinitz, Rybnik, Teschen,·
    Bielitz (Beskiden), Oppeln, Neisse, Neustadt (Oberschles.), Cosel, Gleiwitz
Replacement Training divisions: No. 148: transferred to Metz (Wkr. XII)
                                   No. 158: transferred to Strassburg (Wkr. V)
                                   No. 178: Liegnitz
*Replacement Training regiments:
Replacement Mtz infantry: 85th Mtz: Liegnitz
  Infantry: 18th Mtz: Liegnitz
Training areas: Lamsdorf:
                Neuhammer: Col. STAMMER ( )
Division staffs: 408 z.b.V.: Breslau
             432 z.b.V.: Neisse

---

*The remaining training regiments from this military district have been trans-
ferred for the time being to Alsace-Lorraine; see under Wkr. V and Wkr. XII.

9. Wehrkreis IX (Hq: Kassel)

Part of Thüringen and Hessen
Commander: General Rudolf SCHNIEWINDT (64)
C of S:
Corps mobilized: IX Inf, XXXIX Pz
Divisions mobilized: 1st, 7th (former 2d L) and 20th Pz; 29th Mtz; 9th, 15th,
  52d, 82d, 95th, 129th, 169th, 214th, 251st, 299th, 319th, 328th, 339th and 709th
  Inf
Area Hq : Kassel: Lt Gen PINCKVOSS (56)
  Sub-areas: Kassel I-II, Korbach, Marburg (Lahn), Hersfeld, Siegen, Wetzlar,
    Fulda, Giessen
Area Hq : Frankfurt/Main: Lt Gen DETMERING (55)
  Sub-areas: Frankfurt (Main) I-II, Offenbach (Main), Aschaffenburg, Friedberg,
    Hanau
Area Hq : Weimar:
  Sub-areas: Weimar, Sangerhausen, Gera, Rudolstadt, Mühlhausen (Thür.),
    Erfurt, Eisenach, Gotha, Meiningen
Replacement Training divisions: No. 159: Frankfurt/Main
                                 No. 179: Weimar
Replacement Training regiments:
  Mtz infantry: 81th Mtz: Meiningen
  Infantry: 9th: Siegen?   214th: Hanau
            15th: Kassel   251st: Frankfurt/Main?
            29th Mtz : Erfurt
            52d: Kassel
  Artillery: 9th: 44th:
             15th: 52d:
             29th: Mtz.:
Training areas: Ohrdruf:
                 Schwarzenborn:
                 Wildflecken:
Division staffs: 409 z.b.V.: Kassel

10. Wehrkreis X (Hq: Hamburg)

Schleswig-Holstein and part of Hannover; extended in 1940 to include part of
  Danish Slesvig.
Commander: General Walter RASCHICK (60)
C of S:
Corps mobilized: X Inf, XXXI (Corps Comd)?, XXXX and XXXXVI Pz
Divisions mobilized: 20th Mtz; 22d, 30th, 58th, 83d, 110th, 121st, 170th, 225th,
  269th, 290th, 320th and 710th Inf
Area Hq : Schleswig-Holstein (Hamburg); Maj Gen SCHAUWECKER (61)
  Sub-areas: Naumünster, Rendsburg, Schleswig, Kiel, Eutin, Lübeck
Area Hq : Hamburg: Lt Gen v. WEDDERKOP (60)
  Sub-areas: Hamburg I-VI
Area Hq: Bremen

Sub-areas: Bremen I-II, Stade, Wesermünde, Oldenburg (Oldb.) I-II, Aurich,
   Nienburg (Weser), Lüneburg
Replacement Training divisions: No. 160: transferred to Denmark
   No. 190: Neumünster
*Replacement Training regiments:
  Infantry: 20th Mtz: Hamburg   225th: (Hamburg)*
          22d: Oldenburg   269th: Delmenhorst
          30th: (Lübeck)*
          58th: (Rendsburg?)*
  Artillery: 20th Mtz: Hamburg
          22d: Bremen
          30th: Lübeck
Training areas: Münsterlager:
          Putlos:
Division staffs: 270th "Inf":
          410 z.b.V.: Hamburg Lt Gen POETTER (   )

   11. Wehrkreis XI (Hq: Hannover)

Braunschweig, Anhalt and part of Hannover
Commander: General Wolfgang MUFF (62)
C of S:
Corps mobilized: XI Inf, XIV Pz, XXX Inf, XXXXIII Inf, LI Inf
Divisions mobilized: 13th (former 13th Mtz) and 19th (former 19th Inf) Pz; 31st,
   71st, 96th, 131st, 181st, 216th, 267th, 295th, 321st and 711th Inf
Area Hq : Hannover: Lt Gen v. ZEPELIN (56)
  Sub-areas: Hannover I-II, Braunschweig, Goslar, Hildesheim, Hameln, Gottingen,
   Celle
Area Hq : Magdeburg: Lt Gen OSTERROHT (62)
  Sub-areas: Stendal, Magdeburg I-II, Burg bei Magdeburg, Halberstadt, Dessau,
   Bernburg
Replacement Training divisions: No 171: Hannover
   No 191: Braunschweig
Replacement Training regiments:
  Mtz infantry: 13th Mtz: Magdeburg
  Infantry: 31st: Braunschweig   267th: Hannover?
          71st: Hildesheim
      216th: Hameln?
  Artillery: 13th Mtz: Magdeburg
          19th: Hannover
          31st: Braunschweig
Training areas: Altengrabow:
          Bergen:
          Hillersleben:
          Salchau:

---

*Those regiments marked with an asterisk are at present stationed in Denmark
under No. 160 Div.

Division staffs: 411 z.b.V.: Hannover

12. Wehrkreis XII (Hq:Wiesbaden)

Eifel, part of Hessen, the Palatinate and the Saar area; extended after the Battle
  of France to comprise Lorraine (including the Nancy area)
Commander: General Albrecht STEPPUHN (63)
C of S: Maj Gen Hans MEISSNER (58)
Corps mobilized: XII Inf, XXIV Pz, LIII Inf
Divisions mobilized: 15th Pz (former 33d Inf) and 23d Pz; 36th Mtz; 34th, 72d,
  79th, 112th, 132d, 197th, 246th, 263d, 342d and 712th Inf; 444th "Sicherungs"
Area Hq: Koblenz: Lt Gen v. BERG (61)
  Sub-areas: Trier I-II, Koblenz, Neuwied, Kreuznach, Wiesbaden, Limburg,
    (Lahn), Mainz, Worms, Darmstadt
Area Hq: Mannheim:
  Sub-areas: Saarlautern, Saarbrücken, St. Wendel, Zweibrücken, Kaiserslau-
    tern, Neustadt (Weinstrasse), Ludwingshafen (Rhein) Mannheim I-II, Heidel-
    berg
Area Hq: Metz:
  Sub-areas: (The organization of sub-areas in incorporated Luxemburg and
    Lorraine is not yet known)
*Replacement Training divisions: No. 172: Mainz.
                                   No. 148:(from Wkr. VIII): Metz
                                   No. 182: Nancy

Replacement Training regiments:
  Mtz infantry: 12 mot.:
  Infantry: 34th: Heidelberg   246th: Trier
            36th Mtz: Wiesbaden   342d: Kaiserslautern
            112th: Darmstadt
  Artillery: 33d Mtz: Mainz
            34th: Koblenz
  Infantry: 28th: Metz   252d: Mörchingen
            79th: Nancy   263d: Nancy
            239th: Diedenhofen
  Artillery: 28th: Metz
            263d: Nancy
Training areas: Baumholder:
                 Bitsch:

*From late 1939 to late 1940, most of the depot units from this military district
were stationed in Wehrkreis XXI; during that period Div. No. 172 was at Gnesen
and Div. No. 182 at Litzmannstadt.

Division staffs: 412 z.b.V.: Wiesbaden

13. Wehrkreis XIII (Hq: Nürnberg)

Northern Bayern; extended in 1938 to include part of Western Böhmen.
Commander: General Friedrich v. COCHENHAUSEN (63)
C of S: Maj Gen Paul VOIT (66)
Corps moblized: XIII Inf, XXXXV (Corps Comd)
Divisions mobilized: 4th Pz, 10th Mtz (former 10th Inf); 17th, 46th, 73d, 98th,
   113th, 183d, 296th, 323d, 330th and 713th Inf; 231st Inf (since disbanded)
Area Hq: Regensburg: Lt Gen Edler v. KIESLING auf KIESLINGSTEIN (64)
   Sub-areas: Regensburg, Passau, Straubing, Weiden, Amberg
Area Hq: Nürnberg: Lt Gen Frhr. v. PERFALL (59)
   Sub-areas: Nürnberg, I-II, Fürth, Bamberg, Bad Kissingen, Würzburg,
   Ansbach, Coburg, Bayreuth, Bad Mergentheim, Tauberbischofsheim
Area Hq: Eger (at Karlsbad): Lt Gen VOLK (58)
   Sub-areas: Kaaden, Karlsbad, Eger, Mies, Marktredwitz
*Replacement Training divisions: No 173: Nürnberg: Maj Gen v. BEHR (53) (?)
                                  No 193: Regensburg
Replacement Training regiments:
   Mtz infantry: 84: Würzburg
   Infantry: 17th: Nürnberg   95th: Coburg (?)
              42d: 231st:
              46th: Pilsen (Prot.)
              73d: Würzburg
   Artillery: 10th Mtz:
               17th: Nürnberg
Training areas: Grafenwöhr: Lt Gen HEBERLEIN (54)
                Hammelburg:
Division staffs: 413 z.b.V.: Nürnberg

14. Wehrkreis XVII (Hq: Wien)

Ober- and Nieder Donau; extended in 1939 to include the Southern districts of
   Böhmen and Mähren.
Commander: General Alfred STRECCIUS (64)
C of S: Maj Gen Emil ZELLNER (   )
Corps mobilized: XVII Inf, XXXVII (Corps Comd)
Divisions mobilized: 2d and 9th (former 4 L) Pz; 100th L; 44th, 45th, 137th, 262d,
   297th, 327th and 717th Inf
Area Hq: Linz: Lt Gen. RIEBESAM (54)
   Sub-areas: Wels, Ried i. Innkreis, Linz, Steyr, Krummau a.d. Moldau
Area Hq: Wien: Lt Gen. SCHWARZNECKER (57)

---

*Some of the depot units controlled by these divisions are now stationed in the
western districts of the Protectorate.

Sub-areas: Melk, Zwettl, St. Pölten, Krems a.d. Donau, Znaim, Wiener
  Neustadt, Baden, Nikolsburg, Wien I-IV
*Replacement Training divisions: No. 177: Wien: Maj Gen REICHERT (51)
                                 No. 187: Linz: Lt Gen STEPHANUS (59) (?)
Replacement Training regiments:
  Mtz infantry: 82d Mtz: Wien
  Infantry: 45th: Krummau   462d:
            130th: Linz
            131st: Wien
  Artillery: 96th: Wien
             98th: Linz
Training areas: Bruck a.d. Leitha:
                Döllersheim: Maj Gen OFFENBACHER (51)
Division staffs: 417 z.b.V.: Wien

  15. Wehrkreis XVIII (Hq:Salzburg)

Steiermark, Kärnten, Tyrol; extended in 1941 to include the northern districts of
  Slovenia
Commander: General Hubert SCHALLER-KALLIDE (60)
C of S: Colonel Reichsfrhr. v. d. TANN-RATHSAMHAUSEN (57) (?)
Corps mobilized: XVIII and Norway Mtn
Divisions mobilized: 2d, 3d, 5th, 6th and 7th Mtn; 718th Inf
Area Hq: Innsbruck: Lt Gen Frhr. v. WALDENFELS (58)
  Sub-areas: Bergenz, Innsbruck, Salzburg
Area Hq: Graz: Lt Gen GUNZELMANN (55)
  Sub-areas: Spittal, Klagenfurt, Judenburg, Leoben, Graz, Leibnitz, Fürstenfeld,
    Marburg (Maribor), Cilli (Celje), Krainburg (Kranj)
Replacement Training division: No 188: Salzburg: Lt Gen v. HOSSLIN (63) (?)
Replacement Training regiments:
  Mountain rifle: 136th: Landeck
                  137th: Innsburck (?)
                  138th: Leoben
                  139th: Klagenfurt
  Artillery: 100th:
             112th:
             Dachstein:
Training areas: Seethaler Alpe:
                Strass i. Steiermark:
                Wattener Lizum:
Division staffs: 537th Frontier Guard: Innsbruck
                 538th Frontier Guard: Klagenfurt

---

*Some of the replacement training units controlled by these divisions are now
stationed in the eastern districts of the Protectorate.

16. Wehrkreis XX (Hq: Danzig)

Formed after the Polish campaign, comprising the areas of Danzig Free State,
 the Polish Corridor, and the western part of East Prussia.
Commander: General BOCK (62)
C of S:
Corps maintained: XX Inf, XXXXVII Pz
Divisions maintained: 60th Mtz
Area Hq: Danzig: Lt Gen KURZ ( )
 Sub-areas: Danzig, Neustadt, Pr. Stargard, Marienwerder, Graudenz, Brom-
  berg (Bydgoszcz), Thorn (Torun).
Replacement Training Regiments:
 Infantry: 21st: Elbing.
       60th Mtz: Danzig.
Training areas: Thorn (Torun):
Division staffs: 428 z.b.V.: Danzig

17. Wehrkreis (Hq: Posen)

Formed after the Polish campaign, comprising Western Poland.
Commander: General Walter PETZEL (59).
C of S:
Corps maintained: XXXXVIII Pz
Divisions maintained: 50th Inf
Area Hq: Posen (Poznan):
 Sub-areas: Posen (Poznan), Liss, Hohensalza, Leschnau (Leszno), Kalisch
  (Kalisz), Litsmannstadt (Lodz)
Replacement Training Regiments:
 Infantry: 50th: Posen (Poznan),
Training areas: Sieradsch (Sieratz):
        Warthelager:
Division staffs: 429 z.b.V.: Posen (Poznan)
        430 z.b.V.: Gnesen (Gniezno)
        431 z.b.V.: Litzmannstadt (Lodz)

XIII OCCUPIED COUNTRIES

   In the following pages the occupied countries are set out in historical
sequence. The essential structure of German commands and missions therein is
shown under separate headings.

1. AUSTRIA

   Occupied in March 1938, and absorbed into the Reich as Wehrkreise XVII
and XVIII.

RESTRICTED

2. CZECHOSLOVAKIA

First partitioned in September 1938, when the Sudentenland was detached
and incorporated in Wehrkreise IV, VIII and XIII. Finally occupied in March
1939, when the remaining territory was divided between the Protectorate (Reichs-
Protektorat Böhmen-Mähren) and the protected state of Slovakia.

a. Protectorate* (Hq: Prag)

Commander (Wehrmachtsvevollmächtigter): Maj Gen Rudolf TOUSSAINT (50)
C of S: Col Anton LONGIN
Corps mobilized: XLIX Mtn
Divisions mobilized:
Area Hq: Prag: Lt Gen v. PRONDZYNSKI (60)
 Sub-areas: Prag, Budweis, Brünn, Olmütz
Replacement Training areas: Brdy Wald:
                            Hohenelbe:
                            Milowitz:
                            Wischau:
Division staffs: 539th Frontier Guard: Prag: Lt Gen Dr. SPEICH (58)
                 540th Frontier Guard: Brünn: Lt Gen TARBUK v. SENSEN-
                      HORST

b. Slovakia (Hq:Pressburg (Bratislava))

Head of Military Mission (Chef der Heeresmission): Lt Gen SCHLIEPER (50)
C of S:
Commandant of the Protected Area (Kommandant der Schutzzone)
Replacement Training area: Malacky

3. MEMEL DISTRICT

Occupied in March 1939, and incorporated in Wehrkreis I.

4. POLAND

Occupied after the campaign of September 1939. The Western portion incorporated in Wehrkreise I and VIII, and in the newly formed Wehrkreise XX and
XXI. Central Poland established as the General Government (General-Gouverne-
ment).

Commander (Militärbefehlshaber): General Frhr. von GIENANTH (63)
C of S: Lt Gen Josef BRAUNER

*In effect, though not in name, an additional military district (Wehrkreis).

29

General Government (Hq Krakau)

Area Hq: The following have been identified:
  365th Lemberg (Lwow): Lt Gen BEUTTEL (55)
  372d Kielce:
  379th Lublin: Maj Gen Wilhelm v. ALTROCK (52)
  393d Piaseczno: Maj Gen Kurt SIEGLIN (57)
Town Hq (Stadtkommandanturen): The following have been identified:
Krakau: Lt Gen Eugen v. HÖBERTH ( )
Warsaw:

5. DANZIG FREE STATE

Occupied in September 1939 and incorporated subsequently in the newly formed Wehrkreis XX.

6. NORWAY

Occupied after a brief campaign in April 1940 and subsequently allowed a degree of autonomy in internal affairs.
            GERMAN FORCES IN NORWAY (Hq: OSLO)
Commander (Wehrmachtsbefehlshaber*): Col Gen Nikolaus v. FALKENHORST (57)
C of S: Maj Gen Rudolf BAMLER (45)
G-3: Lt Col v. BUTTLAR
Areas: North (Hq Alta): Lt Gen Emmerich NAGY (58)
            (LXXI Corps Comd)
  Sub-areas: **Kirkenes, Alta, Narvik
  Center (Hq Trondhjem): General Georg BRANDT (65) (XXXIII Corps Comd)
  Sub-areas: Mo, Dombaas
  South (Hq Oslo). General Valentin FEUERSTEIN (56) (LXX Corps Comd)
  Sub-areas: Bergen, Stavanger or Christiansand South, Oslo
  Note: The administrative areas are corps commands, each having two or three sub-areas which are division commands. These in turn are each subdivided into three sectors, each under control of an infantry regiment. The commanders of areas and sub-areas are described as Territorial-Befehlshaber, and the commanders of sectors as Abschnittskommandeure.

7. DENMARK

Occupied almost without resistance in April 1940 and subsequently allowed a degree of autonomy in internal affairs.

German Troops in Denmark (Hq: Copenhagen)

Commander (Befehlshaber der deutschen truppen): General Erich LÜDKE (59) (XXXI Corps Comd)

*Also commanding the Army of Norway.
**In the L of C area of the Army of Lapland.

C of S:
Area Hq: Copenhagen
  Sub-areas: Jutland:
              Aalborg: Lt Col GUERKE, CG 930th Infantry Replacement Training
                        Regiment
              Viborg: CG 225th Infantry Replacement Training Regiment
              Kolding: Colonel v. HERTEL, CG 931st Infantry Replacement Train-
                        ing Regiment
              Zeeland:
              Ringsted: CG 58th Infantry Replacement Training Regiment
Replacement Training divisions: No 160: Copenhagen: Maj Gen Frhr. v.
                                 UCKERMANN (50)
                                 No 416: Silkeborg: Maj Gen BRABÄNDER (51)

8. HOLLAND

Occupied in May, 1940, but subsequently allowed a degree of autonomy in internal affairs.

German Forces in Holland (Hq: The Hague)

Commander (Wehrmachtsbefehlshaber): General (GAF) Friedrich CHRISTIAN-
                                       SEN (62)
C of S: Maj Gen (GAF) Walter SCHWABEDISSEN ( )
Area Hq: The Hague
  Sub-areas: The following has been identified:
              674th: Rotterdam.

9. LUXEMBURG

Occupied in May, 1940, and incorporated in Wehrkreis XII.

10. BELGIUM

Occupied in May, 1941; subsequently allowed a degree of autonomy in internal affairs, but for military administration purposes combined with Northern
France east of the River Somme into the unified command "Belgien-Nordfrank-
reich".

Belgium-Northern France (Hq:Brussels)

Commander (Militärbefehlshaber): General Alexander v. FALKENHAUSEN (65)
C of S: Lt Col v. HARBOU
Administrative Hq*: The following have been identified:
  178th: Bruges: 672d: Brussels.

---

*Including Oberfeldkommandanturen, Feldkommandanturen, Ortskommandan-
turen, Kreiskommandanturen.

510th: Bruges: Maj Gen
        SCHEFOLD (54)
520th: Antwerp
611th: Ghent:
Areas: Brabant (Hq?)
      Commander:
      C of S:
      Flanders-Artois (Hq:Tourcoing).
      Commander: General Günther v. POGRELL (62)
        (XXXVII Corps Comd)
      C of S:

681st: Louvain:
701st: Antwerp:
--- : Liege: Maj Gen
        KEIM (61)

Landesschützen Regimental Staffs: The following have been identified:
      115th: Marais
      Wachregiment CLÜWER

11. FRANCE

Partially occupied after the capitulation of June, 1940; allowed a degree of autonomy in matters of local government throughout the occupied area, with the exception of Alsace-Lorraine* which, in fact, though not in name, has been incorporated into the Reich. Divided for purposes of military administration into the areas "France" and "Northern France" (included in Belgium).

France (Hq:Paris - Reported moved to Nancy)

Commander (Militärbefehlshaber): General Otto v. STÜLPNAGEL (63)
C of S: Col Dr. Hans SPEIDEL
Military districts:
   Northern France (West of the River Somme):
   Southwestern France: Lt Gen Frhr. v. ROTBERG (66)
   Southern France: Maj Gen Heinrich Ritter v. FÜCHTBAUER (62)
   Northwestern France: Lt Gen Karl NEUMANN-NEURODE (62)
   Greater Paris: Lt Gen Ernst SCHAUMBURG (61)
Administrative Hq†: The following have been identified:
   515th: Channel Islands
   529th: Amiens
   523d: Nancy
   541st: Biarritz
   549th: Rennes: Maj Gen Alfred JACOBI (57).
   568th: Dijon
   575th: Paris
   588th: Tours

*See under Wehrkreise V and XII.

† Including Oberfeldkommandanturen, Feldkommandanturen, Ortskommandanturen, Kreiskommandanturen.

```
590th:  Bar-le-Duc
591st:  Nancy
592d:   Laon
602d:   Laon
605th:  La Roche s/Yon: Maj Gen KURNATOWSKI (61)
670th:  Lille:  Lt Gen Heinrich NIEHOFF (58)
677th:  Poitiers
678th:  Arras
680th:  Melun:  Col Ritter v. XYLANDER
723d:   Caen
734th:  Paris area
754th:  Flers
755th:  Le Mans
```

Areas:
  Normandy East (Hq:Rouen): Commander:
          (XXXII Corps Comd)
  Burgundy (Hq:Dijon): Commander: General Kurt v. GREIFF (65)
          (XXXXV Corps Comd)
  Normandy West (Hq:Caen): Commander:
          (LX Corps Comd)
  Brittany (Hq:Angers): Commander:
          (? Corps Comd)
  Guyenne-Gascony (Hq:Bordeaux) Commander:
          (? Corps Comd)
Landesschützen Regimental Staffs: The following have been identified:
  64 z.b.V.: Angers   137th: Lure
  65th: Viroflay   138th: Tours
  113th: Rouen
  122d: Troyes
  125th: Besancon

12. ITALY

Entered the war on 11 June, 1940, since which date German infiltration has continued with growing intensity.

Head of Military Mission and Military Attache: General Enno v. RINTELEN (51)
C of S:

13. ROUMANIA

Under virtual German domination since November, 1940.

Head of Military Mission: Maj Gen HAUFFE (49)
C of S:

14. BULGARIA

Passively associated with Germany since March, 1941.

Head of Military Mission:
C of S:

15. HUNGARY

Allied to Germany since summer, 1940. Since the autumn of that year German dominance has increased. The Hungarians retain, however, a much greater degree of independence than the Roumanians.

Head of Military Mission:
C of S:

16. YUGOSLAVIA

Occupied in May, 1941. Portions of the country ceded to Italy, Hungary and Bulgaria, the rest divided into German, Italian and Bulgarian spheres of influence. Part of Slovenia incorporated into Wehrkreis XVIII.

   a. Serbia (Hq: Belgrade)

Commander (Militärbefehlshaber): General (GAF) DANCKELMANN (54)
C of S:
Corps Command: LXV
   Commander: General Paul BADER (57)
   C of S:

   b. Croatia (Hq: Zagreb)

Head of Military Mission: Maj Gen Edmund GLAISE v. HORSTENAU
Administrative Hq: The following has been identified:
   735th: Agram (Zagreb); Commander: Maj Gen Dr. Karl PRUGEL (65)

17. GREECE

Occupied after the campaign of May, 1940. Portions ceded to Bulgaria. The rest divided into German and Italian spheres of influence.

   a. Northern Greece (Hq: Salonika)

Commander (Feldkommandant): Maj Gen Kurt v. KRENZKI (55)
C of S:
Administrative Hq: The following has been identified:
   808th: Salonika

34

b. Southern Greece (Hq:Athens)

Commander (Befehlshaber): General (GAF) Helmuth FELMY (56)
C of S: Lt Col MEYER-RICKS

c. Crete (Hq:Heraklion)

Divided into German and Italian spheres under a military administration inde-
pendent of the mainland.
Commander: General (GAF) Waldemar ANDRAE (51)
C of S:
Administrative Hq: The following has been identified:
  606th: Heraklion.

18. FINLAND

Allied to Germany since June, 1941. The Army of Lapland (see Part C)
controls German forces in northern Finland, any German forces in southern
Finland come under the Finnish High Command to which a German Military
Mission is accredited.

Head of Military Mission: General Waldemar ERFURTH (62)
C of S: Lt Col HOLTER

19. U. S. S. R.

Attacked in June, 1941; the Baltic States (collectively termed the Ostland)
and portions of South Russia have since been placed under German military administration. Portions of Eastern Poland have been placed under the General
Government.

a. Ostland

Commander:
C of S:

b. Ukraine

Commander (Befehlshaber): General (GAF) Karl KITZINGER (56)
C of S:

XIV THEATER OF WAR

1. In the theater of war the place of the Wekrkreis organization is to some
extent taken by the L of C area command. Each army group has a Befehlshaber
des rückwärtigen Heeresgebiets, and each army   a Kommandant des rückwärtigen
Armeegebiets (Commander of Army Group L of C area, Commandant of Army

L of C Area), whose main task is to supervise the administration of the L of C so that the army group or army commander can concentrate exclusively on the course of operations.

2. The commander of army group L of C District has the additional charge over "Sicherungs" (L of C) units--specially organized divisions and regiments formed to undertake "mopping-up" operations in the rear of the combat zone. He is also in charge of such administrative Hq as may be set up within the area assigned to him, and of all guard units and supply organizations of the GHQ pool stationed within the area.

3. His functions, therefore, correspond very closely to those of the military commanders of occupied countries and on the close of active operations he may in fact remain as military commander over the country or portion of a country which he has hitherto commanded as an L of C District.

4. The functions of the army L of C area commander are less wide, and his status compares more closely with that of the area commander within an occupied country.

PART C--ORGANIZATIONS AND COMMANDERS

_____

CONTENTS

PART C

I INTRODUCTION

1. This Part consists of classified lists of German units from army groups down to divisions, with the names of their commander (where known) and particulars of their composition, followed by brief notes on the campaigns in which they have taken part.

2. In the case of divisions, units the number of which can be deduced with certainty are included, even though they may not yet have been identified. English instead of German terms are employed for the different types of unit--in both cases the departure from the principles adopted in the text, "Order of Battle of the German Army," is deliberate, in order to make this Part of greater utility to the reader who is not a specialist, and who wishes to see, at a glance, the composition of any particular German formation. The latter book will serve as an index to the various units which are given under their divisions only in the following lists.

3. It should be noted that the ages shown in brackets after the names of commanders are those reached in 1942.

4. A German task force is a military force composed of the necessary arms and services under one commander for the accomplishment of a definite mission. Standard German organizations, such as divisions, corps, and armies, are the frameworks around which task forces are formed. Thus, in almost every case, the composition of a German unit in combat will be different, particularly in the larger organizations from the divisions upwards. The German method of organization for combat may be illustrated by the following diagram.

5. It·must be emphasized that under the German system, command is extremely fluid and the Order of Battle of higher formations is liable to change from day to day during the course of active operations, in accordance with the needs of the immediate situation. Armies may be transferred from one army group to another, corps from army to army, divisions from corps to corps, and units of the GHQ pool from one formation to another. In particular, there is no standard equation such as "2 divisions=1 corps" or "2 corps=1 army."

II ARMY GROUPS (As constituted in June 1942)

1. Army Group Center
   Commander: Field Marshal Günther v. KLUGE (60)
   C of S:
   G-3:

2. Army Group A
   Commander: Field Marshal Wilhelm LIST (62)
   C of S:
   G-3:

3. <u>Army Group B (Stalingrad)</u>
   Commander: Field Marshal Fedor v. BOCK (62)
   C of S: General v. SODENSTERN (53)
   G-3:

4. <u>Army Group North</u>
   Commander: Field Marshal Georg v. KÜCHLER (61)
   C of S: General Kurt BRENNECKE (52)
   G-3:

5. <u>Army Group West</u>
   Commander: Field Marshal Gerd v. RUNDSTEDT (67)
   C of S: General Max v. VIEBAHN (54) (?)
   G-3:

III ARMIES (For PANZER ARMIES see Section IV)

First Army (A.O.K.1)

Commander: Col General Johannes BLASKOWITZ (59)
C of S:
G-3:
   Formed on mobilization. Took part in the Western campaign, and has
   subsequently remained in France.

Second Army

Commander: Col General Maximilian, Frhr. v. WEICHS (61)
C of S:
G-3:
   Formed on mobilization. Took part in the Polish, Western, and Balkan
   campaigns. In Russia since June 1941.

Third Army

(Formed on mobilization. Took part, under v. KÜCHLER, in the Polish
   campaign. Not identified since 1939, and probably disbanded.)

Fourth Army

Commander: Col General Richard RUOFF (57)
C of S:
G-3:
   Formed on mobilization. Took part in the Polish and Western campaigns.
   In Russia since June 1941.

Fifth Army

(Formed on mobilization, for service in the West during the Polish campaign. Not identified since 1939, and probably disbanded.)

Sixth Army

Commander: General Fr iedrich PAULUS (52)
C of S:
G-3:
   Formed early in 1940. Took part, under v. REICHENAU, in the Western campaign. In Russia since June 1941.

Seventh Army

Commander: Col Gen Friedrich DOLLMANN (60)
C of S: Lt Gen Eduard WAGNER (48) (?)
G-3:
   Formed on mobilization. Took part in the Western campaign, and has subsequently remained in France.

Eighth Army

(Formed on mobilization. Took part, under BLASKOWITZ, in the Polish campaign. Probably disbanded.)

Ninth Army

Commander: Col Gen Walter MODEL (51)
C of S:
G-3:
   Formed in spring, 1940. Took part in the Western campaign in Russia since June, 1941.

Tenth Army

(Formed on mobilization. Took part, under v. REICHENAU, in the Polish campaign. Not identified since 1939, and probably disbanded.)

Eleventh Army

Commander: Field Marshal Fritz Erich v. LEWINSKI gen. v.
                     MANSTEIN (55)
C of S:
G-3:
   Probably formed late in 1940. In Russia since June, 1941.

Twelfth Army

Commander:
C of S: Maj Gen Hermann FOERTSCH (47)
G-3:
  Probably formed in spring, 1940. Took part in the Western and Balkan
  campaigns, and has remained in the Balkans.

Fourteenth Army

(Formed on mobilization. Took part, under LIST, in the Polish campaign.
  Not identified since 1939, and probably disbanded.)

Fifteenth Army

Commander: Col Gen Curt HAASE (61)
C of S:
G-3:
  Probably formed late in 1940; in France thereafter.

Sixteenth Army

Commander: Col Gen Ernst BUSCH (57)
C of S:
G-3:
  Formed in spring, 1940. Took part in the Western campaign, and in
  Russia since June, 1941.

Seventeenth Army

Commander: Col Gen Hermann HOTH (58)
C of S:
G-3:
  Probably formed late in 1940. In Russia since June, 1941.

Eighteenth Army

Commander: General Georg LINDEMANN (58)
C of S:
G-3:
  Formed in spring, 1940. Took part in the Western campaign, and in
  Russia since June, 1941.

Army of Lapland (A.O.K. Lapland)

Commander: Col Gen Eduard DIETL (52)
C of S: Maj Gen BUSCHENHAGEN ( )
G-3:
  Formed in winter, 1941-1942, in North Finland, to control operations on

the Murmansk front.

Army of Norway (A.O.K. Norwegen)

Commander: Col Gen Nikolaus v. FALKENHORST (57)
C of S: Maj Gen Rudolf BAMLERI (47)
G-3:
    Formed on mobilization as XXI Inf Corps, taking part as such in the
    Polish campaign. As Gruppe XXI organized the conquest of Norway.
    Expanded to an army during summer, 1941. Until the formation of the
    Army of Lapland, it was responsible for German operations in Finland
    as well as for the control of Norway.

IV PANZER ARMIES

First Panzer Army (Pz. A.O.K.1)

Commander: Col Gen Edwald v. KLEIST (61)
C of S: Col ZEITZLER ( )
G-3:
    Formed on, or shortly before mobilization as XXII Inf Corps, taking
    part as such in the Polish campaign. Fought in the west as Gruppe
    Kleist; in the Balkans as Panzergruppe 1; and toward the end of 1941
    became First Panzer Army in Russia.

Second Panzer Army

Commander: Col Gen Rudolf SCHMIDT (56)
C of S: Col Kurt, Frhr. v. LIEBENSTEIN ( )
G-3:
    As XIX Mtz Corps, part (since May, 1939) of the peace-time standing
    army. Fought as such in the Polish campaign; in the West as Gruppe
    Guderian; and in the early stages of the campaign in Russia as Panzer-
    gruppe 2. Became Second Panzer Army at the close of 1941.

Third Panzer Army

Commander: Col Gen Georg Hans REINHARDT (55)
C of S: Maj Gen Julius v. BERNUTH (45)
G-3:
    As XV Mtz Corps part of the peace-time standing army. Fought as such
    in the Polish campaign; in the West as Gruppe Hoth; and in the early
    stages of the campaign in Russia as Panzergruppe 3. Became Third
    Panzer Army at the close of 1941.

Fourth Panzer Army

Commander: Col Gen Erich HOEPPNER (56)
C of S: Col CHALES de BEAULIEU (   )
G-3:
As XVI Mtz Corps part of the peace-time standing army. Fought as such
in Poland and in the West; and as Panzergruppe 4 in the early months
of the campaign in Russia. Became Fourth Panzer Army at the close
of 1941.

Panzer Army of Africa (Pz.A.O.K. Afrika)

Commander: Field Marshal Erwin ROMMEL (51)
C of S: Maj Gen GAUSE (49)
G-3:
Formed in June, 1941, as Panzergruppe Afrika to control the Africa
Corps and Italian formations in Cyrenaica. Became a Panzer army at
the close of 1941.

V INFANTRY CORPS

I Infantry Corps (I.A.K.)

Commander: General Philipp KLEFFEL (54)
C of S:
Home station: Königsberg (Wkr. I).
Part of the peace-time standing army.
Campaigns: Polish, Western, Russian.

II Infantry Corps

Commander: General Walter, Graf v. BROCKDORFF-AHLEFELDT (55)
C of S: Col SCHMIDT-RICHBERG (   )
Home station: Stettin (Wkr. I I)
Part of the peace-time standing army.
Campaigns: Polish, Western, Russian.

III Infantry Corps--see III Pz. Corps (Section VI)

IV Infantry Corps

Commander: General Viktor v. SCHWELDER (57)
C of S: Col Otto BEUTLER (   )
Home station: Dresden (Wkr. IV)
Part of the peace-time standing army.
Campaigns: Polish, Western, Russian.

V Infantry Corps

Commander:
C of S:
Home station: Stuttgart (Wkr. V)
  Part of the peace-time standing army.
  Campaigns: Western, Russian.

VI Infantry Corps

Commander: General Otto FÖRSTER (57)
C of S:
Home station: Münster (Wkr. VI)
  Part of the peace-time standing army.
  Campaigns: Western, Russian.

VII Infantry Corps

Commander:
C of S:
Home station: Munich (Wkr. VII)
  Part of the peace-time standing army.
  Campaigns: Polish, Western, Russian.

VIII Infantry Corps

Commander: **General Walter HEITZ** (64)
C of S:
Home station: Breslau (Wkr. VIII)
  Part of the peace-time standing army.
  Campaigns: Polish, Western, Russian.

IX Infantry Corps

Commander: General Hermann GEYER (60)
C of S: Col GRIMMELS (   )
Home station: Kassel (Wkr. IX)
  Part of the peace-time standing army.
  Campaigns: Western, Russian.

X Infantry Corps

Commander: General Christian HANSEN (57)
C of S:
Home station: Hamburg (Wkr. X)
  Part of the peace-time standing army.
  Campaigns: Polish, Western, Russian.

XI Infantry Corps

Commander: General Joachim v. KORTZFELEISCH (52)
C of S:
Home station: Hannover (Wkr. XI)
  Part of the peace-time standing army.
  Campaigns: Polish, Western, Russian.

XII Infantry Corps

Commander: General Walther SCHROTH (56)
C of S:
Home station: Wiesbaden (Wkr. XII)
  Part of the peace-time standing army.
  Campaigns: Western, Russian.

XIII Infantry Corps

Commander: General Hans FELBER (54)
C of S:
Home station: Nuremburg (Wkr. XIII)
  Part of the peace-time standing army.
  Campaigns: Polish, Western, Russian.

XIV Corps--see XIV Pz. Corps (Section VI)
XV Corps--see Third Panzer Army (Section IV)
XVI Corps--see Fourth Panzer Army (Section IV)

XVII Infantry Corps

Commander: General Werner KIENITZ (57)
C of S:
Home station: Vienna (Wkr. XVII)
  Part of the peace-time standing army, since April, 1938.
  Campaigns: Polish, Western, Russian.

XVIII Corps--See XVIII Mtn Corps (Section III)

XIX Corps--See Second Panzer Army (Section IV)

XX Infantry Corps

Commander:
C of S:
Home station: Danzig (Wkr. XX)
  Formed shortly before mobilization.
  Campaigns: Polish, Russian.

XXI Infantry Corps--see Army of Norway (Section III)
XXII Infantry Corps--see First Panzer Army (Section IV)

XXIII Infantry Corps

Commander: General Albrecht SCHUBERT (56)
C of S:
Home station: Bonn (Wkr. VI)
  Part of the peace-time standing army (as "Eifel Frontier Corps").
  Campaigns: Western, Russian.

XXIV Infantry Corps--see **XXIV** Pz Corps (Section VI)

XXV Infantry Corps

Commander:
C of S:
Home station: Baden-Baden (Wkr. V)
  Part of the peace-time standing army (as "Upper Rhine Frontier Corps").
  Campaign: Western.

XXVI Infantry Corps

Commander: General Albert WODRIG (59)
C of S:
Home station: (Wkr. I)
  Formed on mobilization.
  Campaigns: Polish, Western, Russian.

XXVII Infantry Corps

Commander: General Alfred WÄGER (59)
C of S:
Home station: (Wkr. VII)
  Formed on mobilization.
  Campaigns: Western, Russian.

XXVIII Infantry Corps

Commander: General Friedrich MATERNA (57)
C of S:
Home station: (Wkr. III)
  Formed in early summer 1940.
  Campaign: Russian.

XXIX Infantry Corps

Commander: General Hans v. OBSTFELDER (56)
C of S:
Home station: (Wkr. IV)
  Formed in early summer of 1940.
  Campaign: Russian.

XXX Infantry Corps

Commander: General Maximilian FRETTER-PICO (51)
C of S:
Home station: (Wkr. XI)
  Formed on mobilization.
  Campaigns: Polish, Western, Balkan, Russian.

XXXI-XXXVII Corps

See XXXI-XXXVII Corps (Commands) (Section VIII)

XXXVIII Infantry Corps

Commander:
C of S:
Home station: (Wkr. VIII?)
  Formed on mobilization.
  Campaigns: Polish, Western, Russian.

XXXIX-XXXXI Corps

See XXXIX-XXXXI Pz Corps (Section VI)

XXXXII Infantry Corps

Commander: General Bruno BIELER (53)
C of S:
Home station: (Wkr. III)
  Formed on mobilization.
  Campaigns: Polish, Western, Russian.

XXXXIII Infantry Corps

Commander:
C of S: Col Otto SCHULZ ( )
Home station: Hannover (Wkr. XI)
  Formed in early summer of 1940.
  Campaigns: Western, Russian.

XXXXIV Infantry Corps

Commander:
C of S:
Home station: Dresden (Wkr. IV)
  Formed in early summer of 1940.
  Campaigns: Western, Russian.

XXXXV Corps

See XXXXV Corps (Command)(Section VIII)

XXXXVI-XXXXVIII Corps

See XXXXVI-XXXXVIII Pz Corps (Section VI)

XXXXIX Corps

See XXXXIX Mtn Corps (Section VII)

L Infantry Corps

Commander: General Herbert v. BOCKMANN (55)
C of S:
Home station: (Wkr. V)
  Formed late in 1940.
  Campaigns: Balkan, Russian.

LI Infantry Corps

Commander: General Hans REINHARD (54)
C of S:
Home station: (Wkr. XI)
  Formed late in 1940.
  Campaigns: Balkan, Russian.

LII Infantry Corps

Commander:
C of S:
Home station: (Wkr. III)
  Formed late in 1940.
  Campaign: Russian.

LIII Infantry Corps

Commander: General Erich CLÖSSNER (56)
C of S: Col BORK ( )
Home station: (Wkr. XII)
  Formed late in 1940.
  Campaign: Russian.

LIV Infantry Corps

Commander: General Erik HANSEN (53)
C of S:
Home station:

Formed as a corps command in 1940, and became a field unit in the
spring of 1941.
Campaign: Russian.

LV Infantry Corps

Commander: General Erwin VIEROW (53)
C of S:
Home station:
Probably formed in the spring of 1941.
Campaign: Russian.

LVI-LVII Corps

See LVI-LVII Pz Corps (Section VI)

LVIII Infantry Corps--not yet reported

LIX Infantry Corps

Commander: General Kurt v. d. CHEVALLERIE (51)
C of S:
Home station:
Probably formed in the spring of 1941.
Campaign: Russian.

LX-LXXI Corps

See LX-LXXI Corps (Commands) (Section VIII)

VI PANZER CORPS

III Panzer Corps (III Pz.K.)

Commander: General Eberhard v. MACKENSEN (53)
C of S:
Home station: Berlin (Wkr. III)
Part of the peace-time standing army.
Campaigns: Polish and Western (as III Inf Corps), Russian.

XIV Panzer Corps

Commander: General Gustav v. WIETERSHEIM (58)
C of S:
Home station: Magdeburg (Wkr. XI)
Part of the peace-time standing army.
Campaigns: Polish and Western (as XIV Mtz Corps), Balkan, Russian.

XXIV Panzer Corps

Commander: General Leo, Frhr. GEYR v. SCHWEPPENBURG (56)
C of S:
Home station: Kaiserslautern (Wkr. XII)
   Part of the peace-time standing army (as "Saar-Palatinate Frontier
   Corps").
   Campaigns: Polish and Western (as XXIV Inf Corps), Russian.

XXXIX Panzer Corps

Commander: General Josef HARPE (52) (?)
C of S:
Home station: (Wkr. IX)
   Formed late in 1939.
   Campaigns: Western, Russian.

XXXX Panzer Corps

Commander: General Georg STUMME (56)
C of S: Lt Col HESSE ( )
Home station: (Wkr. X)
   Formed late in 1939.
   Campaigns: Western, Balkan, Russian.

XXXXI Panzer Corps

Commander: General Friedrich KIRCHNER (57)
C of S:
Home station:
   Formed late in 1939.
   Campaigns: Western, Balkan, Russian.

XXXXVI Panzer Corps

Commander: General Heinrich v. VIETINGHOFF gen SCHEEL (55)
C of S:
Home station: (Wkr. X)
   Formed in early summer, 1940.
   Campaigns: Balkan, Russian.

XXXXVII Panzer Corps

Commander: General LEMELSEN (54).
 C of S:
Home station: Danzig (Wkr. XX)
   Formed in early summer, 1940.
   Campaign: Russian.

XXXXVIII Panzer Corps

Commander: General Weiner KEMPF (55)
C of S:
Home station: Posen (Wkr. XXI)
  Formed in early summer, 1940.
  Campaign: Russian.

LVI Panzer Corps

Commander: General Frhr. v. LANGERMANN v. ERLENCAMP (52) (?)
C of S:
Home station: (Wkr. VI)
  Formed late in 1940.
  Campaign: Russian.

LVII Panzer Corps

Commander: General Adolf KUNTZEN (53)
C of S:
Home station: (Wkr. II)
  Formed late in 1940.
  Campaign: Russian.

Africa Panzer Corps (Pz. K. Afrika)

Commander: General Walter NEHRING (50)
C of S: Colonel BAYERLEIN (   )
Home station: Berlin (Wkr. III)
  Formed (as the German Africa Corps) in the spring of 1941.
  Campaigns: Libya and Egypt.

VII MOUNTAIN CORPS

XVIII Mountain Corps (XVIII Geb. K.)

Commander: General Franz BÖHME (57)
C of S:
Home stations: Salzburg (Wkr. XVIII)
  Part of the peace-time standing army since April, 1938.
  Campaigns: Polish, Western, Balkan.

XXXXIX Mountain Corps

Commander: General Rudolf KONRAD (51)
C of S:
Home station: Prague (Protectorate).
  Formed in early summer, 1940.
  Campaigns: Balkan, Russian.

Norway Mountain Corps (Geb. K. Norwegen)

Commander: General Ferdinand SCHÖRNER (48)
C of S:
Home station:
  Formed in summer, 1940, in North Norway.
  Campaigns: Murmansk front.

VIII CORPS COMMANDS*

XXXI Corps Command (Höh. Kdo. z. b. V. XXXI)

Commander:
C of S:
Home station: (Wkr. X?)
  Probably formed shortly after mobilization.
  In Denmark since April, 1940.

XXXII Corps Command

Commander:
C of S:
Home station:
  Probably formed shortly after mobilization.
  In France.

XXXIII Corps Command

Commander:
C of S:
Home station: (Wkr. VI)
  Probably formed shortly after mobilization.
  In Norway since summer, 1940.

XXXIV Corps Command

Commander:
C of S:
Home station: (Wkr. III)
  Probably formed shortly after mobilization.
  In Poland from late in 1939, until June, 1941; thereafter operating as an
    infantry corps in Russia.

---

*These are special task forces for defensive missions usually in occupied areas.
While not composed of a high percentage of offensive combat arms, they can
give a good account of themselves in battle. In some cases, they have been used
for offensive missions.

XXXV Corps Command

Commander: General Rudolf KAEMPFE (59)
C of S:
Home station: (Wkr. VIII)
  Probably formed shortly after mobilization.
  In Poland from late in 1939 until June, 1941; thereafter operating as an
  infantry corps in Russia.

XXXVI Corps Command

Commander:
C of S:
Home station: (Wkr. II)
  Probably formed shortly after mobilization.
In Norway from summer, 1940, until June, 1941; thereafter operating as
  an infantry corps in North Finland.

XXXVII Corps Command

Commander:
C of S:
Home station: Vienna (Wkr. XVII)
  Probably formed shortly after mobilization.
  In France.

XXXXV Corps Command

Commander:
C of S:
Home station: (Wkr. XIII).
  Probably formed early in 1940.
  In France.

LX Corps Command

Commander:
C of S:
Home station:
  Probably formed late in 1940.
  In France.

LXIII Corps Command

Commander:
C of S:
Home station:
  Probably formed late in 1940.
  Present whereabouts unknown.

LXIV Corps Command

Commander:
C of S:
Home station:
  Date of formation uncertain.
  Present whereabouts unknown.

LXV Corps Command

Commander:
C of S:
Home station: (Wkr. II)
  Probably formed early in 1941.
  In Serbia since May, 1941.

LXVII Corps Command

Commander:
C of S:
Home station:
  Date of formation uncertain.
  Present whereabouts unknown.

LXX Corps Command

Commander:
C of S:
Home station:
  Formed in Norway in autumn, 1941.
  In South Norway.

LXXI Corps Command

Commander:
C of S:
Home station:
  Formed in Norway in spring, 1942.
  In North Norway.

IX PANZER DIVISIONS

1st Panzer Division (1 Pz. D.)

Commander: Maj Gen Walter KRÜGER (51)
Composition: 1st Tank Regt , 1st Mtz Inf Brig (1st Mtz Inf Regt , 113th Mtz Inf
Regt, 1st Mtrcl Bn), 73d Arty Regt, Pz Arty Obsn Btry, 4th Pz
Rcn Bn, 37th AT Bn, 37th Pz Engr Bn, 37th Pz Sig Bn

Auxiliary unit number*: 81
Home station: Weimar (Wkr.IX)
    Active division: Personnel from Thuringia and Saxony with draftees from
other parts of Germany. Fought well in Central Poland and Throughout the operations of May-June, 1940. Continuously engaged in Russia, at first in the
North and subsequently in the Center. Suffered considerable losses in the autumn of 1941.

2d Panzer Division

Commander:
Composition: 3d Tank Regt, 2d Mtz Inf Brig, (2d Mtz Inf Regt, 304th Mtz Inf
Regt, 2d Mtrcl Bn); 74th Arty Regt, 320th Pz Arty Obsn
Btry, 5th Pz Rcn Bn, 38th AT Bn, 38th Pz Engr Bn,38th Pz Sig
Bn

Auxiliary unit number: 82
Home Station: Vienna (Wkr. XVII)
    Active division: Personnel Austrian, with considerable number of draftees
from different parts of Germany. Suffered heavy losses in S Poland. Not so
consipicuous as the other armored divisions during the operations in France.
Fought in the Balkan campaign and has been engaged in Russia with the Center
Group since September, 1941.

3d Panzer Division

Commander: Maj Gen Hermann BREITH (49)
Composition: 6th Tank Regt, 3d Mtz Inf Brig (3d Mtz Inf Regt, 394th Mtz Inf
Regt, 3d Mtrcl Bn); 75th Arty Regt, 327th Pz Arty Obsn Btry, Pz
Rcn Bn, AT Bn, 39th Pz Engr Bn, 39th Pz Sig Bn

Auxiliary unit number: 83
Home Station: Berlin (Wkr. III)

    Active divisions: Personnel mainly Prussian. Fought well in Poland and in
Belgium and France. Continuously engaged in Russia since the outset of the
campaign, first in the Central and subsequently in the Southern Sector.

---

    * This is the number carried by the auxiliary units such as the med bn,
vet co, and other services.

4th Panzer Division

Commander:

Composition: 35th Tank Regt, 4th Mtz Inf Brig (12th Mtz Inf Regt, 33d Mtz Inf Regt,
34th Mtrcl Bn), 103d Arty Regt, 324th Pz Arty Obsn Btry, 7th Pz
Rcn Bn, 49th AT Bn, 79th Pz Engr Bn, 79th Pz Sig Bn

Auxiliary unit number: 84

Home station: Würzburg (Wkr. XIII)

Active division: Personnel Bavarian, with draftees from other parts of
Germany. Suffered heavy losses in Poland; had much hard fighting to do in
Belgium and France. Continuously engaged in the Russian campaign in the
Center Group.

5th Panzer Division

Commander:

Composition: 31st Tank Regt, 5th Mtz Inf Brig (13th Mtz Inf Regt, 14th Mtz Inf
Regt, 55th Mtrcl Bn); 116th Arty Regt, Pz Arty obsn Btry, 8th Pz
Rcn Bn, 53d AT Bn, 89th Pz Engr Bn, 77th Pz Sig Bn

Auxiliary unit number: 85

Home station: Oppeln (Wkr. VIII)

Active division (formed late in 1938): Personnel mainly Silesian or
Sudeten German. Inconspicuous in Poland, but prominent in the Battle of France,
where it shared with 7th Panzer Division in the advance on Le Havre. Took part
in the Balkan campaign, both in Yugoslavia and Greece, and has been continuously engaged in Russia with the Center Group.

6th Panzer Division

Commander:

Composition: 11th Tank Regt, 6th Mtz Inf Brig (4th Mtz Inf Regt, 114th Mtz
Inf Regt, 6th Mtrcl Bn), 76th Arty Regt, Pz Arty Obsn Btry, 57th Pz
Rcn Bn, 41st AT Bn, 57th Pz Engr Bn, 82d Pz Sig Bn

Auxiliary unit number: 57

Home station: Wuppertal (Wkr. VI)

Active division (formerly 1st Light Div): Personnel mainly Westphalian.
Fought hard and suffered corresponding losses, in Poland and in France Has
been continuously engaged in the Russian campaign, first in the North and later
in the Center Group, where it apparently suffered serious losses. Transferred

to France for rest and refit in May, 1942.

7th Panzer Division

Commander: Maj Gen Hans Frhr. v. FUNCK (47)

Composition: 25th Tank Regt, 7th Mtz Inf Brig (6th Mtz Inf Regt, 7th Mtz Inf Regt, 7th Mtrcl Bn); 78th Arty Regt, 325th Pz Arty Mtrcl Obsn Btry, 37th Pz Rcn Bn, 42d AT Bn, 58th Pz Engr Bn, 83d Pz Sig Bn

Auxiliary unit number: 58

Home station: Gera (Wkr. IX)

Active division (formerly 2d Light Div). Personnel mainly Thuringian or Saxon. Fought in Poland and with outstanding dash in France, where it was mainly responsible for the successful advance to Le Havre. During these operations it was commanded by Maj Gen Rommel. Continuously engaged in Russia, in the Center Group, where it appears to have sustained appreciable casualties. Transferred to France for rest and refit in May, 1942.

8th Panzer Division

Commander: Maj Gen Erich BRANDENBERGER (49)

Composition: 10th Tank Regt, 8 Mtz Inf Brig (8th Mtz Inf Regt, 9th Mtz Inf Regt, 8th Mtrcl Bn); 80th Arty Regt, Pz Arty Obsn Btry, 59th Pz Rcn Bn, 43d AT Bn, 59th Pz Engr Bn, 59th Pz Sig Bn

Auxiliary unit number: 59

Home Station: Cottbus (Wkr. III)

Active division (formerly 3d Light Div). Personnel mainly Prussian. Fought well in Poland and in France. In Yugoslavia during the Balkan campaign, but no evidence that it took any particular part in the operations. Continuously and heavily engaged on the Northern Russian front up to the end of 1941.

9th Panzer Division

Commander: Lt Gen Dr. Alfred HUBICKI (55)

Composition: 33d Tank Regt, 9th Mtz Inf Brig (10th Mtz Inf Regt, 11th Mtz Inf Regt, 9th Mtrcl Bn); 102d Arty Regt, Pz Arty Obsn Btry, 9th Pz Rcn Bn, 50th AT Bn, 86th Pz Engr Bn, 81st Pz Sig Bn

Auxiliary unit number: 49

Home station: Vienna (Wkr. XVII)

Active division (formerly 4th Light Div). Personnel Austrian, with draftees from other parts of Germany. Fought well and suffered heavy casualties in Poland. Continuously engaged throughout the operations in the West, covering a greater distance than any other armored division. Took part in the Balkan campaign, both in Yugoslavia and Greece, and was continuously engaged in Russia during the advance through the Ukraine.

10th Panzer Division

Commander: Maj Gen Wolfgang FISCHER (51)

Composition: 7th Tank Regt, 10th Mtz Inf Brig (69th Mtz Inf Regt, 86th Mtz Inf Regt, 10th Mtrcl Bn); 90th Arty Regt, Pz Arty Obsn Btry, 90th Pz Rcn Bn, 90th AT Bn, Pz Engr Bn, 90th Pz Sig Bn

Auxiliary unit number: 90

Home station: Stuttgart (Wkr. V)

Composite division, made up of active units from various parts of Germany. Fought well in Poland. Spearhead in the breakthrough at Sedan, taking only a minor part in subsequent operations. Believed to have suffered considerable casualties. Heavily engaged in the Russian campaign in the Center Group up to the end of 1941. Transferred to France for rest and refit in May, 1942.

11th Panzer Division

Commander: Maj Gen Günther ANGERN (50)

Composition: 15th Tank Regt, 11th Mtz Inf Brig (110th Mtz Inf Regt, 111th Mtz Inf Regt, 61st Mtrcl Bn); 119th Arty Regt; Pz Arty Obsn Btry, 231st Pz Rcn Bn, AT Bn, Pz Engr Bn, 85? Pz Sig Bn

Auxiliary unit number: 61?

Home station: Görlitz (Wkr. VIII)

Formation completed after the Battle of France during which the 11th Inf Brig (Mtz) fought and distinguished itself as an independent command. Took part in the Balkan campaign. Has been continuously engaged in Russia, first of all in the advance through the Ukraine and subsequently in the Center Group.

12th Panzer Division

Commander:

Composition: 29th Tank Regt, 12th Mtz Inf Brig, (5th Mtz Inf Regt, 25th Mtz Inf Regt, 22d Mtrcl Bn) 2d Arty Regt, Pz Arty Obsn Btry, 2d Pz Rcn Bn, 2d AT Bn, 32d Pz Engr Bn, 2d Pz Sig Bn

Auxiliary unit number: 2

Home station: Stettin (Wkr. II)

Originally 2d Motorized Division, belonging to the peace-time army, with mainly Prussian personnel. As such saw little fighting in Poland, but was actively engaged in France. Reorganized as 12th Panzer Division in the autumn of 1940. Was continuously engaged in Russia, first in the Center Group and subsequently in the North, up to the end of 1941 when after sustaining considerable losses, it was withdrawn to Estonia for rest and refit.

13th Panzer Division

Commander:

Composition: 4th Tank Regt, 13th Mtz Inf Brig (66th Mtz Inf Regt, 93d Mtz Inf Regt, 43d Mtrcl Bn); 13th Arty Regt, Pz Arty Obsn Btry, 13th Pz Rcn Bn, 13th AT Bn, 4th Pz Engr Bn, 13th Pz Sig Bn

Auxiliary unit number: 13

Home station: Magdeburg (Wkr. XI)

Formed in the autumn of 1940 out of the former 13th Motorized Division, which had fought with great distinction in Poland and in France. Passed the winter of 1940-41 in Roumania. Continuously engaged on the Southern Russian front, where it took part in the encirclement of Kiev.

14th Panzer Division

Commander: Maj Gen Friedrich KÜHN (52)

Composition: 36th Tank Regt, 14th Mtz Inf Brig (103d Mtz Inf Regt, 108th Mtz Inf Regt, 64th Mtrcl Bn); 4th Arty Regt, Pz Arty Obsn Btry, 40th Pz Rcn Bn, 4th AT Bn, 13th Pz Engr Bn, 4th Pz Sig Bn

Auxiliary unit number: 4

Home station: Dresden (Wkr. IV)

Originally 4th Infantry Division, belonging to the peace-time army, with personnel from Saxony and Sudetenland. As such fought well in Poland and in the Battle of France and was reorganized as 14th Panzer Division in the late summer of 1940. Fought in Yugoslavia in the Balkan campaign and has been continuously engaged on the Southern Russian front, where it appears to have suffered serious losses.

15th Panzer Division

Commander: Maj Gen Gustav v. VAERST (49)

Composition: 8th Tank Regt, 115th Mtz Inf Regt, 33d Arty Regt, 33d Pz Rcn Bn, 33 AT Bn, 33d Pz Engr Bn, 78th Pz Sig Bn

Auxiliary unit number: 33

Home station: Kaiserslautern (Wkr. XII)

Originally 33d Infantry Division, belonging to the peace-time army, with Bavarian personnel from the Palatinate. As such, was on the Ardennes front in January, 1939, and fought well during the Battle of France. Reorganized as 15th Panzer Division in the autumn of 1940. Transferred to Libya in the spring of 1941.

16th Panzer Division

Commander: Lt Gen Hans HUBE (52)

Composition: 2d Tank Regt, 16th Mtz Inf Brig (64th Mtz Inf Regt, 79th Mtz Inf Regt, 16th Mtrcl Bn); 16th Arty Regt, Pz Arty Obsn Btry, 16th Pz Rcn Bn, 16th AT Bn, 16th Pz Engr Bn, 16th Pz Sig Bn

Auxiliary unit number: 16

Home station: Münster (Wkr. VI)

Originally, 16th Infantry Division belonging to the peace-time army with personnel from Westphalia, and some E. Prussians. As such, was on the Saar front for a period, and later took part in the attack on Sedan in support of armored formations. Reorganized as 16th Panzer Division in the late summer of 1940. First identified in action during the early weeks of the Russian campaign and has since been continuously engaged on the Southern front.

17th Panzer Division

Commander: Maj Gen Wilhelm Ritter v. THOMA (50)

Composition: 17th Tank Regt, 17th Mtz Inf Brig (40th Mtz Inf Regt, 63d Mtz Inf Regt, 17th Mtrcl Bn); 27th Arty Regt, Pz Arty Obsn Btry; 27th Pz Rcn Bn, 27th AT Bn, 27th Pz Engr Bn, 27th Pz Sig Bn

Auxiliary unit number: 27

Home station: Augsburg (Wkr. VII)

Originally 27th Infantry Division, belonging to the peace-time army, with Bavarian personnel. As such, fought and marched extremely well, both in Poland and in France, and proved a good fighting division during these operations.

Reorganized as 17th Panzer Division in the autumn of 1940. First identified in
action on the Central Russian front in late June, 1941, and since that time has
been continuously in action. Suffered considerable casualties during autumn, 1941

18th Panzer Division

Commander:

Composition: 18th Tank Regt, 18th Mtz Inf Brig (52d Mtz Inf Regt, 101st Mtz Inf
Regt, 18th Mtrcl Bn); 88th Arty Regt, Pz Arty Obsn Btry, 88th Pz
Rcn Bn, 88th AT Bn, 98th Pz Engr Bn, 88th Pz Sig Bn

Auxiliary unit number: 88

Home station: (Wkr. IV)

Formed in the autumn of 1940. First identified in action on the Central
Russian front in late June, 1941. Continuously in action since that time.

19th Panzer Division

Commander: Lt Gen v. KNOBELSDORFF (54)

Composition: 27th Tank Regt, 19th Mtz Inf Brig (73d Mtz Inf Regt, 74th Mtz Inf Regt
19th Mtrcl Bn); 19th Arty Regt, Pz Arty Obsn Btry, 19th Pz Rcn
Bn, 19th AT Bn, 19th Pz Engr Bn, 19th Pz Sig Bn

Auxiliary unit number: 19

Home station: Hannover (Wkr. XI)

Originally 19th Infantry Division, belonging to the peace-time army, and recruited mainly in Hannover area. As such, fought well and suffered heavy
casualties in the Battle of the Bzura, and fought well against the BEF in Bel-
guim. Not identified during the Battle of France and was reorganized as 19th
Panzer Division in the autumn of 1940. Took part in the attack on Russia, where
it operated with the Center Group and was involved in heavy fighting during the
autumn of 1941.

20th Panzer Division

Commander: Lt Gen Horst STUMPFF (54)

Composition: 21st Tank Regt, 20th Mtz Inf Brig (59th Mtz Inf Regt, 112th Mtz Inf
Regt, 20th Mtrcl Bn); 92d Arty Regt, 335th Pz Arty Obsn Btry,
92d Pz Rcn Bn. 92d AT Bn, 92d Pz Engr Bn, 92 Pz Sig Bn.

Auxiliary unit number: 92

Home station: Gotha (Wkr. IX)

Formed in the autumn of 1940. First identified in action on the Central Russian front at the outset of the campaign, where it has been continuously engaged. Suffered heavy casualties, both at Vitebsk and during the final attempt on Moscow.

21st Panzer Division

Commander:

Composition: 5th Tank Regt, 104th Mtz Inf Regt; 155th Arty Regt, 3d Pz Rcn Bn, 39th AT Bn, 200th Pz Engr Bn, 200 Pz Sig Bn

Auxiliary unit number: 200

Home Station: Berlin (Wkr. III)

At first known as 5th Light Division (Mtz). Formed after the Battle of France partly from former 3d Panzer Division. Reorganized as a Panzer Division in Africa during the summer, 1941.

22d Panzer Division

Commander: Maj Gen Wilhelm v. APELL (49)

Composition: 204th Tank Regt, 22d Mtz Inf Brig (129th Mtz Inf Regt, 140th Mtz Inf Regt, 24th Mtrcl Bn); 140th Arty Regt, Pz Arty Obsn Btry, Pz Rcn Bn, AT Bn, 140th Pz Engr Bn, 140th Pz Sig Bn

Auxiliary unit number: 140

Home Station:

Formed in France in October, 1940. Transferred to Russia (Southern Front) early in 1942, and thrown immediately into action, when it suffered heavy casualties.

23d Panzer Division

Commander: Maj Gen Wilhelm Frhr. v. BOINEBURG-LENGSFELD (53)

Composition: 201st Tank Regt, 23d Mtz Inf Brig (126th Mtz Inf Regt, 128th Mtz Inf Regt, 23d Mtrcl Bn); 128th Arty Regt, Pz Arty Obsn Btry, Pz Rcn Bn, AT Bn, 128th Pz Engr Bn, 128th Pz Sig Bn

Auxiliary unit number: 128

Home Station: (Wkr. XII)

Formed in France in October, 1940. Transferred to Russia in the spring of 1942, and identified in action in Kharkov area.

24th Panzer Division

Commander: Maj Gen Ritter v. HAUENSCHILD (48)

Composition: Tank Regt, 24th Mtz Inf Brig (Mtz Inf Regt, Mtz Inf Regt, Mtrcl Bn), Arty Regt, Pz Arty Obsn Btry, Pz Rcn Bn, At Bn, Pz Engr Bn, Pz Sig Bn

Auxiliary unit number:

Home Station: (Wkr. I)

Formed in France in February, 1942, largely from the former 1st Cav Div , which had fought as a brigade in Poland and as a division in France and the Russian campaign. Not yet identified in action.

25th Panzer Division

Commander: Lt Gen HAARDE (53)

Composition: Tank Regt, 25th Mtz Inf Brig (Mtz Inf Regt,   Mtz Inf Regt, Mtrcl Bn); Arty Regt, Pz Arty Obsn Btry, Pz Rcn Bn,   AT Bn, Pz Engr Bn, Pz Sig Bn

Auxiliary unit number:

Home Station:

Formed in France early in 1942. Not yet identified in action.

X MOTORIZED DIVISIONS

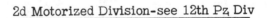

2d Motorized Division-see 12th Pz Div

3d Motorized Division (3d J.D. (mot)

Commander:
Composition: 8th Inf Regt, 29th Inf Regt, 3d Arty Regt, 53 Pz Rcn Bn, 3d AT Bn, 3d Engr Bn (Mtz), 3 Sig Bn (Mtz)
Auxiliary unit number: 3
Home station: Frankfurt/Oder (Wkr. III)
Originally 3d Inf Div, an active division mainly recruited in Prussia. As such it took part in the Polish campaign and the Battle of France, without winning any special distinction. Motorized in autumn, 1940. Fought in Russia from the

beginning. Last identified in the Center Group.

10th Motorized Division

Commander:
Composition: 20th Inf Regt, 41st Inf Regt, 10th Arty Regt,
             10th Pz Rcn Bn, 10th AT Bn, 10th Engr Bn (Mtz) 10th Sig Bn (Mtz)
Auxiliary unit number: 10
Home station: Regensburg (Wkr. XIII)
   Originally 10th Inf Div, an active division with personnel from N Bavaria and
W Sudetenland. As such, it was actively engaged in Poland, less so in France.
Motorized in autumn, 1940. Fought in the Balkan campaign. Operated in Russia
with the Center Group from the beginning. Sustained heavy casualties.

13th Motorized Division - see 13th Pz. Div.

14th Motorized Division

Commander: Maj Gen Friedrich FÜRST (52)
Composition: 11th Inf Regt, 53d Inf Regt, 14th Arty Regt, 14th Pz
             Rcn Bn, 14th AT Bn, 14th Engr Bn (Mtz),
             14th Sig Bn, (Mtz)
Auxiliary unit number: 14
Home station: Leipzig (Wkr. IV)
   As 14th Inf Div, a Saxon division belonging to the peace-time army, it took
part in the campaigns in Poland and France, without winning special distinction.
Motorized in autumn, 1940. Identified early in the Russian campaign in the
battle for Vitebsk. Since then, continuously in action with the Center Group.

16th Motorized Division

Commander:
Composition: 60th Inf Regt, 156th Inf Regt, 146th Arty Regt,
             341st Pz Rcn Bn, AT Bn, 146th Engr Bn (Mtz), Sig Bn (Mtz)
Auxiliary unit number: 146
Home station: Rheine (Wkr. VI)
   Formed in late summer, 1940, from elements of the 16th Inf Div. An active
division with personnel mainly Westphalian but partly Prussian. On the Saar
front for a period and later took part in the attack on Sedan in support of Panzer units. Engaged in the Balkan campaign and later in the Ukraine. Has since
remained with the Southern Group.

18th Motorized Division

Commander: Maj Gen Werner v. ERDMANNSDORF (50)
Composition: 30th Inf Regt, 51st Inf Regt, 18th Arty Regt, 18th Pz
             Rcn Bn, 18th AT Bn, 18th Engr Bn (Mtz), 18th Sig Bn (Mtz)
Auxiliary unit number: 18
Home station: Liegnitz (Wkr. VIII)
   Formerly 18th Inf Div, an active division with Silesian personnel. As such,
it fought in Poland and in North France, winning distinction and sustaining con-

siderable casualties. Motorized in autumn, 1940. Fought in Russia since the beginning of the campaign, first in the Center and later in the Northern Group.

20th Motorized Division

Commander:
Composition: 76th Inf Regt, 90th Inf Regt. 20th Arty Regt, 20th Pz
Rcn Bn, 20th AT Bn, 20th Engr Bn (Mtz), 20th Sig Bn (Mtz)
Auxiliary unit number: 20
Home station: Hamburg (Wkr. X)
  Active division. Recruited mainly in Hamburg. Fought hard and well in Poland. In France it covered great distances but saw less action. Morale very high. First identified in Russia in the Minsk area, and later with the Northern Group. Many reports of heavy casualties.

25th Motorized Division

Commander: Lt Gen Sigfrid HEINRICI (54)
Composition: 35th Inf Regt, 119th Inf Regt, 25th Arty Regt, 25th Pz
Rcn Bn, 25th AT Bn, 25th Engr Bn (Mtz), 25th Sig Bn (Mtz)
Auxiliary unit number: 25
Home station: Ludwigsburg (Wkr.V)
  Originally 25th Infantry Division, an active division recruited in Württemberg, which took little part in active operations. Motorized in autumn, 1940. Has fought in the Center Group since the beginning of the Russian Campaign.

29th Motorized Division

Commander: Maj. Gen. Walter v. BOLTENSTERN (51)
Composition: 15th Inf Regt, 71st Inf Regt, 29th Arty Regt, 29th Pz Rcn Bn, 29th
AT Bn, 29th Engr Bn (Mtz), 29th Sig Bn (Mtz)

Auxiliary unit number: 29
Home station: Erfurt (Wkr. IX)
  Active division. Personnel mainly Thuringian, with draftees from other parts of Germany. Moved great distances and fought hard in Poland and France. Identified at Smolensk in July, 1941. Has remained in the Center Group, without achieving any particular success.

36th Motorized Division

Commander: Maj Gen GOLLNICK (50)
Composition: 87th Inf Regt, 118th Inf Regt, 36th Arty Regt, 36th Pz Rcn
Bn, 36th AT Bn, 36th Engr Bn (Mtz), 36th Sig Bn (Mtz)
Auxiliary unit number: 36
Home Station: Wiesbaden (Wkr. XII)
  As 36th Infantry Division (peace-time army: personnel mainly Bavarian from the Palatinate) it earned some distinction in France, but without a great deal of fighting. Motorized in the autumn of 1940. Entered Russia via the Baltic States

and first underwent heavy fighting at Kalinin in October, 1941, when severe casualties were reported. Engaged in further heavy fighting during the winter.

60th Motorized Division

Commander: Lt Gen EBERHARDT (51)
Composition: 92d Inf Regt, 120th Inf Regt, 160th Arty Regt, 160th Pz Rcn Bn,
　　　　　　160th AT Bn, 160th Engr Bn (Mtz), 160th Sig Bn (Mtz)
Auxiliary unit number: 160
Home station. Danzig (Wkr. XX)
　　Originally 60th Infantry Division formed at Danzig in August, 1939, and embodies the Danzig "Heimwehr." Took part as such in the attack on the Hela Peninsula in September, 1939, and in the Battle of France. In late summer, 1940 it provided a nucleus for the formation of 60th Motorized Division, which fought in Yugoslavia in April, 1941. On the Southern front in Russia, but has apparently not been heavily engaged.

SS Division ADOLF HITLER

Commander: SS General Sepp DIETRICH (50)
Composition: SS Regt Wisch, SS Regt Witt, SS Arty Regt, Mtrcl Bn, AT Bn,
　　　　　　Engr Bn, Sig Bn
Home station: Berlin (Lichterfelde)
　　Formed in 1934 as bodyguard regiment for Hitler. Took part in the Polish and Western campaigns as an independent motorized regiment and was expanded into a division by the spring of 1941. Fought in the Balkan campaign and has subsequently been heavily engaged on the Southern Russian front. Moved to France in July, 1942.

SS Division PRINZ EUGEN

Commander: SS Lt Gen KRUGER (?)
Composition:
Home station:
　　Formed in the spring of 1942. It is believed that this division contains a large percentage of German settlers in foreign countries, particularly from Hungary and the Balkans.

SS Division REICH

Commander: SS Maj Gen Matthias KLENHEISTERKAMP (49)
Composition: SS Regt Deutschland, SS Regt Der Führer, SS Arty Regt, Mtrcl
　　　　　　Bn, AT Bn, Engr Bn, Sig Bn.
Home station: SS Regt Deutschland—Munich.
　　　　　　　SS Regt Der Führer—— Vienna.
　　Formed in the winter, 1940-41 from two regiments of the former SS Verfügungs Division. Fought in the Balkans and heavily engaged on the Central Russian front since the outset of the campaign. Transferred to France in July, 1942.

SS TOTENKOPF Division

Commander: SS Lt Gen Theodor EICKE (49)
Composition: SS Totenkopf Inf Regts 1 and 3, SS Totenkopf Arty Regt, Mtrcl
            Bn, AT Bn, Engr Bn, Sig Bn.
Home station: Berlin (Oranienburg)
  Formed in October, 1939, mainly from existing concentration camp guard units.
Hotly engaged throughout fighting in Flanders and France. Has fought on the
Northern Russian front since the outset of the campaign.

SS Division Wiking

Commander: SS Lt Gen Felix STEINER (46)
Composition: SS Regt Germania, SS Regt Nordland, and SS Regt Westland, 5th
            SS Arty Regt, Mtrcl Bn, AT Bn, Engr Bn, Sig Bn
Home station: SS Regt Germania——Hamburg
             SS Regt Nordland——Klagenfurt
             SS Regt Westland——Klagenfurt
  Formed in the winter of 1940/41 from one regiment of the former SS
Verfügungs Div and from Scandinavian and Flemish volunteers. Continuously
engaged on the Southern Russian front.

XI LIGHT DIVISIONS

5th Light Division (5 le D.)

Commander:
Composition: 56th R Regt, 75th R Regt, 5th Arty Regt, 5th Cyclist Bn, 5th AT
            Bn, 5th Engr Bn, 5th Sig Bn
Auxiliary unit number: 5
Home station: Konstanz (Wkr. V)

  Active division (as 5th Inf Div). Recruited in Baden and Württemberg. Not
actively engaged before the battle of France, where it played a minor role. Identified in Russia during the summer of 1941. After suffering heavy casualties in
the Vyasma sector, withdrawn to France during December for rest and conversion to a light division. Returned to Russia (Northern Group) in February, 1942.

8th Light Division

Commander: Maj Gen Gustav HÖHNE (50)
Composition: 38th R Regt, 84th R Regt, 8th Arty Regt, 8th Cyclist Bn, 8th AT Bn,
            8th Engr Bn, 8th Sig Bn
Auxiliary unit number: 8
Home station: Neisse (Wkr. VIII)

  Active division (as 8th Inf Div). Personnel from Silesia. Fought well in Poland
and in France. Took part in the Russian campaign, as an infantry division, from
the beginning. After suffering heavy casualties, withdrawn to France in December, 1941, for rest and conversion to a light division. Returned to Russia
(Center Group) in early spring, 1942.

28th Light Division

Commander: Lt Gen SINNHUBER (54)
Composition: 49th R Regt, 83d R Regt, 28th Arty Regt, 28th Cyclist Bn, 28th AT Bn,
            28th Engr Bn, 28th Sig Bn
Auxiliary unit number: 28
Home Station: Breslau (Wkr. VIII)

  Active division (as 28th Inf Div). Personnel Silesian, with some German Poles.
Actively engaged in the Polish campaign and in the operations in the west. First
identified in Russia during the late summer of 1941 in the Center Group. Withdrawn to France in November for rest and conversion to a light division. Returned to Russia at the end of the winter and took part in operations in the Kerch
sector during May, 1942.

90th Light Division

Commander: Maj Gen Werner KLEEMANN (48)
Composition: 155th L Inf Regt, 200th L Inf Regt, 361st L Inf Regt, 580th Mixed
            Rcn Co, 190th AT Bn, 190th AA Co, 900th Engr Bn, 190th Sig Bn
Auxiliary unit number:
Home station: (Wkr. III)

Formed as "Africa Division z.b.V." early in 1941. First identified in Africa during the autumn. Renamed "90th Light Division" in November, 1941. Again reorganized in March, 1942. Played a prominent role in operations during June, 1942.

97th Light Division

Commander: Maj Gen BLUMENTRITT (49)
Composition: 204th Inf Regt, 207th Inf Regt, 81st Arty Regt, 97th Rcn Bn, 97th AT Bn, 97th Engr Bn, 97th Sig Bn
Auxiliary unit number: 97
Home Station: (Wkr. VII)

Formed in December, 1940. First identified in action on the Southern Russian front during the summer of 1941.

99th Light Division see 7th Mtn Div (Section XII)

100th Light Division

Commander: Lt Gen SANNE (52)
Composition: 54th Reinf Inf Regt, 369th Reinf Inf Regt, 100th Rcn Bn, 100th AT Bn, 100th Engr Bn, 100th Sig Bn
Auxiliary unit number: 100
Home Station: (Wkr.XVII)
Formed in December, 1940. First identified in action during the summer of 1941 on the Southern Russian front. Includes a Croat battalion.

101st Light Division

Commander:
Composition: 228th Inf Regt, 229th Inf Regt,   Arty Regt, 101st Rcn Bn, 101 AT Bn, 101st Engr Bn, 101st Sig Bn
Auxiliary unit number: 101
Home station: (Wkr. V)
Formed in December, 1940. First identified in action on the Southern Russian front during the summer of 1941.

XII MOUNTAIN DIVISIONS

1st Mountain Division (1 Geb. D.)

Commander: Maj Gen Hubert LANZ (45)
Composition: 98th Mtn R Regt, 99th Mtn R Regt, 79th Mtn Arty Regt, 54th Cyclist
            Bn, 44th AT Bn, 54th Mtn Engr Bn, 54th Mtn Sig Bn
Auxiliary unit number: 54
Home station: Garmisch (Wkr. VII)
   Active division. Personnel mainly Bavarian, with some Austrians. Fought with
great distinction in South Poland. Less prominent during the Battle of France.
Played a minor role in the Yugoslavian campaign of 1941. Has operated through-
out the Russian campaign on the Southern front.

2d Mountain Division

Commander: Maj Gen Ritter v. HENGL ( )
Composition: 136th Mtn R Regt, 137th Mtn R Regt, 111th Mtn Arty Regt, 67th
            Cyclist Bn, 47th AT Bn, 82d Mtn Engr Bn, 67th Mtn Sig Bn
Auxiliary unit number: 67
Home station: Innsbruck (Wkr. XVIII)
   Active division. Personnel Austrians from the Tyrol. Fought well in South
Poland, and during the Norwegian campaign. Part of the Mountain Corps in
North Norway (later expanded to Lapland Army) at the opening of the Russian
campaign. After suffering casualties in operations on the Murmansk front was
withdrawn to North Norway and held in reserve during the winter of 1941-42.

3d Mountain Division

Commander:
Composition: 138th MtnRegt, 139th Mtn R Regt, 112th Mtn Arty Regt, 68th Cyclist
            Bn, 48th AT Bn, 83d Mtn Engr Bn, 68th Mtn Sig Bn
Auxiliary unit number: 68
Home station: Graz (Wkr. XVIII)
   Active division. Personnel Austrian. Fought with distinction in South Poland
and in Norway. Part of the Mountain Corps (later expanded to Lapland Army)
at the opening of the Russian campaign. After a period of rest in Germany, during the winter of 1941-42, returned to the North Finland front. Suffered heavy
casualties during latter part of 1941 in Northern Finland.

4th Mountain Division

Commander: Maj Gen Karl EGLSEER (51)
Composition: 13th Mtn R Regt, 91st Mtn R Regt, 94th Mtn Arty Regt, 94th
            Cyclist Bn, 94th AT Bn, 94th Mtn Engr Bn, 94th Mtn Sig Bn
Auxiliary unit number: 94
Home station: Ulm (Wkr. V)
   Formed in autumn 1940. Personnel mainly South Germans. First identified
during the Balkan campaign, where it played a minor role. Operated in Russia,

on the Southern sector, and was involved in heavy fighting during the autumn of 1941.

5th Mountain Division

Commander: Maj Gen Julius RINGEL
Composition: 85th Mtn R Regt, 100th Mtn R Regt, 95th Mtn Arty Regt, 95th
             Cyclist Bn, 95th AT Bn, 95th Mtn Engr Bn, 95th Mtn Sig Bn
Auxiliary unit number: 95
Home station: Salzburg (Wkr. XVIII)
  Formed in autumn, 1940. Personnel mainly Bavarian, with some Austrians.
First identified in Greece, where it fought well during the Balkan campaign. Subsequently took part in the airborne attack on Crete. Remained in the Aegean area during 1941. Transferred to the Leningrad front early in 1942, and thence to Finland in the late spring.

6th Mountain Division

Commander:Maj Gen Lothar PHILIPP (   )
Composition: 141st Mtn R Regt, 143d Mtn R Regt, 118th Mtn Arty Regt,
             Cyclist Bn,   AT Bn, 91st Mtn Engr Bn, 96th Mtn Sig Bn
Auxiliary unit number:
Home Station: Klagenfurt ? (Wkr. XVIII)
  Formed in winter 1939/40. Took part in the later stages of the Battle of France.
In Greece it played a leading part in the advance on Salonika. Elements took part in the attack on Crete. Transferred in the late summer of 1941 from Greece to Finland, where it operated as part of the Lapland Army.

7th Mountain Division

Commander: Maj Gen Robert MARTINEK (   )
Composition: 144th Mtn R Regt, 206th Mtn R Regt, 82d Mtn Arty Regt, 99th
             Cyclist Bn, 99th AT Bn, 99th Mtn Engr Bn, 99th Mtn Sig Bn
Auxiliary unit number: 99
Home station: (Wkr. XVIII)
  Formed during the winter of 1941/42, mainly by conversion of the former 99th Light Division (formed in December, 1940) which had operated for a time on the Southern Russian front. First in action in Finland in late spring, 1942.

SS Mountain Division NORD

Commander: SS Lt Gen Georg KEPPLER (48)
Composition: SS Mtn R Regt REINHARDT HEYDRICH, SS Mtn R Regt, 7th SS
             Mtn Arty Regt,   Rcn Bn,   AT Bn,   Engr Bn,   Sig Bn
Home Station: Trautenau
  Formed during the summer of 1941 and has taken part in the Russian campaign on the Finnish front.

XIII CAVALRY DIVISIONS

1st Cavalry Division see 24 Pz. Div. (Section IX)

SS Kavallerie Division

Commander: SS Maj Gen Willi BITTRICH (48)
Composition:
Home station: Debica (General Government)
  Not yet in action as a division.

XIV INFANTRY DIVISIONS

1st Infantry Division (1 J.D.)

Commander:
Composition: 1st Inf Regt, 22d Inf Regt, 43d Inf Regt, 1st Arty Regt, 1st Rcn Bn,
1st AT Bn, 1st Engr Bn, 1st Sig Bn
Auxiliary unit number: 1
Home station: Insterburg (Wkr. I)
  Active division. Personnel partly East Prussian, partly from Rhineland.
Fought well in Poland, less actively engaged in France. Engaged on the Northern
Russian front since June, 1941.

3d Infantry Division see 3d Mtz Div (Section X)

4th Infantry Division see 14th Pz Div (Section IX)

5th Infantry Division see 5th L Div (Section XI)

6th Infantry Division

Commander:
Composition: 18th Inf Regt, 37th Inf Regt, 58th Inf Regt, 6th Arty Regt, 6th Rcn
Bn, 5th AT Bn, 6th Engr Bn, 6th Sig Bn
Auxiliary unit number: 6
Home station: Bielefeld (Wkr. VI)
  Active division. Personnel from Westphalia and, in part, East Prussia. Fought
with distinction throughout the Battle of France. Engaged in Russia, Central
Sector, since beginning of campaign.

7th Infantry Division

Commander: Lt Gen Eccard Frhr. v. GABLENZ (50)
Composition: 19th Inf Regt, 61st Inf Regt, 62d Inf Regt, 7th Arty Regt, 7th Rcm,
Bn, 7th AT Bn, 7th Engr Bn, 7th Sig Bn
Auxiliary unit number: 7
Home station: Munich (Wkr. VII)
  Active division. Personnel Bavarian. Heavily engaged in S Poland, suffering
many casualties. Fought against the BEF in Belgium, but took no part in the
Battle of France. A good fighting division. Continuously engaged in Russia
since beginning of campaign and reached Moshaisk area in final attack on
Moscow.

8th Infantry Division see 8th L Div (Section XI)

9th Infantry Division

Commander: Maj Gen Siegmund Frhr. v. SCHLEINITZ (51)
Composition: 36th Inf Regt, 57th Inf Regt, 116th Inf Regt, 9th Arty Regt, 9th Rcn

Bn, 9th AT Bn, 9th Engr Bn, 9th Sig Bn
Auxiliary unit number: 9
Home station: Giessen (Wkr. IX)
 Active division: Personnel from Hessen-Nassau. On the Saar front for a time.
Fought well in France. Engaged in Russia, on the Southern front, since begin-
ning of the campaign.

10th Infantry Division see 10th Mtz Div (Section X)

11th Infantry Division

Commander:
Composition: 2d Inf Regt, 23d Inf Regt, 44th Inf Regt, 11th Arty Regt, 11th Rcn
          Bn, 11th AT Bn, 11th Engr Bn, 11th Sig Bn
Auxiliary unit number: 11
Home station: Allenstein (Wkr. I)
 Active division. Personnel from E Prussia and from the Rhineland. Fought
well, and sustained heavy casualties in Poland. Not identified during the Battle
of France. Engaged in Russia, since beginning of campaign, in the Northern
Sector.

12th Infantry Division

Commander: Maj Gen Hans Jurgen Frhr. v. LUTZOW (49)
Composition: 27th Inf Regt, 48th Inf Regt, 89th Inf Regt, 12th Arty Regt, 12th Rcn
          Bn, 12th AT Bn, 12th Engr Bn, 12th Sig Bn
Auxiliary unit number: 12
Home station: Schwerin (Wkr. II)
 Active division. Personnel mainly Prussian. Fought with distinction in Poland
and in France. Identified in Russia in the Northern Sector, but so far has played
an inconspicuous part.

14th Infantry Division see 14th Mtz Div (Section X)

15th Infantry Division

Commander: Lt Gen Walter BEHSCHNITT (56)
Composition: 81st Inf Regt, 88th Inf Regt, 106th Inf Regt, 15th Arty Regt, 15th
          Rcn Bn, 15 AT Bn, 15th Engr Bn, 15 Sig Bn
Auxiliary unit number: 15
Home station: Kassel (Wkr. IX)
 Active division. Recruited in Frankfurt area with draftees from Austria. Con-
tains a considerable proportion of reservists. On the Saar front for some
months, and later operated in the Luxemburg area. Engaged on the Central
Russian front until April, 1942, and has subsequently been transferred to France.

16th Infantry Division see 16th Pz Div and 16th Mtz Div
(Sections IX and X)

17th Infantry Division

Commander:
Composition: 21st Inf Regt, 55th Inf Regt, 95th Inf Regt, 17th Arty Regt, 17th Rcn
          Bn, 17th AT Bn, 17th Engr Bn, 17th Sig Bn
Auxiliary unit number: 17
Home station: Nuremburg (Wkr. XIII)
  Active division. Personnel Bavarian. Distinguished alike in Poland and in
France. A good fighting division. Engaged in Russia, since beginning of campaign, in the Central Sector.

18th Infantry Division see 18th Mtz Div (Section X)

19th Infantry Division see 19th Pz Div (Section IX)

21st Infantry Division

Commander: Lt Gen Wilhelm BOHNSTEDT (52)
Composition: 3d Inf Regt, 24th Inf Regt, 45th Inf Regt, 21st Arty Regt,   Rcn
          Bn, 21st AT Bn, 21st Engr Bn, 21st Sig Bn
Auxiliary unit number: 21
Home station: Elbing (Wkr. XX)
  Active division. Personnel from E Prussia and from the Rhineland. Fought
well in Poland. Played an inconspicuous part in the Battle of France. Engaged
in Russia in the Northern Sector since beginning of campaign.

22d Infantry Division

Commander: Maj Gen WOLFF (49)
Composition: 16th Inf Regt, 47th Inf Regt, 65th Inf Regt, 22d Arty Regt, 22d Rcn
          Bn, 22d AT Bn, 22d Engr Bn, 22d Sig Bn
Auxiliary unit number: 22
Home station: Oldenburg (Wkr. X)
  Active division. Personnel mainly from E Prussia and Oldenburg. Employed
as "Air-borne Division" in Holland. Played a valuable part in the capture of
Fortress Holland. Morale uneven. Engaged continuously in Russia in the Southern Sector, where it appears to have sustained fairly heavy losses. Moved to
Crete, summer, 1942.

23d Infantry Division

Commander:
Composition: 9th Inf Regt, 67th Inf Regt, 68th Inf Regt, 23d Arty Regt, 23d Rcn
          Bn, 23d AT Bn, 23d Engr Bn, 23d Sig Bn
Auxiliary unit number: 23
Home station: Potsdam (Wkr. III)
  Active division. Personnel mainly from Greater Berlin. Heavily engaged in
Poland, less so in France. Fighting value obscure, but morale likely to be high.
Engaged continuously in Russia, in the Central Sector, where it appears to have

suffered appreciable losses.

24th Infantry Division

Commander: Lt Gen Hans v. TETTAU (53)
Composition: 31st Inf Regt, 32d Inf Regt, 102d Inf Regt, 24th Arty Regt, 24th Rcn
        Bn, 24th AT Bn, 24th Engr Bn, 24th Sig Bn
Auxiliary unit number: 24
Home station: Chemnitz (Wkr. IV)
   Active division. Personnel Saxon. Morale and fighting value very high, to
judge by the Polish campaign. Less prominent during the Battle of France. En-
gaged in Russia since beginning of campaign, on southern front and in the Crimea.

25th Infantry Division see 25th Mtz Div (Section X)

26th Infantry Division

Commander:
Composition: 39th Inf Regt, 77th Inf Regt, 78th Inf Regt, 26th Arty Regt, 26th Rcn
        Bn, 26th AT Bn, 26th Engr Bn, 26th Sig Bn
Auxiliary unit number: 26
Home station: Cologne (Wkr. VI)
   Active division. Personnel mainly from the Rhineland, with draftees from E
Prussia. Took a minor part in the Battle of France. Continuously engaged in
Russia, in the Central Sector, since beginning of campaign.

27th Infantry Division see 17th Pz Div (Section IX)

28th Infantry Division see 28th L Div (Section XI)

30th Infantry Division

Commander: Lt Gen Kurt v. TIPPELSKIRCH (50)
Composition: 6th Inf Regt, 26th Inf Regt, 46th Inf Regt, 30th Arty Regt, 30th Rcn
        Bn, 30th AT Bn, 30th Engr Bn, 30th Sig Bn
Auxiliary unit number: 30
Home station: Lübeck (Wkr. X)
   Active division. Recruited mainly in Schleswig-Holstein. Earned special
distinction and suffered heavy casualties in N Poland. Fought in Belgium, but
took no part (as far as is known) in the Battle of France. Engaged in Russia in
the Northern Sector, since beginning of campaign.

31st Infantry Division

Commander:
Composition: 12th Inf Regt, 17th Inf Regt, 82d Inf Regt, 31st Arty Regt, 31st Rcn
        Bn, 31st Engr Bn, 31st Sig Bn
Auxiliary unit number: 31
Home station: Braunschweig (Wkr. XI)

Active division. Recruited mainly in the Braunschweig area. Took little part in the Polish campaign, but fought hard in Belgium and throughout the Battle of France. Continuously engaged in Russia in the Central Sector, since beginning of campaign.

32d Infantry Division

Commander: Maj Gen v. LEYSER (52)
Composition: 4th Inf Regt, 94th Inf Regt, 96th Inf Regt, 32d Arty Regt, 32d Rcn
        Bn, 32d AT Bn,   Engr Bn, 32d Sig Bn
Auxiliary unit number: 32
Home station: Köslin (Wkr. II)
  Active division. Personnel, Prussians from Pomerania. Fought well in Poland and in France. A good attacking division. Engaged in Russia, in Northern Sector, since beginning of campaign.

33d Infantry Division see 15th Pz Div (Section IX)

34th Infantry Division

Commander:
Composition: 80th Inf Regt, 107th Inf Regt, 253d Inf Regt, 34th Arty Regt, 34th
        Rcn Bn, 34th AT Bn, 34th Engr Bn, 34th Sig Bn
Auxiliary unit number: 34
Home station: Heidelberg (Wkr. XII)
  Active division. Personnel mainly from the Rhineland. On the Saar front for some months, and later took part in the Battle of France, without winning special distinction. Identified on Central Russian Front in August, 1941, where it appears to have been fairly heavily engaged up to January, 1942.

35th Infantry Division

Commander: Maj Gen Rudolf Frhr. v. ROMAN (48)
Composition: 34th Inf Regt, 109th Inf Regt, 111th Inf Regt, 35th Arty Regt, 35th
        Rcn Bn, 35th AT Bn, 35th Engr Bn, 35th Sig Bn
Auxiliary unit number: 35
Home station: Karlsruhe (Wkr. V)
  Active division. Personnel from Baden and Württemberg. Fought against the BEF in Belgium, otherwise saw little active fighting prior to the Russian campaign. Continuously engaged in Russia, in Central Sector, where it has suffered considerable casualties.

36th Infantry Division see 36th Mtz Div (Section X)

44th Infantry Division

Commander: Lt Gen Friedrich SIEBERT (53)
Composition: 131st Inf Regt, 132d Inf Regt, 134th Inf Regt, 96th Arty Regt, 44th
        Rcn Bn, 46th AT Bn, 80th Engr Bn, 64th Sig Bn

Auxiliary unit number: 44
Home station: Vienna (Wkr. XVII)`
Active division. Personnel mainly Austrian. Sustained heavy casualties in Poland. Saw little fighting, but marched great distances in France. Morale less high than that of the other Austrian active divisions. Engaged in Russia, on the Southern front, since beginning of the campaign.

45th Infantry Division

Commander: Maj Gen KÜHLWEIN (49)
Composition: 130th Inf Regt, 133d Inf Regt, 135th Inf Regt, 98th Arty Regt, 45th Rcn Bn, 45th AT Bn, 81st Engr Bn, 65th Sig Bn
Auxiliary unit number: 45
Home station: Linz (Wkr. XVII)
Active division. Personnel mainly Austrian. Fought well in S Poland and in the Battle of France. Continuously engaged in Russia, in the Central Sector, where it appears to have sustained considerable casualties.

46th Infantry Division

Commander:
Composition: 42d Inf Regt, 72d Inf Regt, 97th Inf Regt, 114th Arty Regt, 46th Rcn Bn, 52d AT Bn, 88th Engr Bn, 76th Sig Bn
Auxiliary unit number: 46
Home station: Karlsbad (Wkr. XIII)
Active division, formed at the close of 1938. Personnel partly Bavarian partly Sudeten German. Saw comparatively little active fighting before the Russian campaign where it has been engaged on the Southern front and in the Crimea.

50th Infantry Division

Commander: Lt Gen Conrad SORSCHE (58)
Composition: 121st Inf Regt, 122d Inf Regt, 123d Inf Regt, 150th Arty Regt, 150th Rcn Bn, 150th AT Bn, 150th Engr Bn, 150th Sig Bn
Auxiliary unit number: 150
Home station: Posen (Wkr. XXI)
Active division (as "Küstrin Frontier Command"). Personnel Prussian. Had little fighting to do in Poland, but took an active part in the Battle of France. Continuously engaged on the Southern Russian front and in the Crimea.

52d Infantry Division

Commander:
Composition: 163d Inf Regt, 181st Inf Regt, 205th Inf Regt, 152d Arty Regt, 152d Rcn Bn, 152d AT Bn, 152d Engr Bn, 152th Sig Bn
Auxiliary unit number: 152
Home station: Kassel (Wkr. IX)
Reserve division formed on mobilization. Personnel mainly from Hessen. On the Saar front for some months. Some units fought in France, but the division

may have been sent to Norway. Engaged in Russia, in the Central Sector, since beginning of campaign, but does not appear to have played a very conspicuous part in action.

56th Infantry Division

Commander: Lt Gen Karl v. OVEN (53)
Composition: 171st Inf Regt, 192d Inf Regt, 234th Inf Regt,
             156th Arty Regt, 156th Rcn Bn, 156th AT Bn, 156th Engr Bn, 156th
             Sig Bn
Auxiliary unit number: 156
Home station: Dresden (Wkr. IV)
  Reserve division formed on mobilization. Personnel Saxon. Took part in the Polish campaign. Fought well against the BEF in Belgium. Identified in the Central Sector of the Russian front in November, 1941, where it has been heavily engaged.

57th Infantry Division

Commander: Maj Gen Anton DOSTLER (50)
Composition: 179th Inf Regt, 199th Inf Regt, 217th Inf Regt, 157th Arty Regt,
             157th Rcn Bn, 157th AT Bn, 157th Engr Bn, 157th Sig Bn
Auxiliary unit number: 157
Home station: Bad Reichenhall (Wkr. VII)
  Reserve division formed on mobilization. Personnel mainly Bavarian. Distinguished itself in S Poland an in the operations on the Lower Somme. A good fighting division. Continuously engaged in Russia, on the Southern front, since beginning of campaign.

58th Infantry Division

Commander: Maj Gen Dr. Friedrich ALTRICHTER (51)
Composition: 154th Inf Regt, 209th Inf Regt, 220th Inf Regt, 158th Arty Regt,
             158th Rcn Bn, 158th AT Bn, 158th Engr Bn, 158th Sig Bn
Auxiliary unit number: 158
Home station: Rendsburg ? (Wkr. X)
  Reserve division formed on mobilization. Personnel from N Germany. On the Saar front in April, 1940. Too little active employment for its fighting value to be assessed. Identified in the Northern Sector of the Russian front in December, 1941, but little evidence that it has seen much action.

60th Infantry Division see 60th Mtz Div (Section X)

61st Infantry Division

Commander: Lt Gen Siegfried HAENICKE (63)
Composition: 151st Inf Regt, 162d Inf Regt, 176th Inf Regt, 161st Arty Regt,
             161st Rcn Bn, 161st AT Bn, 161st Engr Bn, 161st Sig Bn
Auxiliary unit number: 161

Home station: Königsberg (Wkr. I)
Reserve division formed on mobilization. Personnel mainly from E Prussia. Fought well against the BEF in Belgium. Identified on Northern Sector of Russian front but little evidence that it has seen much action.

62d Infantry Division

Commander: Lt Gen Walter KEINER (51)
Composition: 164th Inf Regt, 183d Inf Regt, 190th Inf Regt, 162d Arty Regt, 162d Rcn Bn, 162d AT Bn, 162d Engr Bn, 162d Sig Bn
Auxiliary unit number: 162
Home station: Glatz (Wkr. VIII)
Reserve division formed on mobilization with Silesian personnel. Fought well in Flanders and in Poland. Identified on the Southern Russian front but little evidence that it has seen much action.

68th Infantry Division

Commander:
Composition: 169th Inf Regt, 188th Inf Regt, 196th Inf Regt, 168th Arty Regt, 168th Rcn Bn, 168th AT Bn, 168th Engr Bn, 168th Sig Bn
Auxiliary unit number: 168
Home station: Guben (Wkr. III)
Reserve division formed on mobilization. Took part in the operations in France without earning special distinction. Engaged since the beginning of the Russian campaign in the Southern Sector, where it appears to have sustained considerable losses.

69th Infantry Division

Commander: Maj Gen Bruno ORTNER
Composition: 159th Inf Regt, 193d Inf Regt, 236th Inf Regt, 169th Arty Regt, 169th Rcn Bn, 169th AT Bn, 169th Engr Bn, 169th Sig Bn
Auxiliary unit number: 169
Home station: Soest (Wkr. VI)
Reserve division formed on mobilization and recruited mainly from the Ruhr area. Fought well against weak Norwegian forces. Has remained in Norway on occupational and defense duties.

71st Infantry Division

Commander: Maj Gen v. HARTMANN (51)
Composition: 191st Inf Regt, 194th Inf Regt, 211th Inf Regt, 171st Arty Regt, 171st Rcn Bn, 171st AT Bn, 171st Engr Bn, 171st Sig Bn
Auxiliary unit number: 171
Home station; Hildesheim (Wkr. XI)
Reserve division formed on mobilization and recruited mainly from Hannover area. On the Saar front for a period. Fought with distinction in the Sedan area and in the advance on Verdun. Fought in Russia in the Southern Sector for the

first four months of the campaign, then returned to France and left again for the Eastern front during April, 1942.

72d Infantry Division

Commander:
Composition: 105th Inf Regt, 124th Inf Regt, 266th Inf Regt, 172d Arty Regt, 172d Rcn Bn, 172d AT Bn, 172d Engr Bn, 172d Sig Bn
Auxiliary unit number: 172
Home station: (Wkr. XII)
   Formed on mobilization in Wkr. IX and XII, incorporating two active infantry regiments and one reserve. Mainly Rhinelanders and Bavarians. On the Saar front for many months. Not an aggressive division during these operations. Took part in the Balkan campaign and has been continuously engaged in Russia on the Southern front and in the Crimea.

73d Infantry Division

Commander:
Composition: 170th Inf Regt, 186th Inf Regt, 213th Inf Regt, 173d Arty Regt, 173d Rcn Bn, 173d AT Bn, 173d Engr Bn, 173d Sig Bn
Auxiliary unit number: 173
Home station: Wurzburg (Wkr. XIII)
   Reserve division formed on mobilization. Bavarian personnel. Saw little fighting in Poland, less on the Saar front, and was not distinguished during the campaign in France. Took part in the Balkan campaign, and has been continuously engaged on the Southern Russian front and in the Crimea.

75th Infantry Division

Commander: Lt Gen Karl HAMMER (58)
Composition: 172d Inf Regt, 202d Inf Regt, 222d Inf Regt, 175th Arty Regt, 175th Rcn Bn, 175th AT Bn, 175th Engr Bn, 175th Sig Bn
Auxiliary unit number: 175
Home station: Neustrelitz (Wkr. II)
   Reserve division formed on mobilization. Personnel Prussian, mainly from Schwerin area. On the Saar front for several months, and in France in June, 1940. Fighting value unknown. Identified in the Southern Sector of the Russian front but little evidence that it has seen much action.

76th Infantry Division

Commander:
Composition: 178th Inf Regt, 203d Inf Regt, 230th Inf Regt, 176th Arty Regt, 176th Rcn Bn, 176 AT Bn, 176th Engr Bn, 176th Sig Bn
Auxiliary unit number: 176
Home station: Berlin (Wkr. III)
   Reserve division formed on mobilization. Prussian personnel. Fought well in France. Engaged in Russia in the Southern Sector since beginning of campaign.

78th Infantry Division

Commander:
Composition: 195th Inf Regt, 215th Inf Regt, 238th Inf Regt, 178th Arty Regt,
        178th Rcn Bn, 178th AT Bn, 178th Engr Bn, 178th Sig Bn
Auxiliary unit number: 178
Home station: Ulm (Wkr. V)
  Reserve division formed on mobilization. Personnel mainly from Württemberg.
Took part in the Battle of France where its fighting value was indeterminate.
Continuously engaged since beginning of Russian campaign in the Central Sector.

79th Infantry Division

Commander:
Composition: 208th Inf Regt, 212th Inf Regt, 226th Inf Regt, 179th Arty Regt,
        179th Rcn Bn, 179th AT Bn, 179th Engr Bn, 179th Sig Bn
Auxiliary unit number: 179 .
Home station: Koblenz (Wkr. XII)
  Reserve division formed on mobilization. Personnel mainly from the Rhineland.
On the Saar front for a period, but took little part in active operations. Identified
in the Southern Sector of the Russian front but little evidence that it has seen
much action.

81st Infantry Division

Commander: Lt Gen v. LOEPER (54)
Composition: 161st Inf Regt, 174th Inf Regt, 188th Inf Regt, 181st Arty Regt,
        181st Rcn Bn, 181st AT Bn, 181st Engr Bn, 181st Sig Bn
Auxiliary unit number: 181
Home station: (Wkr. VIII)
  Reserve division formed on mobilization. Took part in Battle of France with-
out winning special distinction. Apparently arrived on the Northern Sector of the
Russian front from France in January, 1942.

82d Infantry Division

Commander:
Composition: 168th Inf Regt,   Inf Regt,   Inf Regt, 182d Arty Regt, 182d
        Cyclist Co, 182d AT Bn, 182d Engr Bn, 182d Sig Bn
Auxiliary unit number: 182
Home station: Frankfurt/Main (?) (Wkr. IX)
  Reserve division formed on mobilization. Not identified during the Battle of
France. Identified in Holland late in 1941 but believed to have left, presumably
for Russia, in May, 1942.

83d Infantry Division

Commander:
Composition: Inf Regt, 225th Inf Regt, 227th Inf Regt, 183d **Arty Regt**, 183d Rcn

Bn, 183d AT Bn, 183d Engr Bn, 183d Sig Bn
Auxiliary unit number: 183
Home station: Hamburg (Wkr. X)
   Reserve division formed on mobilization. Took part in the Polish campaign
and the Battle of France without winning special distinction. Left France for
Russia early in 1942 and was identified in the Central Sector during April.

86th Infantry Division

Commander:
Composition: 167th Inf Regt, 184th Inf Regt, 214th Inf Regt, 186th Arty Regt,
              186th Rcn Bn, 186th AT Bn, 186th Engr Bn, 186th Sig Bn
Auxiliary unit number: 186
Home station: (Wkr. VI)
   Reserve division formed on mobilization. Personnel mainly Westphalian. On
the Saar front for two months. Took part in the Battle of France. Continuously
engaged in Russia, in the Central Sector, since the beginning of the campaign.

87th Infantry Division

Commander: Lt Gen Bogislav v. STUDNITZ (55)
Composition: 173d Inf Regt, 185th Inf Regt, 187th Inf Regt, 187th Arty Regt,
              187th Rcn Bn, 187th AT Bn, 187th Engr Bn, 187th Sig Bn
Auxiliary unit number: 187
Home station: (Wkr. IV)
   Reserve division formed in Wkr. IV and Wkr. IX on mobilization. Personnel
mainly Saxon or Thuringian. First in action during Battle of France, when it
fought well. Continuously engaged in Russia, in the Central Sector, since begin-
ning of the campaign.

88th Infantry Division

Commander: Lt Gen Friedrich GOLLWITZER (52)
Composition: 245th Inf Regt, 246th Inf Regt, 248th Inf Regt, 188th Arty Regt,
              188th Rcn Bn, 188th AT Bn, 188th Engr Bn, 188th Sig Bn
Auxiliary unit number: 188
Home station: (Wkr. VII)
   Reserve division. Formed in autumn, 1939. Played an inconspicuous part in
the Battle of France. Left France for Russia early in 1942 and has been identi-
fied on the Southern front.

93d Infantry Division

Commander: Lt Gen TIEMANN (53)
Composition: 270th Inf Regt, 271st Inf Regt, 272d Inf Regt, 193d Arty Regt, 193d
              Rcn Bn, 193d AT Bn, 193d Engr Bn, 193d Sig Bn
Auxiliary unit number: 193
Home station: Berlin (Wkr. III)
   Reserve division formed in September 1939. Personnel Prussian, with some

previous military training. On the Saar front for several months without distinguishing itself. Identified in the Northern Sector of the Russian front, but little evidence that it has seen much action.

94th Infantry Division

Commander: Maj Gen Georg PFEIFFER (52)
Composition: 267th Inf Regt, 274th Inf Regt, 276th Inf Regt, 194th Arty Regt, 194th Rcn Bn, 194th AT Bn, 194th Engr Bn, 194th Sig Bn
Auxiliary unit number: 194
Home station: (Wkr. IV)
Reserve division formed in September, 1939. Personnel mainly Saxon or Sudeten German, with some previous military training. Took some part in the Battle of France. Fighting value indeterminate in these operations. Engaged in Russia in the Southern Sector, where it was first identified in August, 1941.

95th Infantry Division

Commander: Lt Gen Hans Heinrich SIXT v. ARNIM (52)
Composition: 278th Inf Regt, 279th Inf Regt, 280th Inf Regt, 195th Arty Regt, 195th Rcn Bn, 195th AT Bn, 195th Engr Bn, 195th Sig Bn
Auxiliary unit number: 195
Home Station: (Wkr. IX)
Reserve division formed in September, 1939. Personnel mainly Westphalian, with draftees from Thuringia, with some previous military training. Showed initiative and dash on the Saar front. Not identified during the Battle of France. Continuously engaged in Russia, on the Southern front, where it appears to have sustained considerable casualties.

96th Infantry Division

Commander:
Composition: 283d Inf Regt, 284th Inf Regt, 287th Inf Regt, 196th Arty Regt, 196th Rcn Bn, 196th AT Bn, 196th Engr Bn, 196th Sig Bn
Auxiliary unit number: 196
Home station: (Wkr. XI)
Reserve division formed in September, 1939. Personnel mainly with some previous military training. Took part in the Battle of France. Engaged in Russia, in the Northern Sector, but has not been identified since early in 1942.

98th Infantry Division

Commander:
Composition: 282d Inf Regt, 289th Inf Regt, 290th Inf Regt, 198th Arty Regt, 198th Rcn Bn, 198th AT Bn, 198th Engr Bn, 298th Sig Bn
Auxiliary unit number: 198
Home station: (Wkr. XIII)
Reserve division formed in September, 1939. Personnel Bavarian, mainly with some previous military training. Fought well in the Battle of France. Identified

in the Central Sector of the Russian front in November, 1941, where it appears
to have been fairly heavily engaged.

102d Infantry Division

Commander: Maj Gen ANSAT (50)
Composition: 232d Inf Regt, 233d Inf Regt, 235th Inf Regt,   Arty Regt,   Rcn
Bn,   AT Bn,   Engr Bn,   Sig Bn
Auxiliary unit number: 102
Home station: (Wkr. VIII)
  Formed in December, 1940. First identified in action on Central Russian
front in August, 1941. Constantly engaged until February, 1942, when it may have
been withdrawn to Germany to rest. Again on Central front in mid—April.

106th Infantry Division

Commander:
Composition: 239th Inf Regt, 240th Inf Regt, 241st Inf Regt, 89th? Arty Regt,
106th Rcn Bn, 106th AT Bn, 106th Engr Bn, 106th Sig Bn
Auxiliary unit number: 106
Home station: (Wkr. VI)
  Formed in December, 1940. First identified in action on Central Russian
front in August, 1941. Fought in the Center Group throughout the winter, sustaining heavy casualties, particularly in latter half of January, 1942. Has subsequently returned to France for rest and refit.

110th Infantry Division

Commander:
Composition: 252d Inf Regt, 254th Inf Regt, 255th Inf Regt, 120th Arty Regt,
110th Rcn Bn, 110th AT Bn, 110th Engr Bn, 110th Sig Bn
Auxiliary unit number: 110
Home station: Oldenburg (Wkr. X)
  Formed in December, 1940. First identified in action on the Russian front in
August, 1941. Heavily engaged throughout the winter in the Center Group.
Moved to France in Spring, 1942.

111th Infantry Division

Commander:
Composition: Inf Regt, 70th Inf Regt, 117th Inf Regt,   Arty Regt, 111th
Rcn Bn, 111st AT Bn, 111st Engr Bn, 111st Sig Bn
Auxiliary unit number: 111
Home station: (Wkr. III)
  Formed in December, 1940. Has fought in Russia in the Southern Group. Does
not appear to have been much in action.

112th Infantry Division

Commander: Lt Gen MIETH (55)
Composition: 110th Inf Regt, 256th Inf Regt, 258th Inf Regt, 86th Arty Regt, 120th
        Rcn Bn, 112th AT Bn, 112th Engr Bn, 112th Sig Bn
Auxiliary unit number: 112
Home station: Darmstadt (Wkr. XII)
  Formed in December, 1940. With Center Group on Russian front from August,
1941. Heavily engaged till December, when, after severe losses near Tula, it
was withdrawn to rest in Poland. Again in action in mid-March in Center Group.

113th Infantry Division

Commander: Lt Gen GÜNTZEL (53)
Composition: 260th Inf Regt, 261st Inf Regt, 268th Inf Regt, 87th Arty Regt,
        113th Rcn Bn, 113th AT Bn, 113th Engr Bn, 113th Sig Bn
Auxiliary unit number: 113
Home station: (Wkr. XIII)
  Formed in December, 1940. Was in the Balkans on occupational duties during
November and December, 1941. Later transferred to the Southern Sector of the
Russian front where it appears to have been fairly heavily engaged.

114th Infantry Division

Commander:
Composition: Inf Regt,   Inf Regt,   Inf Regt,   Arty Regt,   Rcn Bn,
        AT Bn,   Engr Bn,   Sig Bn
Auxiliary unit number:
Home station:
  Possibly formed in December, 1940. Reported in action on the Central Russian
front from December to March, 1942, though perhaps withdrawn for a short time
to Poland after losses at Tula in late December.

117th Infantry Division

Commander:
Composition: Inf Regt,   Inf Regt,   Inf Regt,   Arty Regt,   Rcn Bn,
        AT Bn,   Engr Bn,   Sig Bn
Auxiliary unit number:
Home station:
  Possibly formed in December, 1940. Reported in Center Group in August, 1941,
but never identified in action.

118th Infantry Division

Commander:
Composition: Inf Regt,   Inf Regt,   Inf Regt,   Arty Regt,   Rcn
        Bn,   AT Bn,   Engr Bn,   Sig Bn
Auxiliary unit number:

Home station:
  Possibly formed in December, 1940. Reported in the Central Sector of the Russian front in February, 1942.

119th Infantry Division

Commander:
Composition: Inf Regt,   Inf Regt,   Inf Regt,   Arty Regt,   Rcn
           Bn,   AT Bn,   Engr Bn,   Sig Bn
Auxiliary unit number:
Home station:
  Possibly formed in December, 1940. Reported in the Southern Sector of the Russian front.

121st Infantry Division

Commander:
Composition: 405th Inf Regt, 407th Inf Regt, 408th Inf Regt, 121st Arty Regt,
           121st Rcn Bn, 121st AT Bn, 121st Engr Bn, 121st Sig Bn
Auxiliary unit number: 121
Home station: (Wkr. X)
  Formed in Wehrkreis X in October 1940. In action in the Northern Sector from the outset of the Russian campaign.

122d Infantry Division

Commander:
Composition: 409th Inf Regt, 411th Inf Regt, 414th (?) Inf Regt
               122d Arty Regt, 122 d Rcn Bn, 122d AT Bn, 122 Engr
               Bn, 122d Sig Bn
Auxiliary unit number: 122
Home Station: (Wkr. II)
   Formed in October, 1940. In action on the Northern Russian front in July,
1941, where it appears to have been fairly heavily engaged up to January, 1942.

123d Infantry Division

Commander:
Composition: 415th Inf Regt, 416th Inf Regt, 418th Inf Regt,
               123d Arty Regt, 123d Rcn Bn, 123d AT Bn,
               123d Engineer Bn, 123d Sig Bn
Auxiliary unit number: 123
Home station: (Wkr.III)
   Formed in October, 1940. In action on the Northern Russian front where it
appears to have been fairly heavily engaged.

125th Infantry Division

Commander:
Composition: 419th Inf Regt, 420th (?) Inf Regt, 421st Inf Regt,
               125th Arty Regt, 125th Rcn Bn, 125 AT Bn, 125th Engr Bn,
               125th Sig Bn
Auxiliary unit number: 125
Home station: (Wkr. V)
   Formed in October, 1940. Engaged on the Southern Russian front since July,
1941, where it sustained considerable losses, particularly during November,
1941.

126th Infantry Division

Commander: Lt Gen Paul LAUX (54)
Composition: 422d Inf Regt, 424th Inf Regt, 426th Inf Regt,
               126th Arty Regt, 126th Rcn Bn, 126th AT Bn,
               126th Engr Bn, 126th Sig Bn
Auxiliary unit number: 126
Home station: (Wkr. VI)
   Formed in October, 1940. In action on Northern Russian front since outset
of campaign, where it appears to have been fairly continuously engaged.

129th Infantry Division

Commander: Maj Gen RITTAU (50)
Composition: 427th Inf Regt, 428th Inf Regt, 430th Inf Regt,

129th Arty Regt, 129th Rcn Bn, 129th AT Bn,
129th Engr Bn, 129th Sig Bn

Auxiliary unit number: 129

Home station: Fulda (Wkr. IX)

Formed in October, 1940, and has been continuously engaged on the Central Russian front since the beginning of the campaign.

131st Infantry Division

Commander: Lt Gen Heinrich MEYER-BUERDORF (53)

Composition: 431st Inf Regt, 432d Inf Regt, 434th Inf Regt, 131st Arty Regt, 131st Rcn Bn, 131st AT Bn, 131st Engr Bn, 131st Sig Bn

Auxiliary unit number: 131

Home station: (Wkr. XI)

Formed in October, 1940. Identified on the Central Russian front in August, 1941, where it appears to have been fairly heavily engaged. May now be transferred to the Southern Sector.

132nd Infantry Division

Commander: Lt Gen Rudolf SINTZENICH (52)

Composition: 436th Inf Regt, 437th Inf Regt, 438th Inf Regt, 132d Arty Regt, 132d Rcn Bn, 132d AT Bn, 132d Engr Bn, 132 Sig Bn

Auxiliary unit number: 132

Home station: (Wkr. XII)

Formed in Wehrkreis VII in October, 1940. Subsequently transferred to Wkr. XII. Engaged on the Southern Russian front and in the Crimea since July, 1941.

134th Infantry Division

Commander:

Composition: 439th Inf Regt, 445th Inf Regt, 446th Inf Regt, 134th Arty Regt, 134th Rcn Bn, 134th AT Bn, 134th Engr Bn, 134th Sig Bn

Auxiliary unit number: 134

Home station: (Wkr. IV)

Formed in Wehrkreis XIII in October, 1940. Subsequently transferred to Wkr. IV. Continuously and heavily engaged on the Central Russian front since the beginning of the campaign.

137th Infantry Division

Commander: Maj Gen DEWITZ gen.v. KREBS

Composition: 447th Inf Regt, 448th Inf Regt, 449th Inf Regt, 137th Arty Regt, 137th Rcn Bn, 137th AT Bn, 137th Engr Bn, 137th Sig Bn

Auxiliary unit number: 137

Home station: (Wkr. XVII)
Formed in October, 1940. Identified on the Central Russian front in August, 1941, where it appears to have been fairly heavily engaged.

161st Infantry Division

Commander:
Composition: 364th? Inf Regt, 371st Inf Regt, 373d? Inf Regt,
              241st Arty Regt, 241st Rcn Bn, 241st AT Bn,
              241st Engr Bn, 241st Sig Bn
Auxiliary unit number: 241
Home station: (Wkr. I)
Formed in January, 1940. Continuously engaged on Central Russian front.

162nd Infantry Division

Commander: Lt Gen Hermann FRANKE (63)
Composition: 303d Inf Regt, 314th Inf Regt, 329th? Inf Regt,
              236th Arty Regt, 236th Rcn Bn, 236th AT Bn,
              236th Engr Bn, 236th Sig Bn
Auxiliary unit number: 236
Home station: Rostock? (Wkr. II)
Formed in January, 1940. Continiously engaged on Central Russian front from the beginning of the campaign until the end of 1941.

163rd Infantry Division

Commander: Lt Gen Erwin ENGELBRECHT (51)
Composition: 307th Inf Regt, 310th Inf Regt, 324th Inf Regt,
              234th Arty Regt, 234th Cyclist Co, 234th AT Bn,
              234th Engr Bn, 234th Sig Bn
Auxiliary unit number: 234
Home station: Berlin (Wkr. III)
Formed in January, 1940. Personnel mainly Prussian. Fought well in the Gudbransdal during the Norwegian campaign. Was transferred to Finland at beginning of Russian campaign where it has fought fairly continiously.

164th Infantry Division

Commander:
Composition: 382d Inf Regt, 433d Inf Regt, 440th Inf Regt,
              220th Arty Regt, 220th Rcn Bn, 220th AT Bn,
              220th Engr Bn, 220th Sig Bn
Auxiliary unit number: 220
Home station: Leipzig (Wkr. IV)
Formed in January, 1940. In reserve on the Western front, it was first identified in action in Greece. Has remained in the Aegean, and since the close of the Balkan campaign based at first in Salonika, and since early in 1942, on Crete. Transferred to Panzer Army Africa during summer of 1942.

167th Infantry Division

Commander: Maj Gen SCHARTOW (51)
Composition: 315th Inf Regt, 331st Inf Regt, 339th Inf Regt,
             238th Arty Regt, 238th Rcn Bn, 238th AT Bn,
             238th Engr Bn, 238th Sig Bn
Auxiliary unit number: 238?
Home station: (Wkr. VII)
  Formed in January, 1940. Personnel Bavarian. First in action during the
Battle of France. Continuously engaged on the Central Russian front since the
beginning of the campaign.

168th Infantry Division

Commander:
Composition: 417th Inf Regt, 429th Inf Regt, 442nd Inf Regt,
               248th Arty Regt, 248th Rcn Bn, 248th AT Bn,
               248th Engr Bn, 248th Sig Bn
Auxiliary unit number: 248
Home station: (Wkr. VIII)
  Formed in January, 1940. Identified on the Southern Russian front in July,
1941, but does not appear to have seen much action.

169th Infantry Division

Commander: Lt Gen Hermann TITTEL (53)
Composition: 378th Inf Regt, 379th Inf Regt, 392d Inf Regt,
               230th Arty Regt, 230th Rcn Bn, 230th AT Bn,
               230th Engr Bn, 230th Sig Bn
Auxiliary unit number: 230
Home Station: (Wkr. IX)
  Formed in January, 1940. First in action during Battle of France. Apparently
arrived in Finland from Norway during the early stages of the Russian campaign
and has been in action on the Kandalaksha front .

170th Infantry Division

Commander: Lt Gen Walter WITTKE (53)
Composition: 391st Inf Regt, 399th Inf Regt, 401st Inf Regt,
               240th Arty Regt, 240th Rcn Bn, 240th AT Bn,
               240th Engr Bn, 240th Sig Bn
Auxiliary unit number: 240
Home Station: Bremen (Wkr. X)
  Formed in January, 1940. Fairly continuously engaged on the Southern Russian
front and in the Crimea since the beginning of the campaign.

181st Infantry Division

Commander: Lt Gen BAYER (55)

Composition: 344th Inf Regt, 349th Inf Regt, 359th Inf Regt,
222d Arty Regt, 222d Cyclist Bn, 222d AT
Bn, 222d Engr Bn, 222d Sig Bn
Auxiliary unit number: 222
Home Station: (Wkr. XI)
Formed in January, 1940. Employed in Norway (Trondhjem-Dombaas area) since April, 1940.

183d Infantry Division

Commander: Maj Gen Richard STEMPEL (57)
Composition: 343d (?) Inf Regt, 351st Inf Regt, 402d Inf Regt,
219th Arty Regt, 219th Rcn Bn, 219th AT
Bn, 219th Engr Bn, 219th Sig Bn
Auxiliary unit number: 219
Home station: (Wkr. XIII)
Formed in January, 1940. Identified on Central Russian front late in 1941, but does not appear to have seen much action.

196th Infantry Division

Commander: Maj Gen Dr. Friedrich FRANEK (51)
Composition: 340th Inf Regt, 345th Inf Regt, 362d Inf Regt,
233d Arty Regt, 233d Cyclist Bn, 233d AT
Bn, 233 Engr Bn, 233 Sig Bn
Auxiliary unit number: 233
Home station: Bielefeld (Wkr.VI)
Formed early in 1940. Fought well during Norwegian campaign and stayed on as a garrison division in Central Norway.

197th Infantry Division

Commander: Lt Gen Hermann MEYER-RABINGEN (53)
Composition: 321st Inf Regt, 332d Inf Regt, 347th Inf Regt, 229th Arty Regt, 229th
Rcn Bn, 229th AT Bn, 229th Engr Bn, 229th Sig Bn
Auxiliary unit number: 229
Home station: Speyer (Wkr.XII)
Formed early in 1940. Identified on Central Russian front in August, 1941, where it has been fairly continuously in action.

198th Infantry Division

Commander:
Composition: 305th Inf Regt, 326th Inf Regt, Inf Regt,
235th Arty Regt, 235th Rcn Bn, 235th AT
Bn, 235th Engr Bn, 235th Sig Bn
Auxiliary unit number: 235
Home station: (Wkr.V)

Formed early in 1940. Identified on Southern Russian front in July, 1941, where it appears to have been fairly continuously engaged.

199th Infantry Division

Commander: Lt Gen Hans v.KEMPSKI (57)
Composition: 341st Inf Regt, 357th Inf Regt, 410th Inf Regt,
             199th Arty Regt, 199th Rcn Bn, 199th AT Bn,
             199th Engr Bn, 199th Sig Bn
Auxiliary unit number: 199
Home station: Düsseldorf (Wkr.VI)
  Formed in the spring, 1940. In southern Norway from end of 1940 till med-May 1941, when it was moved to Northern Norway. During latter half of 1941 it may have been for a time in Finland but did not do any fighting. Since December, 1941, in Central Norway (Tromsö area).

205th Infantry Division

Commander: Lt Gen RICHTER (53)
Composition: 335th Inf Regt, 353d Inf Regt, 358th Inf Regt,
             205th Arty Regt, 205th Cyclist Co,
             205th AT Bn, 205th Engr Bn, 205th Sig Bn
Auxiliary unit number: 205
Home station: Ulm (Wkr. V)
  Formed on mobilization with a high proportion of Landwehr personnel, from Baden and Württemberg. Identified in France in August, 1941, and left for Russia early in 1942. In action in the Central Sector during March and April. Personnel now more uniformly distributed in age groups..

206th Infantry Division

Commander: Lt Gen Hugo HÖFL (63)
Composition: 301st Inf Regt, 312th Inf Regt, 330th Inf Regt,
             206th Arty Regt, 206th Cyclist Co, 206th AT Bn,
             206th Engr Bn, 206th Sig Bn
Auxiliary unit number: 206
Home station: Gumbinnen (Wkr.I)
  Formed on mobilization. Personnel mainly E Prussian, of Landwehr age group. Fairly continuously engaged on Central Russian front since the beginning of the campaign. Personnel now of normal age groups.

207th Infantry Division-see 207th "Sicherungs" (L of C) Div. (Section XV)

208th Infantry Division

Commander: Lt Gen ANDREAS (56)
Composition: 309th Inf Regt, 337th Inf Regt, 338th Inf Regt,
             208th Arty Regt, 208th Cyclist Co, 208th AT Bn,

208th Engr Bn, 208th Sig Bn
Auxiliary unit number: 208
Home station: Cottbus (Wkr. III)
Formed on mobilization. Personnel Prussian, originally mainly Landwehr. Identified in France in April, 1941, and was transferred to Russia, probably in December, where it has been continuously engaged with the Center Group since January, 1942. Personnel age groups now normal.

(209th Infantry Division)

(Landwehr division formed in Wkr. IV on mobilization, with Saxon personnel. Disbanded after the Battle of France.)

211th Infantry Division

Commander: Lt Gen Theodor RENNER (55)
Composition: 306th Inf Regt, 317th Inf Regt, 366th Inf Regt,
211th Arty Regt, 211 Rcn Bn, 211th AT Bn,
211th Engr Bn, 211 Sig Bn
Auxiliary unit number: 211
Home station: Cologne (Wkr. VI)
Formed on mobilization. Personnel mainly from Cologne area and of Landwehr age group. In SW France during most of 1941. Moved east at the beginning of 1942 and has fought on the Central front. Personnel now normal.

212th Infantry Division

Commander: Lt Gen Theodor ENDRES (65)
Composition: 316th Inf Regt, 320th Inf Regt, 323d Inf Regt,
212th Arty Regt, 212th Cyclist Co, 212th AT Bn,
212th Engr Bn, 212th Sig Bn
Auxiliary unit number: 212
Home station: Munich (Wkr. VII)
Formed on mobilization, with personnel mainly from Southern Bavaria, and of Landwehr age group. On the Saar front for a time, later in France. Morale believed to be uneven. Left France for Russia late in 1941 where it has been identified in the Center Group but does not appear to have been much in action. Personnel age groups now normal.

213th Infantry Division-see 213th "Sicherungs" (L of C)
Div. (Section XV)

214th Infantry Division

Commander: Lt Gen Max HORN (53)
Composition: 355th Inf Regt, 367th Inf Regt, 388th Inf Regt,
214th Arty Regt, 214th Rcn Bn, 214th AT Bn,
214th Engr Bn, 214th Sig Bn

Auxiliary unit number: 214
Home station: Hanau (Wkr. IX)
   Formed on mobilization, with personnel from the Frankfurt area. Saar front
till December, 1939. In Southern Norway since May, 1940. From September,
1941, 388th Inf Regt has been detached for service in North Finland.

215th Infantry Division

Commander:
Composition: 380th Inf Regt, 390th Inf Regt, 435th Inf Regt,
               215th Arty Regt, 215th Rcn Bn, 215th AT Bn,
               215th Engr Bn, 215th Sign Bn
Auxiliary unit number: 215
Home station: Heilbronn (Wkr.V)
   Formed on mobilization. Personnel mainly Landwehr, from Baden and
Württemberg. On the Saar front in May, 1940. Fighting value unknown. In
Central France during the summer of 1941, but left for Russia late in that
year and has been identified subsequently in the Northern Group. Personnel
age groups now normal.

216th Infantry Division

Commander: Maj Gen Werner Frhr. v.u.zu GILSA (52)
Composition: 348th Inf Regt, 396th Inf Regt, 398th Inf Regt,
               216th Arty Regt, 216th Rcn Bn, 216th AT
               Bn, 216th Engr Bn, 216th Sig Bn
Auxiliary unit number: 216
Home station: Hannover (Wkr. XI)
   Formed on mobilization. Personnel mainly Landwehr from Hannover area.
Fought in Holland and Belgium. Fighting value unknown. Apparently arrived
on the Central Russian front from France early in January, 1942, and went im-
mediately into action. Personnel now normal.

217th Infantry Division

Commander: Lt Gen Willy BALTZER (56)
Composition: 311th Inf Regt, 346th Inf Regt, 413th Inf Regt, 217th Arty Regt,
       217th Rcn Bn, 217th AT Bn, 217th Engr Bn, 217th Sig Bn
Auxiliary unit number: 217
Home station: Allenstein (Wkr. I)
  Formed on mobilization. Personnel mainly East Prussian, of Landwehr age group. Fought in Poland and in Flanders. Identified on Northern Russian front in July, 1941. Employed on coastal defense duties and has apparently suffered appreciable casualties in fighting round Leningrad. Personnel now normal.

218th Infantry Division

Commander:
Composition: 323d Inf Regt, 386th Inf Regt, 397th Inf Regt, 218th Arty Regt,
       218th Rcn Bn, 218th AT Bn, 218th Engr Bn, 218th Sig Bn
Auxiliary unit number: 218
Home station: Berlin (Wkr. III)
  Formed on mobilization. Personnel mainly of the Landwehr age-group. Distinguished itself both in Poland and France, but has been reorganized since those campaigns with draft of younger men. In Denmark from May, 1941, till January, 1942, when it left for the Eastern front.

221st Infantry Division—see 221st "Sicherungs" (L of C) Div (Section XV)

223d Infantry Division

Commander: Lt Gen Willy KÖRNER (61)
Composition: 344th Inf Regt, 385th Inf Regt, 425th Inf Regt, 223d Arty Regt,
       223d Rcn Bn, 223d AT Bn, 223d Engr Bn, 223 Sig Bn
Auxiliary unit number: 223
Home station: Dresden (Wkr. IV)
  Formed on mobilization. Personnel Saxon, mainly Landwehr. No evidence for active operations prior to the Russian campaign. Identified in Southwestern France in May, 1941, where it remained until transferred to Russia at the end of the year. Personnel now normal.

225th Infantry Division

Commander:
Composition: 333d Inf Regt, 376th Inf Regt, 377th Inf Regt, 225th Arty Regt,
       225th Rcn Bn, 225th AT Bn, 225th Engr Bn, 225th Sig Bn
Auxiliary unit number: 225
Home station: Hamburg (Wkr. X)
  Formed in greater Hamburg district on mobilization. Personnel mainly of Landwehr age groups. Arrived on Northern Russian front from France in January, 1942, having been transported by sea from Danzig to Riga. Appears to have suffered appreciable casualties on the Leningrad front during March and April. Personnel now normal.

227th Infantry Division

Commander: Lt Gen ZICKWOLFF (53)
Composition: 328th Inf Regt, 365th Inf Regt, 412th Inf Regt, 227th Arty Regt,
227th Cyclist Co, 227th AT Bn, 227th Engr Bn, 227th Sig Bn
Auxiliary unit number: 227
Home station: Düsseldorf (Wkr. VI)
Formed on mobilization, Personnel mainly of Landwehr age group. Took part
in active operations in Belgium. In NE France in latter part of 1941. Identi-
fied on Norther Russian front in April, 1942. Personnel now normal.

228th Infantry Division

Commander:
Composition: 325th Inf Regt, 356th Inf Regt, 400th Inf Regt, 228th Arty Regt,
228th Rcn Bn, 228th AT Bn, 228th Engr Bn, 228th Sig Bn
Auxiliary unit number: 228
Home station: Lötzen (Wkr. I)
Formed in Elbing area on mobilization. Personnel mainly Landwehr. Dis-
tinguished itself in North Poland; later in action in Holland and Belgium. In the
Protectorate during the winter of 1940-41. First identified on the Central
Russian front in September, 1941, where it appears to have been held in reserve.
Personnel now normal.

(231st Infantry Division)

(Landwehr division formed in Wkr. XIII on mobilization. No evidence of any
active operations. Disbanded after theFrench Campaign.)

239th Infantry Division

Commander: Lt Gen Ferdinand NEULING (56)
Composition: 327th Inf Regt, 372d Inf Regt, 444th Inf Regt, 239th Arty Regt,
239 Rcn Bn, 239th AT Bn, 239th Engr Bn, 239th Sig Bn
Auxiliary unit number: 239
Home Station: Oppeln (Wkr. VIII)
Formed on mobilization. No evidence of any active operations prior to the
Russian campaign. In the Protectorate during the winter of 1940-41. Con-
tinuously engaged on the Southern front since the beginning of the campaign.

246th Infantry Division

Commander:
Composition: 313th Inf Regt, 352d Inf Regt, 404th Inf Regt, 246th Arty Regt,
246th Cyclist Co, 246th AT Bn, 246th Engr Bn, 246th Sig Bn
Auxiliary unit number: 246
Home Station: Trier (Wkr. XII)
Formed on mobilization. On the Saar front for a time. In SW France between
August, 1941, and mid-January, 1942, when it left for the Eastern front.

250th Infantry Division (Blue Division)

Commander: (Spanish) Gen. Estaban INFANTES
Composition: 262d Inf Regt, 263d Inf Regt, 269th Inf Regt, 250th Arty Regt
Auxiliary unit number: 250
   Formed in August, 1941, from Spanish volunteers, at Grafenwöhr (Wkr. XIII).
Originally destined for the Southern Russian front, it was eventually sent to the
Northern Sector, where it has been since late 1941. Has suffered considerable
casualties both in battle and from frost-bite.

251st Infantry Division

Commander:
Composition: 451st Inf Regt, 459th Inf Regt, 471st Inf Regt, 251st Arty Regt,
           251st Rcn Bn, 251st AT Bn, 251st Engr Bn, 251st Sig Bn
Auxiliary unit number: 251
Home Station: (Wkr. IX).
   Formed on mobilization from men already serving in Ergänzungs units in
Hessen and Thüringen. First identified on Central Russian front in July, 1941,
where it has been fairly heavily and continuously engaged.

252d Infantry Division

Commander:
Composition: 452d Inf Regt, 461st Inf Regt, 472d Inf Regt, 252d Arty Regt, 252d
           Rcn Bn, 252d AT Bn, 252d Engr Bn, 252d Sig Bn
Auxiliary unit number: 252
Home Station: Neisse (Wkr. VIII)
   Formed on mobilization from Silesians already serving in Ergänzungs units.
On the Saar front for several months. Later distinguished itself in the attack on
the Maginot Line. Morale high. Continuously and heavily engaged on Central
Russian front since the beginning of the campaign.

253d Infantry Division

Commander: Lt Gen Fritz KÜHNE (58)
Composition: 453d Inf Regt, 464th Inf Regt, 473d Inf Regt, 253d Arty Regt, 253d
           Rcn Bn, 253d AT Bn, 253d Engr Bn, 253d Sig Bn
Auxiliary unit number: 253
Home Station: Cologne (Wkr. VI)
   Formed on mobilization from men already serving in Westphalian Ergänzungs
units. Took part in the Battle of France. First identified on the Northern
Russian front in July, 1941, but subsequently transferred to the Center Group.
Appears to have sustained considerable casualties.

254th Infantry Division

Commander:
Composition: 454th Inf Regt, 474th Inf Regt, 484th Inf Regt, 254th Arty Regt,
           254th Rcn Bn, 254th AT Bn, 254th Engr Bn, 254th Sig Bn

Auxiliary unit number: 254
Home Station: Dortmund (?) (Wkr. VI)
Formed on mobilization from men already serving in Westphalian Ergänzungs units. Took part in active operations in Holland, Belgium and N France. Identified on Northern Russian front in July, 1941, where it was in action during November and December.

255th Infantry Division

Commander: Lt Gen WETZEL (54)
Composition: 455th Inf Regt, 465th Inf Regt, 475th Inf Regt, 255th Arty Regt, 255th Rcn Bn, 255th AT Bn, 255th Engr Bn, 255th Sig Bn
Auxiliary unit number: 255
Home Station: Löbau (Wkr. IV)
Formed on mobilization from men already serving in Saxon Ergänznugs units. Also contains a proportion of Sudeten Germans. Took an inconspicuous part in the Battle of France. Identified on Central Russian front in August, 1941, where it has been fairly continuously engaged.

256th Infantry Division

Commander: Lt Gen KAUFFMANN (51)
Composition: 456th Inf Regt, 476th Inf Regt, 481st Inf Regt, 256th Arty Regt, 256th Rcn Bn, 256th AT Bn, 256th Engr Bn, 256th Sig Bn
Auxiliary unit number: 256
Home Station: Meissen (?) (Wkr. IV/XIII)
Formed in Wkr. IV and XIII on mobilization from men already serving in Ergänzungs units. Personnel Saxon, Bavarian and Sudeten Germans. Fought in Holland and Belgium. Continuously engaged in Russia, with the Center Group, since the beginning of the campaign.

257th Infantry Division

Commander:
Composition: 457th Inf Regt, 466th Inf Regt, 477th Inf Regt, 257th Arty Regt, 257th Rcn Bn, 257th AT Bn, 257th Engr Bn, 257th Sig Bn
Auxiliary unit number: 257
Home Station: Frankfurt/Oder (Wkr. III)
Formed on mobilization from men already serving in Ergänzungs units. Personnel Prussian. On the Saar front for a time. Identified on the Southern Russian front in July, 1941, where it has been continuously and heavily engaged.

258th Infantry Division

Commander: Lt Gen WOLIMANN (51)
Composition: 458th Inf Regt, 478th Inf Regt, 479th Inf Regt, 258th Arty Regt, 258th Rcn Bn, 258th AT Bn, 258th Engr Bn, 258th Sig Bn
Auxiliary unit number: 258
Home Station: Rostock (Wkr. II)

Formed in Wkre. II and III on mobilization from men already serving in Ergänzungs units. Personnel Prussian. On the Saar front for some months, and took part in the attack on the Maginot Line. Continuously engaged on Central Russian front since the beginning of the campaign and suffered considerable losses during the final attack on Moscow.

260th Infantry Division

Commander:
Composition: 460th Inf Regt, 470th Inf Regt, 480th Inf Regt, 260th Arty Regt,
260th Rcn Bn, 260th AT Bn, 260th Engr Bn, 260th Sig Bn
Auxiliary unit number: 260
Home Station: Karlsruhe (Wkr. V)
Formed on mobilization from men already serving in Ergänzungs units in Baden and Württemberg. No evidence of active operations prior to the Russian campaign. Continuously and heavily engaged on the Central front.

262d Infantry Division

Commander: Lt Gen Edgar THEISEN (53)
Composition: 462d Inf Regt, 482d Inf Regt, 486th Inf Regt, 262d Arty Regt, 262d
Rcn Bn, 262d AT Bn, 262 Engr Bn, 262 Sig Bn
Auxiliary unit number: 262
Home Station: Vienna (Wkr. XVII)
Formed on mobilization from men already serving in Ergänzungs units in Austria. On the Saar front for several months. Identified on the Central Russian front in September, 1941, where it has been continuously engaged.

263d Infantry Division

Commander: Maj Gen Ernst HAECKEL (51)
Composition: 463d Inf Regt, 483d Inf Regt, 485th Inf Regt, 263d Arty Regt, 263d
Rcn Bn, 263d AT Bn, 263d Engr Bn, 263d Sig Bn
Auxiliary unit number; 263
Home Station: Idar-Oberstein (Wkr. XII)
Formed on mobilization from men already serving in Ergänzungs units. Personnel mainly Bavarians from the Palatinate. Fought with distinction during the Battle of France. Identified on Central Russian front in July, 1941, where it has been fairly heavily engaged.

267th Infantry Division

Commander: Lt Gen Friedrich Karl v. WACHTER (52)
Composition: 467th Inf Regt, 487th Inf Regt, 497th Inf Regt, 267th Arty Regt,
267th Rcn Bn, 267th AT Bn, 267th Engr Bn, 267th Sig Bn
Auxiliary unit number: 267
Home Station: (Wkr. XI)
Formed on mobilization from men already serving in Ergänzungs units in the Hannover-Braunschweig area. Identified on Central Russian front in July, 1941,

where it has been fairly continuously engaged.

268th Infantry Division

Commander: Lt Gen Erich STRAUBE (54)
Composition: 468th Inf Regt, 488th Inf Regt, 499th Inf Regt, 268th Arty Regt,
              268th Rcn Bn, 268th AT Bn, 268th Engr Bn, 268th Sig Bn
Auxiliary unit number: 268
Home Station: Munich (Wkr. VII)
   Formed in Wehrkreise VII and XVII on mobilization from men already serving
in Ergänzungs units. On the Saar front for several months. Continuously en-
gaged since the beginning of the Russian campaign on the Central front, where it
appears to have suffered appreciable casualties.

269th Infantry Division

Commander:
Composition: 469th Inf Regt, 489th Inf Regt, 490th Inf Regt, 269th Arty Regt,
              269th Rcn Bn, 269th AT Bn, 269th Engr Bn, 269th Sig Bn
Auxiliary unit number: 269
Home Station: Delmenhorst (Wkr. X)
   Formed on mobilization from men already serving in Ergänzungs units. Personnel N German. Fought in N France, Transferred to Denmark in the late
summer of 1940, where it remained until May, 1941. Heavily engaged in Russia,
in the Northern Group until early 1942, when it appears to have been withdrawn
for rest.

270th Infantry Division

Commander:
Home Station: (Wkr. X)
   Formed before midsummer, 1940. Probably only a local defense or admini-
strative division staff.

272d Infantry Division

Commander:
Home Station: Neustrelitz (Wkr. II)
   Formed before midsummer, 1940. Probably only a local defense or administra-
tive division staff.

276th Infantry Division

Commander:
Home Station: (Wkr. VI)(?)
   Formed before midsummer, 1940. Probably only a local defense or administra-
tive division staff.

277th Infantry Division

Commander: Maj Gen Friedrich HÜHNLEIN (68)
Home Station: Augsburg (?) (Wkr. VII)
Formed before midsummer, 1940. Probably only a local defense or administrative division staff.

290th Infantry Division

Commander: Lt Gen Max DENNERLEIN (56)
Composition: 501st Inf Regt, 502d Inf Regt, 503d Inf Regt, 290th Arty Regt,
290th Rcn Bn, 290th AT Bn, 290th Engr Bn, 290th Sig Bn
Auxiliary unit number: 290
Home Station: (Wkr.X)
Formed in March/April, 1940, from newly trained personnel. First in action in June, 1940, during the Battle of France, where its fighting value was unknown. Heavily engaged on the Northern Russian front since July, 1941, and appears to have suffered considerable casualties.

291st Infantry Division

Commander: Lt Gen Kurt HERZOG (54)
Composition: 504th Inf Regt, 505th Inf Regt, 506th Inf Regt, 291st Arty Regt,
291st Rcn Bn, 291st AT Bn, 291st Engr Bn, 291st Sig Bn
Auxiliary unit number: 291
Home Station: Insterburg (Wkr. I)
Formed in March/April, 1940, from newly trained Prussian personnel. First in action during the Battle of France, when it had little hard fighting to do. Identified on the Northern Russian front in July, 1941, but does not appear to have been much in action.

292d Infantry Division

Commander: Maj Gen SEEGER (51)
Composition: 507th Inf Regt, 508th Inf Regt, 509th Inf Regt, 292d Arty Regt,
292d Rcn Bn, 292d AT Bn, 292d Engr Bn, 292d Sig Bn
Auxiliary unit number: 292
Home Station: (Wkr. II)
Formed in March/April, 1940, from newly trained Prussian personnel. Experience in the Battle of France similar to that of 291st Division. Identified on the Central Russian front in August, 1941.

293d Infantry Division

Commander: Lt Gen Justin v. OBERNITZ (57)
Composition: 510th Inf Regt, 511th Inf Regt, 512th Inf Regt, 293d Arty Regt,
293d Rcn Bn, 293d AT Bn, 293d Engr Bn, 293d Sig Bn
Auxiliary unit number: 293
Home Station: (Wkr. III)
Formed in March/April, 1940, from newly trained Prussian personnel. Experience in the Battle of France similar to that of 291st Division. Identified

on the Central Russian front in July, 1941, where it has been continuously and heavily engaged and appears to have suffered appreciable losses.

294th Infantry Division

Commander:
Composition: 513th Inf Regt, 514th Inf Regt, 515th Inf Regt, 294th Arty Regt, 294th Rcn Bn, 294th AT Bn, 294th Engr Bn, 294th Sig Bn
Auxiliary unit number: 294
Home Station: (Wkr. IV)
    Formed in March/April, 1940, from newly trained Saxon personnel. First identified in action during the Balkan campaign and has fought on the Russian front, with the Southern Group, since September, 1942.

295th Infantry Division

Commander:
Composition: 516th Inf Regt, 517th Inf Regt, 518th Inf Regt, 295th Arty Regt, 295th Rcn Bn, 295th AT Bn, 295th Engr Bn, 295th Sig Bn
Auxiliary unit number: 295
Home Station: (Wkr. XI)
    Formed in March/April, 1940, from newly trained personnel. Not identified in action prior to the Russian campaign, where it was continuously engaged on the Southern front from July, 1941, until February, 1942.

296th Infantry Division

Commander: Lt Gen Wilhelm STEMMERMANN (53)
Composition: 519th Inf Regt, 520th Inf Regt, 521st Inf Regt, 296th Arty Regt, 296th Rcn Bn, 296th AT Bn, 296th Engr Bn, 296th Sig Bn
Auxiliary unit number: 296
Home Station: Nuremburg (?) (Wkr. XIII)
    Formed in March/April, 1940, from newly trained men from N Bavaria and W Sudetenland. Not identified in action prior to the Russian campaign, where it has operated with the Center Group and was involved in particularly heavy fighting around Tula late in 1941.

297th Infantry Division

Commander: Lt Gen Max PFEFFER (57)
Composition: 522d Inf Regt, 523d Inf Regt, 524th Inf Regt, 297th Arty Regt, 297th Rcn Bn, 297th AT Bn, 297th Engr Bn, 297th Sig Bn
Auxiliary unit number: 297
Home Station: Vienna (Wkr. XVII)
    Formed in March/April, 1940, from newly trained Austrian personnel. Not identified in action prior to the Russian campaign where it has operated with the Southern Group since July, 1941.

298th Infantry Division

Commander: Gen GRAESSNER (50)
Composition: 525th Inf Regt, 526th Inf Regt, 527th Inf Regt, 298th Arty Regt,
        298th Rcn Bn, 298th AT Bn, 298th Engr Bn, 298th Sig Bn
Auxiliary unit number: 298
Home Station: (Wkr. VIII)
   Formed in March/April, 1940, from newly trained Silesian personnel. Not
identified in action prior to the Russian campaign, where it has operated with
the Southern Group since July, 1941.

299th Infantry Division

Commander: Lt Gen Willi MOSER (53)
Composition: 528th Inf Regt, 529th Inf Regt, 530th Inf Regt, 299th Arty Regt,
        299th Rcn Bn, 299th AT Bn, 299th Engr Bn, 299th Sig Bn
Auxiliary unit number: 299
Home Station: Weimar (Wkr. IX)
   Formed in March/April, 1940, from newly trained men from Hessen and
Thüringen. First in action during the Battle of France in June, 1940. Continuous-
ly engaged in Russia, on the Southern front, until early in 1942.

302d Infantry Division

Commander:
Composition: 570th Inf Regt, 571st (?) Inf Regt, 572d (?) Inf Regt, 302d Arty
        Regt, 302d Rcn Co, 302d AT Bn, 302d Engr Bn, 302 Sig Co
Auxiliary unit number: 302
Home Station: (Wkr. II)
   Probably formed late in 1940, but not reliably identified till early in 1942 in
N France, where it has remained.

304th Infantry Division

Commander:
Composition: 573d Inf Regt, 574th Inf Regt, 575th (?) Inf Regt, 304th Arty Regt,
        304th Rcn Co, 304th AT Bn, 304th Engr Bn, 304th Sig Co
Auxiliary unit number: 304
Home Station: (Wkr. IV)
   Probably formed early in 1940. Since April, 1942, in Belgium.

305th Infantry Division

Commander:
Composition: 576th Inf Regt, 577th Inf Regt, 578th Inf Regt, 305th Arty Regt,
        305th Rcn Co, 305th AT Bn, 305th Engr Bn, 305th Sig Co
Auxiliary unit number: 305
Home Station: (Wkr.V)
   Date of formation uncertain. In W France from end of 1941 until beginning of
May, 1942, when it left, presumably for the Russian front.

306th Infantry Division

Commander:
Composition: 579th Inf Regt, 580th Inf Regt,581st Inf Regt, 306th Arty Regt, 306th
       Rcn Co, 306th AT Bn, 306th Engr Bn, 306th Sig Co
Auxiliary unit number: 306
Home Station: (Wkr. VI)
 Date of formation uncertain. In Belgium since late 1941.

311th Infantry Division

Commander: Lt Gen Albrecht BRAND (54)
Classification and composition uncertain.
Home Station: (Wkr. I)

319th Infantry Division

Commander:
Composition: 582d Inf Regt, 583d Inf Regt, 584th Inf Regt, 319th Arty Regt, 319th
       Rcn Co, 319th AT Bn, 319th Engr Bn, 319th Sig Co
Auxiliary unit number: 319
Home Station: (Wkr. IX)
 Date of formation uncertain. In Brittany since August, 1941.

320th Infantry Division

Commander:
Composition: 585th Inf Regt, 586th Inf Regt, 587th Inf Regt, 320th Arty Regt,
       320th Rcn Co, 320 AT Bn, 320th Engr Bn, 320th Sig Co
Auxiliary unit number: 320
Home Station: (Wkr. X)
 Date of formation uncertain. Moved early in January, 1942, from Belgium to
Brittany. Transferred early April to NE France.

321st Infantry Division

Commander:
Composition: 588th Inf Regt, 589th Inf Regt, 590th Inf Regt, 321st Arty Regt,
       321st Rcn Co, 321st AT Bn, 321st Engr Bn, 321st Sig Co
Auxiliary unit number: 321
Home Station: (Wkr. XI)
 Date of formation uncertain. In NE France since end of 1941.

323d Infantry Division

Commander:
Composition: 591st Inf Regt, 592d Inf Regt, 593d Inf Regt, 323d Arty Regt,
       323d Rcn Co, 323d AT Bn, 323d Engr Bn, 323d Sig Co
Auxiliary unit number: 323
Home Station: (Wkr. XIII)
 Date of formation uncertain. In NW France from end of 1941 until early May,

1942, when it left, presumably for Russia.

327th Infantry Division

Commander:
Composition: 595th Inf Regt, 596th Inf Regt, 597th Inf Regt, 327th Arty Regt,
327th Rcn Co, 327th AT Bn, 327th Engr Bn, 327th Sig Co
Auxiliary unit number: 327
Home Station: (Wkr. XVII)
  Date of formation uncertain. In E France in latter half of 1941, and in SW
France from January, 1942, onwards.

328th Infantry Division

Commander:
Composition: Inf Regt,   Inf Regt,   Inf Regt, 328th Arty Regt, 328th Rcn
Co, 328th AT Bn, 328th Engr Bn, 328th Sig Co
Auxiliary unit number: 328
Home Station: (Wkr. IX)
  Date of formation uncertain. First identified in March 1942, and probably in
reserve on the Central Russian front.

330th Infantry Division

Commander: Lt Gen Karl GRAF (59)
Composition: 554th Inf Regt, 555th Inf Regt, 556th Inf Regt, 330th Arty Regt,
330th Cyclist Bn, 330th AT Bn, 330th Engr Bn, 330th Sig Co
Auxiliary unit number: 330
Home Station: (Wkr. XIII)
  Date of formation uncertain. First identified in February, 1942, and has sub-
sequently been in action on the Central Russian front.

331st Infantry Division

Commander:
Composition: 557th Inf Regt, 558th Inf Regt, 559th Inf Regt, 331st Arty Regt,
331st Rcn Co, 331st AT Bn, 331st Sig Co
Auxiliary unit number: 331
Home Station:
  Date of formation uncertain. First identified in February, 1942, and now in
reserve on the Central Russian front.

332d Infantry Division

Commander:
Composition: 676th Inf Regt, 677th Inf Regt, 678th Inf Regt, 332d Arty Regt,
332d Rcn Co, 332d AT Bn, 332 Engr Bn, 332 Sig Co
Auxiliary unit number:
Home Station: (Wkr. VIII)

106

Formed in January, 1941, In Normandy since August, 1941.

333d Infantry Division

Commander:
Composition: 679th Inf Regt, 680th Inf Regt, 681st Inf Regt, 333d Arty Regt,
333d Cyclist Co, 333d AT Bn, 333d Engr Bn, 333 Sig Co
Auxiliary unit number: 333
Home Station: Berlin (Wkr. III)
Formed in January, 1941. Moved in May, 1941, from Wkr. III to SW France.
Transferred to Brittany in March, 1942.

335th Infantry Division

Commander:
Composition: 682d Inf Regt, 683d Inf Regt, 684th Inf Regt, 335th Arty Regt,
335 Rcn Co, 335th AT Bn, 335th Engr Bn, 335th Sig Co
Auxiliary unit number: 335
Home Station: (Wkr. V)
Formed in January, 1941. First identified in N France in October, 1941.
Moved in to Brittany February, 1942.

336th Infantry Division

Commander: Maj Gen Walther LUCHT (59)
Composition: 685th Inf Regt, 686th Inf Regt, 687th Inf Regt, 336th Arty Regt,
336th Rcn Co, 336th AT Bn, 336th Engr Bn, 336th Sig Co
Auxiliary unit number: 336
Home Station: Rheine (Wkr. VI)
Formed in January, 1941, with cadres from 256th Inf Div and moved to
Normandy. Transferred end of March 1942, to Brittany. Left for Eastern
front end of May, 1942.

337th Infantry Division

Commander:
Composition: 688th Inf Regt, 689th Inf Regt, 690th Inf Regt, 337th Arty Regt,
337th Rcn Co, 337th AT Bn, 337th Engr Bn, 337th Sig Co
Auxiliary unit number: 337
Home Station: (Wkr. VII)
Formed in January, 1941. In Central France from August, 1941, until May,
1942, when it left for the Eastern front.

339th Infantry Division

Commander:
Composition: 691st Inf Regt, 692d Inf Regt, 693d Inf Regt, 339th Arty Bn,
339th Rcn Co, 339th AT Bn, 339th Engr Bn, 339th Sig Co

Auxiliary unit number: 339
Home Station: Jena (Wkr. IX)
  Formed in January, 1941. In Central France until it left for the Russian front at the end of 1941. Has subsequently been in action in the Center Group.

340th Infantry Division

Commander: Maj Gen BUTZE (50)
Composition: 694th Inf Regt, 695th Inf Regt, 696th Inf Regt, 340th Arty Regt,
        340th Rcn Co, 340th AT Bn, 340th Engr Bn, 340th Sig Co
Auxiliary unit number: 340
Home Station: (Wkr. I)
  Formed in January, 1941, but first identified in April, 1942, in NE France.

342d Infantry Division

Commander: Maj Gen Kurt HOFFMANN (50)
Composition: 697th Inf Regt, 698th Inf Regt, 699th Inf Regt, 342d Arty Regt,
        342d Rcn Co, 342d AT Bn, 342d Engr Bn, 342 Sig Co
Auxiliary unit number: 342
Home Station: Kaiserslautern (Wkr. XII)
  Formed in January, 1940. Engaged in "mopping up" operations in Yugoslavia from late in 1941 until February, 1942, when it was transferred to the Central Sector of the Russian front.

358th Infantry Division

Landwehr division formed late in 1939 and believed disbanded after the Battle of France

365th Infantry Division

Landwehr division formed late in 1939 and believed disbanded after the Battle of France.

372d Infantry Division

Landwehr division formed late in 1939 and believed disbanded after the Battle of France

379th Infantry Division

Formed after mobilization. Believed converted to L of C command.

383d Infantry Division

Commander: Maj Gen Eberhard v. FABRICE (50)
Composition: 531st (?) Inf Regt, 532d (?) Inf Regt, 533d (?) Inf Regt, 383d Arty
        Regt, 383d Rcn Co, 383d AT Bn, 383d Engr Bn, 383d Sig Co

Auxiliary unit number:
Home Station:
  Formed in winter 1941-42. Not yet reported in action.

384th Infantry Division

Commander:
Composition: 534th (?) Inf Regt, 535th (?) Inf Regt, 536th (?) Inf Regt, 384th
              Arty Regt, 384th Rcn Co, 384th AT Bn, 384th Engr Bn, 384th Sig Co
Auxiliary unit number:
Home Station:
  Formed in winter 1941-42. In action on the Southern Russian front in May, 1942.

385th Infantry Division

Commander:
Composition: 537th (?) Inf Regt, 538th (?) Inf Regt, 539th Inf Regt, 385th Arty Regt,
              385th Rcn Co, 385th AT Bn, 385th Engr Bn, 385th Sig Co
Auxiliary unit number:
Home Station:
  Formed in winter 1941-42. In action on the Central Russian front since May,
1942.

386th Infantry Division

Commander:
Composition: 540th Inf Regt, 541st Inf Regt,   Inf Regt, 386th Arty Regt, 386th
              Rcn Co, 386th AT Bn, 386th Engr Bn, 386th Sig Co
Auxiliary unit number:
Home Station: (Wkr. VI)
  Formed late in 1939. Not identified since summer, 1940.

387th Infantry Division

Commander:
Composition: 542d Inf Regt, 543d Inf Regt, 547th Inf Regt, 387th Arty Regt,
              387th Rcn Co, 387th AT Bn, 387th Engr Bn, 387th Sig Co
Auxiliary unit number: 387
Home Station: (Wkr. VII)
  Formed in winter, 1941-42. On the Russian front since May, 1942.

389th Infantry Division

Commander:
Composition: 548th (?) Inf Regt, 549th (?) Inf Regt, 550th (?) Inf Regt, 389th
              Arty Regt, 389th Rcn Co, 389th AT Bn, 389th Engr Bn, 389th Sig Co
Auxiliary unit number:
Home Station: (Wkr. X) (?)
  Formed in winter, 1941-42. In action on the Southern Russian front May, 1942.

393d Infantry Division

Formed late in 1939. Now converted to a L of C Command.

395th Infantry Division

Formed after mobilization and believed disbanded after the Battle of France.

399th Infantry Division

Formed after mobilization and believed disbanded after the Battle of France.

554th Infantry Division

Formed in Wkr. IV early in 1940 and believed disbanded after the Battle of France.

555th Infantry Division

Formed in Wkr. VI in 1940 and probably disbanded after the Battle of France.

557th Infantry Division

Formed in Wkr. V in 1940 and believed disbanded after the Battle of France.

702d Infantry Division

Commander:
Composition: 722d Inf Regt, 742d Inf Regt,   Arty Bn, 702d Rcn Co, 702d
            Engr Bn, 702d Sig Co
Auxiliary unit number: 702
Home Station: (Wkr. II)
   Formed in April and sent to S Norway in May, 1941. Moved at the end of June,
1941, to N Norway. 742d Inf Regt has been under command of 181st Inf Div.

704th Infantry Division

Commander:
Composition: 724th Inf Regt, 734th Inf Regt, 654th Arty Bn, 704th Rcn Co, 704th
            Engr Bn, 704th Sig Co
Auxiliary unit number: 704
Home Station: (Wkr. IV)
   Formed in April, 1941. Known to have been in Yugoslavia between September,
1941, and April, 1942.

707th Infantry Division

Commander: Maj Gen Gustav, Frhr. v. MAUCHENHEIM gen. BECHTOLSHEIM
   (52)
Composition: 727th Inf Regt, 747th Inf Regt,   Arty Bn, 707 Rcn Co, 707th Engr
            Bn, 707th Sig Co

Auxiliary unit number: 707
Home Station: (Wkr. VII)
  Formed in April, 1941. Identified on the Central Russian front in October, 1941, where it has been employed on L of C duties.

708th Infantry Division

Commander: Lt Gen Hermann WILCK (57)
Composition: 728th Inf Regt, 748th Inf Regt,   Arty Bn, 708th Rcn Co, 708th
                    Engr Bn, 708th Sig Co
Auxiliary unit number: 708
Home Station: (Wkr. VIII)
  Formed in April, 1941. Probably in Central France in November, 1941, and from December, 1941, onwards in SW France.

709th Infantry Division

Commander:
Composition: 729th Inf Regt, 739th Inf Regt,   Arty Bn, 709th Rcn Co, 709th
                    Engr Bn, 709th Sig Co
Auxiliary unit number: 709
Home Station: (Wkr. IX)
  Formed in April 1941. In Brittany from November to mid-December, 1941, when it left, presumably for the Eastern front.

710th Infantry Division

Commander: Maj Gen PETSCH (54)
Composition: 730th Inf Regt, 740th Inf Regt,   Arty Bn, 710th Rcn Co, 710th
                    Engr Bn, 710th Sig Co
Auxiliary unit number: 710
Home Station: (Wkr. X)
  Formed in April, 1941. In Southern Norway since June, 1941.

711th Infantry Division

Commander:
Composition: 731st Inf Regt, 744th (?) Inf Regt,   Arty Bn, 711th Rcn Co,
                    711th Engr Bn, 711th Sig Co
Auxiliary unit number: 711
Home Station: (Wkr. XI) (?)
  Formed in April, 1941. From August to December, 1941, in NE France. From January, 1942, till mid-May, 1942, in W Normandy, although it may have been in SW France during March. Left in mid-May, presumably for Eastern front.

712th Infantry Division

Commander:
Composition: 732d Inf Regt, 745th Inf Regt,   Arty Bn, 712th Rcn Co,

712th Engr Bn, 712th Sig Co
Auxiliary unit number: 712
Home Station:
 Formed in April, 1941.

713th Infantry Division

Commander:
Composition: 733d Inf Regt, 746th Inf Regt,   Arty Bn, 713th Rcn Co, 713th
            Engr Bn, 713th Sig Co
Auxiliary unit number: 713
Home Station   (Wkr. XIII)
 Formed in April, 1941. Part in Crete and part in S Greece since autumn, 1941.

714th Infantry Division

Commander:
Composition: 721st Inf Regt, 741st Inf Regt,   Arty Bn, 714th Engr Bn, 714th
            Sig Co
Auxiliary unit number: 714
Home Station: (Wkr. 1)
 Formed in April 1941. Engaged in "mopping up" duties in Yugoslavia since
November, 1941.

715th Infantry Division

Commander:
Composition: 715th Inf Regt, 735th Inf Regt,   Arty Bn, 715th Rcn Co, 715th
            Engr Bn, 715th Sig Co
Auxiliary unit number: 715
Home Station: (Wkr. V)
 Formed in April, 1941. Since August, 1941, in SW France.

716th Infantry Division

Commander:
Composition: 726th Inf Regt, 736th Inf Regt,   Arty Bn, 716th Rcn Co, 716th
            Engr Bn, 716th Sig Co
Auxiliary unit number: 716
Home Station: (Wkr. VI (?))
 Formed in April, 1941, and identified in February, 1942, in Brittany. Since
beginning of April, 1942, in NE France.

717th Infantry Division

Commander:
Composition: 737th Inf Regt, 749th Inf Regt, 670th Arty Bn, 717th Rcn Co,
            717th Engr Bn, 717th Sig Co
Auxiliary unit number: 717

Home Station: (Wkr. XVII)
  Formed in April, 1941. Engaged in "mopping-up" operations in Yugoslavia since September, 1941.

718th Infantry Division

Commander: Maj Gen Johann FORTNER (58)
Composition: 718th Inf Regt, 750th Inf Regt,   Arty Bn, 718th Rcn Co, 718th
              Engr Bn, 718th Sig Co
Auxiliary unit number: 718
Home Station: (Wkr. XVIII)
  Formed in April, 1941. Stationed in Yugoslavia since summer, 1941.

719th Infantry Division

Commander:
Composition: 723d Inf Regt, 743d Inf Regt,   Arty Bn, 719th Rcn Co, 719th
              Engr Bn, 719th Sig Co
Auxiliary unit number: 719
Home Station: (Wkr. III)
  Formed in April, 1941. No evidence of its subsequent history.

SS "Police" Division

Commander: SS Maj Gen WÜNNENBERG
Composition: 1st Police R Regt, 2d Police R Regt, 3d Police R Regt, SS Police
              Arty Regt, Rcn Bn, AT Bn, Engr Bn, and Sig Bn
  Formed in October, 1939, with draftees from police units in all parts of Germany. Training completed in February, 1940. Has taken part in Western and Russian campaigns, incurring heavy casualties in the latter.

XV "SICHERUNGS" (L of C) DIVISIONS

207th Sicherungs (L of C) Division
(207 Sich.D.)

Commander:
Composition: 322d Reinf Inf Regt, 368th Reinf Inf Regt, 207th Cyclist
        Co, 207th AT Bn, 207th Engr Bn, 207th Sig Co
Auxiliary unit number: 207
Home station: Stargard (Wkr. II)
  Formed on mobilization as 207th Infantry Division with Prussian personnel
from Pomerania. Fought with distinction in Poland. Converted in winter, 1940-
41, when it lost one infantry regiment and its artillery staff. Employed on L of
C duties on the Northern Russian front since the outset of the campaign.

213th "Sicherungs" (L of C) Division

Commander: Lt Gen Rene de l'HOMME de COURBIERE (55)
Composition: 318th Reinf Inf Regt, 354 Reinf Inf Regt, 213th Cyclist Co,
        213th AT Bn, 213th Engr Bn, 213th Sig Co
Auxiliary unit number: 213
Home Station: Glogau (Wkr. VIII)
  Formed on mobilization as 213th Infantry Division in the Breslau area. Con-
verted in winter, 1940-41, when it lost one infantry regiment and its artillery
staff. No evidence for its part in active operations prior to the Russian campaign,
where it appears to have been employed on L of C duties, first in the Southern
Group and subsequently in the Center.

221st "Sicherungs" (L of C) Division

Commander: Lt Gen Johann PFLUGBEIL (59)
Composition: 350th Reinf Inf Regt, 375 Reinf Inf Regt, 221st Cyclist Bn,
        221 AT Bn, 221 Engr Bn, 221 Sig Co
Auxiliary unit number: 221
Home Station: Breslau (Wkr. VIII)
  Formed on mobilization as 221st Infantry Division with Silesian personnel.
Saw active fighting in Poland. Converted in winter, 1940-41, when it lost one
infantry regiment and its artillery staff. Employed first on the Central Russian
front and subsequently in the South, where it appears to have seen some action.

285th "Sicherungs" (L of C) Division
Commander: Lt Gen Wolfgang Edler Herr u. Frhr. v. PLOTHO (62)
Composition: (Normally consisting of two reinforced infantry regiments.)
Home Station:
  Date of formation uncertain. On the L of C, Northern Group, since early 1941.

286th "Sicherungs" (L of C) Division

Commander:

Composition: (Normally consists of two reinforced infantry regiments.)
Home Station:
  Date of formation uncertain. On the L of C Center Group, since autumn,1941.

403d "Sicherungs" (L of C) Division

Commander:
Composition: (Normally consists of two reinforced infantry regiments.)
Home Station: Berlin (Wkr.III)
  Formed in spring, 1940, as a z.b.V. division staff. Converted during the Russian campaign and employed on the L of C Center Group since November, 1941, later moving to the South.

441st "Sicherungs" (L of C) Division

Commander:
Composition: (Normally consists of two reinforced infantry regiments.)
Home Station:
  Formed early in 1940. No evidence for its history.

442d "Sicherungs" (L of C) Division

Commander:
Composition: (Normally consists of two reinforced infantry regiments.)
Home Station:
  Formed early in 1940. In Russia on the L of C of Army Group Center.

444th "Sicherungs" (L of C) Division

Commander:
Composition: (Normally consists of two reinforced infantry regiments.)
Home Station: (Wkr.XII)
  Formed early in 1940. On the L of C of Army Group South since autumn, 1941.

445th "Sicherungs" (L of C) Division

Commander:
Composition: (Normally consists of two reinforced infantry regiments.)
Home Station:
  Formed early in 1940.

454th "Sicherungs" (L of C) Division

Commander:
Composition: (Normally consists of two reinforced infantry regiments.)
Home Station:
  Date of formation uncertain. On the L of C of Army Group South since autumn, 1941.

455th "Sicherungs" (L of C) Division

Commander:

Composition: (Normally consists of two reinforced infantry regiments.)

Home Station:

Date of formation uncertain. On the L of C of Army Group South since autumn, 1941.

(GAF) ANTIAIRCRAFT UNITS.
(Flakkorps)

XVI AAA CORPS

I AA Corps

Commander: Major Gen Walther v AXTHELM ( )
   Operated in France in 1940. In Russia 1941-42, at first on the Central and later on the Southern front.

II AA Corps

Commander: General Otto DESSLOCH ( )
   Operated in France in 1940. In Russia 1941-42, at first on the Southern and later on the Central front.

XVII AAA DIVISIONS (Flakdivisionen)

1st AA Division

Commander: Lt Gen SPIESS ( ) (?)
Hq: Berlin

2d AA Division (mtz)

Commander:
  Transferred from the Paris area to Russia (Northern front) early in 1942.

3d AA Division

Commander:
Hq: Hamburg

4th AA Division

Commander:
Hq: Düsseldorf

5th AA Division

Commander:
Hq: Frankfurt/Main

6th AA Division

Commander:
  Believed to be stationed in Western Europe (probably Belgium and Northern France).

7th AA Division

Commander:
  Believed to be stationed in Western Germany (Luftgau VI).

8th AA Division

Commander:
Hq: Bremen

9th AA Division (Mtz)

Commander:
  Transferred from the Paris area to Russia (Central front) early in 1942.

10th AA Division (Mtz)

Commander: Lt Gen SEIFERT ( )
  Controlled all AAA in Roumania and Bulgaria in 1941. In Russia (Southern front) since early in 1942.

11th AA Division

Commander:
Hq: Rennes

12th AA Division (Mtz)

Commander: Maj Gen Rudolf EIBENSTEIN ( )
  Operating in Russia (Central front) since late in 1941.

13th AA Division

Commander:
Hq: Cherbourg (?)

14th AA Division

Commander:
Hq: Leipzig

15th AA Division (Mtz)

Commander:
  Believed to have been formed in Roumania by expansion of III AAA Brigade late in 1941. Transferred to Russia (Southern front) early in 1942.

16th AA Division

Commander:
  Not yet identified.

17th AA Division (Mtz)

Commander:
  Transferred from Germany to Russia (Southern front) early in 1942.

18th AA Division (Mtz)

Commander:
  Operating on the Central front in Russia since early in 1942.

PART D--MISCELLANEOUS UNITS

CONTENTS

Page

PART D

I INTRODUCTION

1. In Part D the principal units of the GHQ pool are described as far as they are known. They are listed as far as possible according to the German classification (e.g., under Infanterie or Landesschützen-Einheiten, Sections II and XIV below). The only deliberate departure from that system has been to place the various types of parks at the end of the sections which they serve (e.g., Heergeräte-Park at the end of Section III below), instead of in a single group among the administrative units (Section XVI below) to which they are formally assigned.

2. For division units and corps troops, reference should be made to the current issue of "Order of Battle of the German Army".

3. There is one unit which defies classification, and must, therefore, be described here, namely Lehr-Regiment Brandenburg z.b.V. 800 (800th Brandenburg Special Mission Demonstration Regt). This unit was formed on the outbreak of war as Bau-Lehr-Bataillon 800) (800th Construction Demonstration Bn), and expanded to a regiment during the summer of 1940. Its home station is at Brandenburg (Wkr. III), where its recruits are trained, but detachments from it may be encountered wherever German forces are operating. Its primary function is sabotage (whether by companies, platoons or individuals). Its personnel contains a high proportion of Germans who have lived abroad and speak foreign languages fluently. Different companies of the regiment specialize in preparation for operations in specific countries. Its members often operate in civilian clothes, in some cases dropping by parachute in enemy-occupied country. Though they hold military rank, the unit is under the direct control of the Intelligence Branch of the Defense Ministry (O.K.W. Abwehr) as regards its policy and organization.

4. The following table gives an alphabetical list of the types of units described in Part D, with references to the sections and paragraphs under which they will be found. In this list, the most usual German abbreviation are employed. For the expansion of the abbreviation, and an American equivalent, reference should be made to the place in which it is described.

Type	¶	Section	Type	¶	Section
A.Bekl.Amt.	1i	XVI	A.V.A.	1e	XVI
A.Briefstelle	1h	XVI	A.Vet.Pk.	4	XII
A. Feldlaz.	4	XI	Art.Lehr.Rgt.	1	V
A. Kartenlager	11	V	Art.Pk.	12	V
5 A.K.P.	11	IX	15 Astr.Mess-Zug	9	V
A.Nachr.Pk.	13	VIII	Aufkl.Lehrabt.	2	III
			Ball.Bttr.	7	V
A.Pf.Laz.	1	XII	Bäck.Kp.	1a	XVI
A.Pf.Pk.	3	XII	Bau-Btl.	3	XV
A.San.Abt.	1	XI	20 Betr.Kol.	2e	IX
10 A.San.Pk.	14	XI	Betr.Verw.Kp.	2g	XVI

	Br.Baubtl.	4	XV		Fstgs.Nachr.		
	Bruko	1f	VII		Kdtr.Stelle	10	VIII
	Dulag	4b	XVI		Fstgs.Pi.Abschn.Gr.	2c	VII
25	Eisb.Baubtl.	3c	VII	70	Fstgs.Pi.Kdr.	2a	VII
		7	XV		Fstgs.Pi.Pk.	2e	VII
	Eisb.Betr.Kp.	3b	IX		Fstgs.Pi.St.	2b	VII
	Eisb.Fsp.Kp.	3c	VII		Fstgs.Stammbtl.	2d	VII
	Eisb.Kuchenwagabt.	1c	XVI		Filterkol.	2e	IX
	E.Pz.Zug	5	IV	75	Fla-Btl.		X
30	Eisb.Pf.Baukp.	3c	VII		Fla-Kp.		X
	Eisb.Baukp.	3c	VII		Flak Abt.	2	XVII
	Eisb.Pi.Pk.	3d	VII		Flak Div.	2	XVII
	Eisb.Pi.Rgt.	3a	VII		Flak Korps	2	XVII
	Eisb.Pi.Stb.z.b.V.	3b	VII	80	Flak Rgt.	2	XVII
35	Entg.Abt.	8	VI		Flieger Div.	1	XVIII
	Entl.St.	2b	IX		Flieger Korps	1	XVIII
	Fahrkol.	2e	IX		Frontstalag	4a	XVI
	F.S.Art.Rgt.	1	XVIII		F.Staffel	2	XVIII
	F.S.Fla-Btl.	1	XVIII	85	Fuhr.Begl.Btl.	4	II
40	F.S.Jg.Rgt.	1	XVIII		Fuhrgs.Nachr.Rgt.	6	VIII
	F.S.M.G-Btl.	1	XVIII		Fu.Uberw.Kp.	9	VIII
	F.S.Nachr.Kp.	1	XVIII		Gassch.Ger.Pk.	10	VI
	F.S.Pz.Jg.Abt.	1	XVIII		Geb.Werf.Abt.	7	VI
	F.S.Pi.Btl.	1	XVIII	90	G.F.P.	4	XIII
45	F.S.San.Kp.	1	XVIII		Grz.Sch.		
	F.S.San.Tr.	1	XVIII		Abschn.Kdo.	5	XIV
	Feldbahnkp.	3b	IX		Grz.Sch.U.Abschn.	5	XIV
	Feldeisb.Betr.Amt.	3a	IX		Grz.Wa.	5	XIV
	Feldeisb.Dir.	3a	IX		Grz.Wa.Kp.	5	XIV
50	Feldeisb.			95	Gr.Back.Kp.	1a	XVI
	Masch.Amt.	3a	IX		Gr.Kw.Kol.	2e	IX
	Feldeisb.				Gr.Kw.Kol.f.		
	Werkstättenamt	3a	IX		Wass.Trsp.	1c	IX
	Feldgend.Abt.	1	XIII		H.Betreuungsabt.	1d	XVI
	Feldgend.Tr.	2	XIII		H.Flak		X
	Feldhalblaz.	6	XI	100	H.Flak Abt.	3	V
55	F.K.	3b	XVI		H.Flak Lehrabt.	2	V
	Feldlaz.	5	XI		H.J.G.Kp.	9	II
	F.N.K.	5	VIII		H.P.K.	1m	IX
	F.P.A.	1g	XVI		H.Nachr.Rgt.	7	VIII
	Feld-Werkst.	1j	IX	105	H.Pfd.Laz.	1	XII
60	Feld-Werkst.Zg.	1k	IX		H.San.Abt.	1	XI
	Fz.Btl.	2d	XVI		H.Verpfl.Amt.	1f	XVI
	Fz.Kdo.	2a	XVI		H.Ger.Pk.	6	III
	Fz.St.	2c	XVI		Heim.Eisb.Pi.Pk.	3d	VII
	Fernschreibkp.	9	VIII	110	Heim.Wachtbtl.	4	XIV
65	Fernspr.Baukp.	9	VIII		Horchkp.	9	VIII
	Fsp.Betr.Zg.	9	VIII		H.Staffeln	2	XVIII
	Fstgs.Baubtl.	5	XV		Inf.Btl.z.b.V.	5	II

No.	Unit		
	Inf.Lehr.Rgt.	1	II
115	Inf.Pk.	12	II
	Inf.Regt."Grossdeutschland"	2	II
	Jagdkdo.	7	II
	Kav.Brig.	3	III
	Kav.Lehr.Abt.	1	III
120	Kav.Rgt.	4	III
	Kesselwg.Kol.f.Betr. Stoff	2e	IX
	Kl.Kw.Kol.	2e	IX
	Komb.Kol.	2e	IX
	Kdr.der Bau.Tr.	2	XV
125	Kdr.der.Nachr.Tr.	2	VIII
	Kf.Pk.Kp.	1n	IX
	Kfz.Inst.Abt.	1d	IX
	Kfz.Inst.Kp.	1f	IX
	Kw.Trsp.Abt.	1b	IX
130	Kw.Trsp.Kol.	1c	IX
	Kw.Trsp.Rgt.	1a	IX
	Kw.Wkst.Zg.	1h	IX
	Kr.Kw.Zg.	10	XI
	Kr.Trsp.Abt.	9	XI
135	Kreiskdtr.	3b	XVI
	Krgf.Bau-u.Arb.Btl.	9	XV
	Krgs.Laz.	7	XI
	Krgs.Laz.Abt.	2	XI
	Landesbau-Btl.	10	XV
140	Ldsch.Btl.	2	XIV
	Ldsch Rgt.	1	XIV
	Laz.Zg.	11	XI
	le Störungstr.	12	VIII
	Leichtkr.Krgs.Laz.	8	XI
145	Leichtkranken Zug	12	XI
	Lg.St.	3	XVII
	Luft.Nachr.Abt.(H.) mot.	3	XVIII
	Marine Bau Btl.	8	XV
	M.G.-Btl.	8	II
150	Mun.Verw.Kp.	2f	XVI
	Nachr.Abt.St.z.b.V.	4	VIII
	Nachr.Aufkl.Kp.	9	VIII
	Nachr.Fü.z.b.V.	4	VIII
	Nachr.Helf. Einsatzabt.	11	VIII
155	Nachr.Lehr.Rgt.	1	VIII
	Nachr.Rgt.Stab. z.b.V.	3	VIII
	Nachsch.Btl.	2a	IX
	Nachsch.Kol.Abt.	2c	IX
	Nachsch.Kol.Abt. z.b.V.	2d	IX
160	Nachsch.Stab.z.b.V.	2b	IX
	Nbl.Lehr.Rgt.	1	VI
	Nbl.Werf.Abt.	5	VI
	Nbl.Werf.Battr.	6	VI
	Nbl.Werf.Rgt.	3	VI
165	Nbl.Werf.Rgt.z.b.V.	2	VI
	Ob.Baustb.	1	XV
	Ob.F.K.	3a	XVI
	Ob.Fz.St.	2b	XVI
	Oflag	4c	XVI
170	Ortskdtr.	3b	XVI
	Pz.Abt.Fl.W.	2	IV
	Pz.Inst.Abt.	1e	IX
	Pz.Inst.Kp.	1g	IX
	Pz.Lehr.Rgt.	1	IV
175	Pfd.Trsp.Kol.	2	XII
	Pi.Btl.z.b.V.	1c	VII
	Pi.Landgskp.	1d	VII
	Pi.Lehr.Btl.	1a	VII
	Pi.Lehr.Btl.z.b.V.	1a	VII
180	Pi.Masch.Zg.	1j	VII
	Pi.Pk.	1h	VII
	Pi.Pk.Kp.	1i	VII
	Pi.Rgts.Stab.	1b	VII
	Pi.Rgt.z.b.V.	1b	VII
185	Prop.Kp.	8	VIII
	Radf.Abt.	5	III
	Rgts.Stab der Nbltr.	2	VI
	R.R.	4	III
	Res.Krgs.Laz.Abt.	3	XI
190	Schlächt.Einheiten	1b	XVI
	s.Pz.Jg.Abt.	4	IV
	s.Werf.Rgt.	4	VI
	Sich.Rgt.(mot.)	6	II
	Sd.Btl	11	II
195	Sd.Verbd.288	3	II
	Staffeln	2	XVIII
	Stalag	4d	XVI
	Str.Baubtl.	6	XV
	Strass.Entg.Abt.	9	VI
200	Sturmbootkp.	1e	VII
	Sturmbootkdo.	2e	VII
	Stu.Gesch.Abt.	4	V
	Stu.Gesch.Battr.	5	V
	Stu.Rgt.	1	XVIII
205	Techn.Btl.	1g	VII

Tr.Entg.Kp.	13	XI
V° Mess Zg	8	V
Verkehrsregl.Btl.	3	XIII
Verl. St.	2b	IX
210 Verm.u.Kart.Abt.	6	V
Vers. Btl.	10	II
Wa. Blt.	4	XIV
Wa.R.	3	XIV
Werkst.Kp.mot.	1i	IX
Werf.Abt.	5	VI
Werf.Battr.	6	VI
Werf.Regt.	3	VI
Wett.Peilzg.	10	V
Z.E.L.	2e	XVI

II INFANTRY (Infanterie)

White piping, the distinguishing color of the infantry arm, is also worn by Landeschützen units, Army AAA battalions and companies (but not batteries, which wear red--see Section V), and certain administrative units (see Sections X, XIV, and XVI). For division infantry reference should be made to the current issue of Order of Battle of the German Army. The following paragraphs outline various miscellaneous infantry units which may be encountered.

1. Infanterie-Lehr-Regiment (Infantry Instruction Regt). This regiment is normally stationed at the Infantry School at Doberitz (Wkr.III), providing demonstrations of tactics and carrying out experiments with new infantry weapons. It performs the same function as the 29th Infantry in connection with the Infantry School and the Infantry Board. It is possible that it may be found, in whole or part, on active service in the field.

2. Infanterie-Regiment "Grossdeutschland" (Greater Germany Infantry Regt). In peace-time this regiment was stationed in Berlin. It is a corps d'elite, its personnel being drawn from all over Germany. After a period of service in it, the personnel were normally promoted and transferred to other units. It is fully motorized, and includes a number of companies not found in the normal infantry regiment-reconnaissance, armored assault guns, antiaircraft and signal. In addition it has an artillery battalion, a heavy smoke company and its own supply columns. Recently, it was enlarged to a motorized division. This unit should not be confused with the SS Regiment Deutschland (in SS Div Reich). Identification: Gothic "GD" woven on the shoulder strap.

3. Sonderverband 288 (Special Unit 288). This is a small, self-contained group consisting of a Hq Co and 8 Cos as follows:

1 Rifle?	5 AT
2 Mtn Rifle	6 AAA
3 Rifle	7 Engineer
4 MG	8 Signal

124

The 5th Co includes an armored assault gun platoon and an armored car platoon. There are in addition (unnumbered), a medical detachment and a supply echelon. The unit was formed in the summer of 1941, and has seen service with the Africa Panzer Army.

4. **Führrersbegleitbataillon** (Führer's Escort Battalion). This unit was formed after the Polish campaign, from picked personnel, to serve as Hitler's escort in the field. It is fully motorized, and consists of a Hq and three Cos as follows:

1 Wach (Guard)	3 schwere Sicherungs (Heavy
2 Schnelle (Mobile)	Protective)

In addition, it has a supply column.

5. Infanterie-Bataillon z. b. V. (Special Duty Infantry Battalion) · An army Hq may have an independent, fully motorized infantry battalion for special duty (not at present definable). Units of this type so far identified carry the numbers 100 and 500.

6. Sicherungs-Regiment (mtz) (L of C Regiment). In addition to a number of converted infantry divisions, commanders of army group L of C areas have at their disposal, in some cases, special mopping-up regiments, which are controlled either by "Sicherungs" (L of C) division staffs or by special brigade staffs. Units of this type are numbered in a separate series (4 is the highest number so far noted), and have special war establishments, including cyclist companies and MT echelons. Identification: Latin "S" with an Arabic number on shoulder strap.

7. Jagdkommando (Raiding detachment). During the winter of 1941-42, a number of units of this type were formed for service on the Russian front. They are numbered in a separate series (5 is the highest number so far reported).

8. Maschinengewehr-Bataillon (mtz)(MG Battalion). For a list of identifications see Order of Battle of the German Army. MG battalions may be incorporated, for a greater or lesser period, in an infantry division, or employed as GHQ troops.

9. Heeres Infanterie-Geschütz-Kompanie or schwere I.G.Kp. (GHQ, Heavy Infantry Gun Co). Ten or twelve units of this type, numbered in the series 701-, have been identified. They are most commonly found attached to the mtz infantry brigade of a Panzer division. They are equipped with 150 mm (5.91 in.) guns mounted on Pz.Kw. II chassis.

10. Versuchs-Bataillon (Experimental Battalion). Details of the composition and station of this unit are not yet available.

11. Sonderbataillon (Special Battalion). This is a penal unit, to which soldiers guilty of certain offenses may be transferred. It was formed in the winter 1941-42 and sent to the area of Army Group North.

12. Infanterie-Park (Infantry Equipment Park). Each army has an infantry park, carrying a number selected at random from the series 501-. The officers wear the color of their arm, but other ranks wear light blue piping, in each case with the Arabic number of the park.

It should be noted that the mtz infantry of the Panzer divisions are classified as Panzertruppen (see Section IV).

The following figures show the tactical signs for infantry units:-

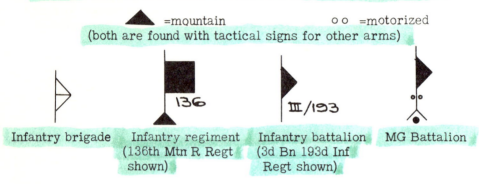

=mountain   o o =motorized
(both are found with tactical signs for other arms)

Infantry brigade   Infantry regiment   Infantry battalion   MG Battalion
(136th Mtn R Regt   (3d Bn 193d Inf
shown)   Regt shown)

Note: A complete list of German military symbols is in the process of preparation.

III CAVALARY (Kavallerie)

Yellow piping is the distinguishing color of the cavalry (including horsed and partly horsed cavalry regiments and cyclist battalions). It is also reported to be worn, in place of pink, by units of the 24th Panzer Division (recently formed by conversion of the former 1st Cavalry Division). It is worn by reconnaissance units (with the exception of the Panzer reconnaissance units of Panzer and motorized divisions, which wear copper-brown), which receive their personnel from the cavalry depot units. The following types of unit may be encountered apart from the division reconnaissance units (for which see Order of Battle of the German Army).

1. Kavallerie-Lehr-Abteilung (Cavalry Instruction Battalion). Stationed at the Cavalry School at Hannover (Wkr. XI), but potentially available for service in the field.

2. Aufklärungs-Lehr-Abteilung (Reconnaissance Instruction Battalion). Likewise stationed at the Cavalry School.

3. Kavallerie-Brigade (Cavalry Brigade): The former 1st Cavalry Division contained two cavalry brigades, each probably of two cavalry regiments. It is possible that there may still be a number of independent cavalry brigades in the

GHQ pool.

4. Kavallerie-Regiment (Cavalry Regiment, part mechanized) and Reiter-Regiment (Cavalry Rgt, horsed). For a list of identifications see Order of Battle of the German Army.

5. Radfahr-Abteilung (Cyclist Battalion): Some division reconnaissance units have been reorganized recently as cyclist battalions. In addition, there are some (numbered in the series 401-) in the GHQ pool, which may be found operating in the spearhead of the attack. The cyclist battalion includes a motorcycle company, so that motorcyclists may still be seen wearing yellow piping.

6. Heeresgeräte-Park (Heavy Transport Equipment Park). One such park with each army (excluding Panzer armies), serving its heavy transport columns as well as cavalry units. Such parks are numbered on the same principle as infantry parks, the officers wearing the color of their arm and other ranks light blue piping with the Arabic number of the park.

The following figures show the tactical signs for cavalry units:-

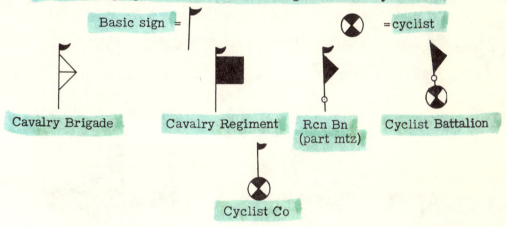

Basic sign =   = cyclist

Cavalry Brigade   Cavalry Regiment   Rcn Bn (part mtz)   Cyclist Battalion

Cyclist Co

IV ARMORED TROOPS (Panzertruppen)

Tank units and antitank battalions wear pink piping, the latter with the addition of the letter "P" on the shoulder strap. Motorized infantry wear grass green, and Panzer reconnaissance units and motorcycle battalions copper brown. For division units see Order of Battle of the German Army. In addition, the following types may also be encountered.

1. Panzer-Lehr-Regiment (Tank Instruction Regt). This regiment, stationed at the Tank School at Wünsdorf (Wkr. III) consists of I and II Tank and III Antitank Bns. Like other demonstration units, it is potentially available for service in the field.

127

2. Panzerabteilung **Flammenwerfer** (Tank Flame Thrower Bn). The GHQ pool includes a number of independent flame thrower tank battalions (series 100-) which will normally be found employed under Panzer corps in the spearhead of the attack.

3. Non-division tank units. The GHQ pool also includes a number of independent tank regiments and battalions, which may be found either under Panzer corps or under Panzer brigade staffs, or on occasion supporting or assigned to infantry divisions.

4. Schwere Panzerjäger-Abteilung, S.Pz.Jg.Abt. (Heavy Antitank Bn). Among the GHQ antitank battalions, several are classified as heavy. Such units are equipped in some cases with 75 mm (2.95 in) antitank guns, and in others with 88 mm (3.46 in) antiaircraft guns for use in an antitank role. The 75 mm gun in such cases, is on a self-propelled mount, while the 88 mm weapon is either tractor drawn or on a SP mount. Other GHQ antitank units are equipped with the 47 mm. (1.85 in) gun (SPM) which is rated as a medium caliber weapon.

5. Eisenbahn-Panzerzug, E.Pz.Zug (Armored Train). Numbered in series 1-50 (half a dozen identified to date). The personnel wear pink piping with the letter "E" on the shoulder strap.

The following figures show the tactical signs for units in this category:-

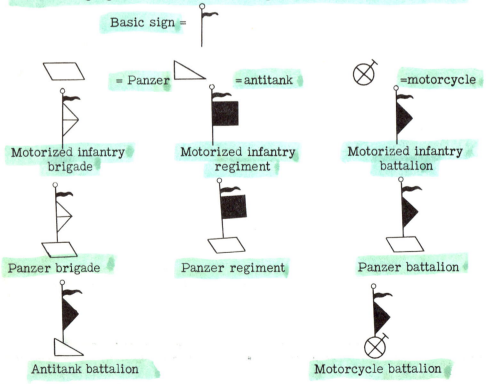

Basic sign =

= Panzer   = antitank   =motorcycle

Motorized infantry brigade   Motorized infantry regiment   Motorized infantry battalion

Panzer brigade   Panzer regiment   Panzer battalion

Antitank battalion   Motorcycle battalion

V ARTILLERY (Artillerie)

Red is the color of the artillery arm, including armored assault artillery and army AAA batteries. Artillery observation (sound and flash ranging) units and survey and mapping units are distinguished, in addition, by the Gothic letters "B" or "V" as the case may be. For lists of identified artillery and artillery observation units, and for the employment of GHQ artillery, see Order of Battle of the German Army. The following paragraphs describe various miscellaneous artillery units which may be encountered.

1. Artillerie-Lehr-Regimenter (Artillery Instruction Regts). There are three of these regiments, all stationed at the School of Artillery at Jüterbog (Wkr III). No 1 is horse-drawn, No 2 motorized (including an armored assault artillery battery), and No 3 consists of artillery observation, survey and mapping, range-finding and balloon battalions. Portions of one or more of these regiments may be found serving in the field from time to time.

2. Heeresflak-Lehrabteilung (Army AAA Instruction Bn). Stationed at the Army AAA School in Wkr. II but available for service in the field.

3. Heeresflakabteilung (Army AAA Bn). Units of this type carry numbers in the same series as GAF AAA units (see paragraph 1 Section XVII and Order of Battle of the German Army). Twelve have been identified to date. The battalion consists of three heavy batteries equipped with 88 mm (3.46 in) guns and two batteries of 20 mm (0.79 in) guns, and is fully motorized.

4. Sturmgeschütz-Abteilung (Armored Assault Gun Battalion). Numbered in the main artillery series. Fifteen identified to date, with numbers ranging between 177 and 244. The battery consists of Hq Btry and three six-gun batteries equipped with 75 mm (2.95 in) guns on SP mount.

5. Sturmgeschütz-Batterie (Armored Assault Gun Battery). No 665 and 667 identified.

6. Vermessungs-und Karten-Abteilung, V.u.K.Abt. (Survey and Mapping Units). These units belong to the GHQ pool, from which they may be allocated to army groups or armies. One is numbered 501, and the remainder carry numbers in the series 601-(about a dozen identified to date).

7. Ballon-Batterie (Observation Balloon Battery). In addition to the balloon sub-units of the artillery observation battalions, the GHQ pool contains some independent balloon batteries numbered in series 100-.

8. Velocitäts-Mess-Zug, Vo.Mess-Zug (Velocity Measurement Platoon): Numbered in series 501-.

9. Astronomischer Mess-Zug (Astronomical Survey Platoon). Numbered in series 701-.

10. Wetter-Peilzug (Meteorological Platoon): Numbered in series 501-.

11. Armee-Kartenlager (Army Map Depot): Carrying numbers from the series 501-, allotted arbitrarily.

12. Artillerie-Park (Artillery Equipment Park). One to each army, carrying a number from the series 501-, allotted arbitrarily. The officers wear the color of their arm, and other ranks light blue, in each case with the Arabic number of the park.

The following figures show the tactical signs for artillery units:-

Basic sign =

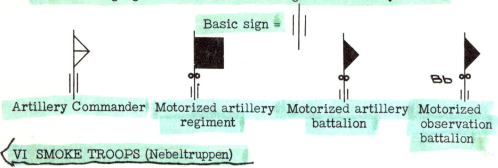

Artillery Commander   Motorized artillery regiment   Motorized artillery battalion   Motorized observation battalion

VI SMOKE TROOPS (Nebeltruppen)

Smoke troops wear maroon piping. They include the following types of unit, all belonging to the GHQ pool. Changes of establishment and nomenclature of units are now in progress. Where alternative designations are given the second can be taken as being in process of superseding the first.

1. Nebel-Lehr-Regiment (Smoke Instruction Regt). Stationed at the Army Smoke School at Celle (Wkr.XI), but liable to serve in whole or in part at the front.

2. Regimentsstab der Nebeltruppen or Nebelwerfer-Regiment z.b.V. (Smoke Regt Staff). Regimental staffs to control smoke battalions in action, numbered in series 1 upwards.

3. Nebelwerfer- or Werfer-Regiment (Smoke Regt). Regiments with Hq and three battalions (numbered I-III). Series 51-54 and 70 identified to date.

4. Schweres Werfer-Regiment (Heavy Smoke Regt). Also, probably, consisting of a Hq and three battalions. No 1 is at present the only one identified.

5. Nebelwerfer- or Werfer-Abteilung (Smoke Battery). Independent battalions which in action may be controlled by smoke regimental staffs. Series 1-8 identified to date.

6. Nebelwerfer-Batterie or Werfer-Batterie (150 mm Werfer 41) (Smoke Battery or Heavy Smoke Battery). Independent batteries equipped with the 150 mm (5.91 in) smoke projector. No 151 has been identified.

7. Gebirgs-Werfer-Abteilung (Mountain Smoke Battalion) A unit of this type is known to exist, but no identification has been made as yet.

8. Entgiftungs-Abteilung (Decontamination Bn). Also equipped for service as a contamination battalion. Series 101-103 identified to date.

9. Strassenentgiftungs-Abteilung (Road Decontamination Bn). Similar to the foregoing type in its functions. No 132 has been identified.

10. Gasschutz-Gerätepark (Antigas Equipment Park). One to each army, allotted numbers at random in the series 501-. Officers wear the color of their arm, other ranks pale blue, in each case with the Arabic number of the park.

The following figures show the tactical signs for smoke units:-

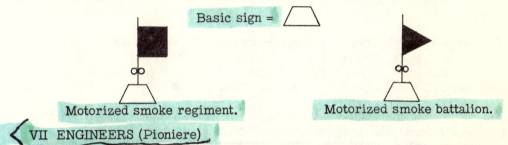

Basic sign =

Motorized smoke regiment.   Motorized smoke battalion.

VII ENGINEERS (Pioniere)

Black, the distinguishing color of the engineer arm, is also worn by various other units of similar type as outlined below. In such cases, a distinguishing letter on the shoulder strap will show what type of unit is in question.

1. General; Without Qualification.

For the employment of engineers in the GHQ pool, and for a list of identifications, see Order of Battle of the German Army. The following are the principle types of unit which may be encountered:

a. Pionier-Lehr-Bataillon (Engineer Instruction Battalion). Nos. 1 and 2 are stationed at No 1 Engineer School (Pionier-Schule 1) at Dessau-Rösslau (Wkr. XI). There is also a Pioner-Lehr-Bataillon z.b.V. at Offenbach on Main (Wkr. IX), which specializes in mining and similar activities. These units may also be found serving in the field.

b. Pionier-Regiment z.b.V. or Pioner-Regimentsstab (Engineer Regt Staff). Some twenty have been identified, carrying numbers selected from the series 501-700. Such staffs are used to control engineer battalions, bridge trains and, if need be, construction units of the GHQ pool under corps or army.

c. Pionier-Bataillon z.b.V. (Engineer Battalion Staff). Nos 300 and 750 have been identified. These consist of staffs controlling independent engineer units.

d. Pionier-Landungskompanie. (Engineer Landing Co). Equipped with assault boats with outboard motors. No. 778 has been identified.

e. Sturmbootkompanie and Sturmbootkommando (Assault Boat Co, Detachment): No companies have been identified as yet, though they are known to exist. The detachments carry numbers in the series 901-.

f. Brückenkolonne or Brüko (Bridge Train): In addition to the bridge trains which form part of the division and GHQ engineer battalions, there are two series of independent bridge trains in the GHQ pool. One series, carrying numbers in the range 401-450, consists of units of two trains (e.g., 1/403, 2/403) which operate independently. The other series, in the range 601-700, consists of single trains. All are fully motorized.

g. Technisches-Bataillon (Technical Battalion). These battalions, supplied with personnel by the Technical Depot Battalion at Pirna (Wkr. IV), are intended for such specialized functions as the production and treatment of mineral oil for coal mining and the like. They are numbered in series 1-50 (a dozen examples identified to date).

h. Pionier-Park (Engineer Equipment Park). One to each army, allotted numbers at random in the series 501 upwards. Officers wear the color of their arm, other ranks light blue , in each case with the Arabic number of the park.

i. Pionier-Parkkompanie (Engineer Park Co). Two are included in each engineer park. Likewise numbered in series 501 upwards.

j. Pionier-Maschinenzug (Engineer Machine Platoon). One is included in each engineer park. Likewise used independently under engineer battalion staffs "z.b.V." (see c above).

2. Festungspioniere (Fortress Engineers)

Fortress engineers wear the letters "Fp" or "F" on their shoulder straps (Gothic "Fp" if the unit existed in peace time; Latin "F" if it was formed on or after mobilization). The following units and staffs may be identified:

a. Festungspionier-Kommandeur (Fortress Engineer Commander): Gothic "Fp" followed by the Roman numeral of a Wehrkreis. In effect, regimental commander and Hq for fortress engineer units in the military district concerned.

b. Festungspionier-Stab (Fortress Engineer Staff): Gothic "Fp" or Latin "F" followed by an Arabic number in series 1-50. A regimental staff, normally controls two sector groups.

c. Festungspionier-Abschnittsgruppe (Fortress Engineer Sector Group). Numbered I or II followed by the Arabic number of the controlling staff (e.g. Fest.Pi.Abs.Gr. II/21). Equivalent in status to a battalion staff.

d. Festungs-Stammbataillon (Fortress Cadre Battalion). A training unit, in Germany, in which personnel from basic training units receive further training while awaiting transfer elsewhere.

e. Festungspionier-Park (Fortress Engineer Equipment Park): One for each area in which fortress engineers are employed extensively.

For fortress signal, transport and construction units, see sections VIII, IX, and XV.

3. RAILWAY ENGINEERS (Eisenbahnpioniere)

Railway engineers wear black piping with the letter "E" (Gothic if the unit existed in peace-time, otherwise Latin) on the shoulder strap. They are not always easy to distinguish from Eisenbahntruppen (Railway troops), for which see paragraph 3 Section IX. The following types of unit may be encountered:

a. Eisenbahnpionier-Regiment (Railway Engineer Regt). Eight exist (Nos. 1-8). Each consists of a Hq and two battalions each of four companies , numbered consecutively (e.g., 7/Eisb.Pi.Rgt. 3 = 3d Co 2d Bn 3d Railway Engineer Regt). In common with the independent companies listed below, they receive personnel from five railway engineer depot battalions (Nos 1-5).

b. Eisenbahnpionierstab z.b.V. (Special Railway Engineer Staff): One unnumbered example has been identified.

c. Eisenbahn (Pioneer)-Baukompanie (Railway (Engineer) Construction Co). Numbered in series 101-200. These are specialist companies, the function of which may be defined by a further title: e.g., Eisb. Pfeilerbaukp. (Railway Pier Construction Co). In others, the special title replaces Bau.: e.g., Eisb. Fernsprechkompanie (Railway Telephone (Construction) Co). By contrast, the Eisenbahn-Baubataillon (Railway Construction Battalion) belongs to the category of construction troops (Section XV).

d. Eisenbahnpionier-Park (Railway Engineer Equipment Park). No 403 has been identified. In addition there is a Heimat-Eisenbahnpionier-Park at Rehagen-Klausdorf (Wkr. III), where the railway engineer school is situated.

The following figures show the tactical signs for engineer units:-

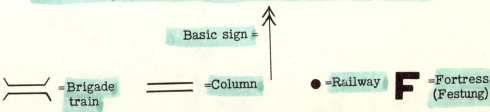

Basic sign =

=Brigade train   =Column   ●=Railway   F =Fortress (Festung)

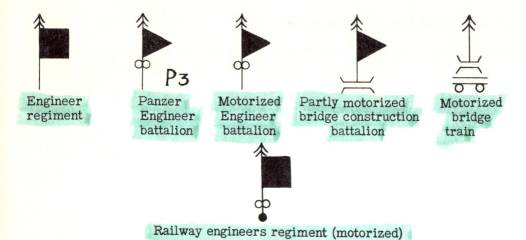

Engineer regiment

Panzer Engineer battalion

Motorized Engineer battalion

Partly motorized bridge construction battalion

Motorized bridge train

Railway engineers regiment (motorized)

VIII SIGNAL TROOPS (Nachrichtentruppen)

Lemon yellow (Zitronen) piping is the distinguishing color of signal units. It should not be confused with the yellow cavalry piping. For a list of identified units, reference may be made to Order of Battle of the German Army. The following types of unit may be encountered. Army, corps and division units are excluded.

1. Nachrichten-Lehr-Regiment (Signal Instruction Regt). Stationed at the Army Signal School at Halle (Wkr. IV), this regiment (like other instruction units) is potentially available for service in the field.

2. Kommandeur der Nachrichtentruppen (CO Signal Troops). A Roman numeral with yellow piping denotes the staff of the Signal Officer in a particular Wehrkreis, he has the status of a regimental commander, and controls both training and army communications within his district. Officers of the same title may also be found in the field.

3. Nachrichten-Regimentsstab z.b.V. (Special Signal Regt Staff). Special regimental staff to command independent battalions and other units in special situations.

4. Nachrichtenführer z.b.V., Nachrichten-Abteilungsstab z.b.V. (Special Signal Commander, Special Signal Bn Staff). Special battalion staffs, formed to control independent signal companies in the field. Mainly numbered in series 651—700.

5. Feldnachrichtenkommandantur (Field Signal Command). A static signal Hq for a sector of occupied territory or in rear areas of the zone of operations. The personnel wear yellow piping and a latin "K" followed by the Arabic number of the unit (series 1-60).

6. Führungsnachrichten-Regiment (Command Signal Regt) Nos 40 and 601, in the main series, have this classification. Their function is to provide and maintain the highest grade signal communications between GHQ, army group, and army Hq.

7. Heeres-Nachrichten-Regiment (GHQ, Signal Regt). Other signal regts, carrying numbers selected from the series 501-700, provide and maintain networks of lesser importance or are allotted to army groups as army group signal regts.

8. Propaganda-Kompanie (Propaganda Co). Provided with personnel from the Propaganda Depot Bn at Berlin(Wkr. III). Propaganda cos include No 501 and at least fifteen carrying numbers selected from the series 601-700. These cos are normally allotted to armies. In addition, there are unnumbered bns and cos (Frankreich, allotted to CG, Occupied France; Belgien, under CG, Belgium and Northern France; Afrika, under Africa Panzer Army). The personnel

are mainly journalists, press photographers or film cameramen in civil life, and their main function is front-line reporting. They are considered as part of the Signal Corps.

9. Independent signal companies etc. The following are the principal types of independent signal companies which may be encountered:

   Fernsprech-Baukompanie, Fsp.Baukp. (Telephone Construction Co)
   Fsp.Betriebszug, Fsp.Betr.Zg. (Telephone Operating Platoon)
   Fernschreibkp. (Teletype Co)
   Horchkp. (Interception Co)
   Nachr. Aufklärungskp. (Signal Rcn Co)
   Funküberwachungskp. (Radio Supervision Co). All carry numbers in the
      series 601 and upwards.

10. Festungsnachrichten-Kommandantur, -Stelle (Fortress Signal Command Station). The command carries the same number as the Festungspionier-Stab (see ¶2 Section VII) to which it is attached. It is not known on what principle the stations are numbered.

11. Nachrichtenhelferinneneinsatzabteilung (Female Signal Operations Bn). As yet, No 52 is the only example of this type of unit to be identified. It probably administers the women telephone operators over a large area, such as Occupied France.

12. Leichter Störungstrupp (Light Repair Detachment). Principles of numbering not yet known.

13. Armee-Nachrichten-Park (Army Sig Equipment Park). One to each army, carrying a number from the series 501--. Officers wear the color of their arm, other ranks light blue, in each case with the Arabic number of the park.

The following figures show the tactical signs for signals units:

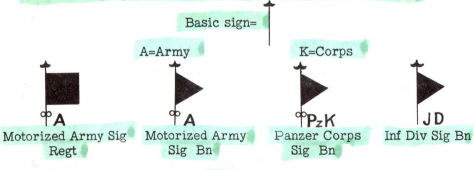

Basic sign=

A=Army   K=Corps

A	A	PzK	JD
Motorized Army Sig	Motorized Army	Panzer Corps	Inf Div Sig Bn
Regt	Sig Bn	Sig Bn	

IX TRANSPORT TROOPS (Fahrtruppen)

The distinguishing color of transport (including supply) units is light blue. The following list includes the main types of unit belonging to this category, with the exception of division and corps units.

1. Transport Units

a. Kraftwagentransport-Regiment, Kw. Trsp. Rgt. (MT Regt). The primary purpose of these regts is to move non-motorized fighting units. They may also be used, however, for the transport of supplies. Examples identified are 360 z. b. V., 501, 602, 605, 606, 616, 982, 985 z.b.V.

b. Kraftwagentransport-Abteilung, Kw. Trsp. Abt. (MT Bn). Independent bns, similar in function to the foregoing units. Examples identified are 503 z.b. V., 795, 979, 987 z.b.V. and 990 z.b.V.

c. Kraftwagentransport-Kolonne, Kw.Trsp.Kol. (MT Column or Train). Independent columns, carrying numbers in the series 601 and upwards. In some cases, the title is more elaborate (e.g., grosse Kraftwagenkolonne für Wassertransport 643 = 643d Hv Water MT Train).

d. Kraftfahrzeuginstandsetzungsabteilung. Kfz. Jnst.Abt. (MT Repair Bn). The following numbers have been identified: 508, 522, 548, 564, 567, 569, 592, 593, 596, 598.

e. Panzerinstandsetzungsabteilung, Pz. Jnst. Abt. (Tank Repair Bn). The following numbers have been identified: 543, 545, 552.

f. Kraftfahrzeuginstandsetzungskompanie. Kfz.Jnst.Kp. (MT Repair Co). These are independent cos numbered in series 101-200 (Nos 134, 138, 140, 145, 164, 166, 169 have been identified) and 301—(No 312 identified).

g. Panzerinstandsetzungskompanie, Pz. Jnst. Kp. (Tank Repair Co). The following number has been identified: 122.

h. Kraftwagenwerkstattzug, Kw.Wkst.Zg. (MT Workshop Platoon). Independent platoons; No 612 has been identified.

i. Werkstattkompanie (mot) (Motorised Workshop Co). Ten or twelve have been identified, carrying numbers in the series 1-200.

j. Feldwerkstatt (Field Workshop). Normally one of these is allotted to each army or Panzer army. They carry numbers, allotted arbitrarily, in the series 501—.

k. Feldwerkstattzug (Field Workshop Platoon). These are independent platoons; Nos 573, 604, and 607 have been identified.

l. Armee-Kraftfahr-Park (Army MT Park). One to each army or Panzer army, numbered arbitrarily in series 501 and upwards.

m. Heeres-Krafthafr-Park, H.K.P. (GHQ MT Park). A separate series, numbered concurrently with the establishments described in 1 above.

n. Kraftfahr-Parkkompanie (MT Park Co). A component sub-unit of the establishments described in 1 and m above and carrying the same number.

2. Supply Units

a. Nachschub-Bataillon (Supply Bn). Two series exist, namely 1-200 (half a dozen identified) which are non-motorised, and 501--700 (26 identified) which are fully motorised. Both types may be found serving as army troops.

b. Nachschubstab z.b.V. (Special Supply Staff). Series 671--750 (a dozen have been identified to date) when employed as loading or unloading staffs at a seaport they are described as Verladestab or Entladestab.

c. Nachschub-Kolonnenabteilung, N.K.A. (Supply Column or Train Bn). Some thirty have been noted, carrying numbers between 5C1 and 950. Their component columns are distinguished by an Arabic number preceding that of the battalion (e.g., 10/N.K.A.529). Some are horse drawn and some have MT. They are assigned to armies as required, and no standard allotment can be given.

d. Nachschubkolonnenabt. z.b.V. (Supply Column Bn, Staff). Special staffs formed to control and administer independent supply columns of the GHQ pool. Nos 671 and 672 and 798 have been identified.

e. Independent supply columns. These include the following types (all carrying numbers from the series 501-999).

gross Kw. Kol. (Hv MT Clm)—capacity 60 tons.
kleine Kw. Kol. (L MT Clm)—capacity 30 tons.
Betriebsstoff-Kolonne (gr. Kw. Kol f.Betr.St., kl.Kw. Kol.f.Betr.St.)
    (Gas and Oil Clm Hv or L)—capacity 50 or 25 cubic meters
    (11,000 or 5,500 gallons).
Kesselwagen-Kolonne f. Betr. St. (Tank Clm for Gas and Oil).
Filterkolonne. (Filter Column). This is believed to be a water column.
Kombinierte-Kolonne. (Combined column). The function of this column is
    not known.
Fahrkolonne (H-Dr Clm).

3. Railway units (Eisenbahntruppen)

a. Operating Staffs: The following railway operating staffs, numbered concurrently in series 1 and upwards, have been identified:

Feldeisb. Direktion (Field Railway Command Station).
Feldeisb. Betriebsamt (Field Railway Operations Office).
Feldeisb. Maschinenamt (Field Railway Machinery Office).

Feldeisb. Werkstättenamt (Field Railway Workshop Office).

The various offices are believed to be sub-divisions of the directorates or command stations which carry the same number.

b. Operating units. Two series of operating units have been identified, as follows:--

Eisenbahnbetriebskompanie (Ry Operations Co) —series 201 and upwards.
Feldbahnkompanie (F Ry Co)—series 301 and upwards.

It is possible that some of the independent companies noted under ¶3 Section VII may come under the control of railway operating staffs on occasion, although their personnel are railway engineers and wear black piping accordingly.

The following figures show the principal tactical signs for transport (including supply) troops:--

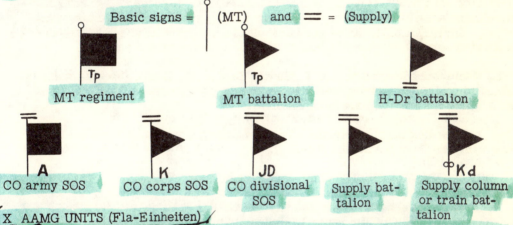

Basic signs = | (MT) and ═ = (Supply)

MT regiment   MT battalion   H-Dr battalion

CO army SOS   CO corps SOS   CO divisional SOS   Supply battalion   Supply column or train battalion

X AAMG UNITS (Fla-Einheiten)

This category consists solely of Fla-Bataillone, numbered consecutively with MG battalions (Section II) and wearing the white infantry piping with the addition of the Gothic letters "Fl" on the shoulder strap. On charts they are grouped with Army AAA batteries under the heading Heeresflak (see Section V). Two series exist:—

Nos 22-66 (ten identified). These consist of six companies, which operate separately. One company is often incorporated in a Panzer division, being attached for administrative purposes to the division AT Bn, but retaining its original number.

Nos 601-620 (eighteen identified). These consist of three companies, and normally operate as battalions.

In addition, the 90th Light Division in North Africa contains a Fla-Kompanie bearing the division auxiliary number 190.

XI MEDICAL UNITS (Sanitäts-Einheiten)

Dark blue is the distinguishing color for medical units. The following varieties may be encountered in addition to division medical units (for which reference may be made to Order of Battle of the German Army).

1. Heeres-or Armee-Sanitätsbteilung (GHQ or Army Medical unit). These units are in some cases fully and in others partly motorized. They carry numbers allotted at random from the series 501-700.

2. Kriegslazarett-Abteilung (War Hospital unit). Carrying numbers in the same series as the foregoing type of unit. They are fully motorized.

3. Reserve Kriegslazarett-Abteilung (Reserve War Hospital Bn). Numbered in the same series, but with a different establishment usually. They are non-motorized.

4. Armee-Feldlazarett (Army Field Hospital). Units of this type carry the number of the army medical battalion preceded by 1, 2, 3 or 4 (e.g., A.-Feldlaz. 3/542). The prefix Armee- will often be dropped, but the type can be recognized by its double numbering.

5. Feldlazarett (Field Hospital). Independent field hospitals in the GHQ pool carry numbers in the series 601-700. Some are motorized, others are not.

6. Feldhalblazarett (Field Half-Hospital). No 716 has been identified.

7. Kriegslazarett (War Hospital). Units of this type carry the number of the War Hospital Bn preceded by 1, 2, 3 or 4 (e.g., Kriegslaz 4/571) or single numbers in series 901--.

8. Leichtkranken-Kriegslazarett (War Hospital for Minor Cases). Some are motorized, others are not. The principles of numbering are not yet known.

9. Krankentransport-Abteilung (Ambulance Bn). Numbered in the series 501-700 and allotted to armies.

10. Kranken-Kraftwagenzug (Motorized Ambulance Platoon). Numbered in series 501-800.

11. Lazarett-Zug (Hospital Train). Numbered in series 501-700.

12. Leichtkranken-Zug (Hospital Train for Slightly Wounded Cases).

13. Truppenentgiftungskompanie (Personnel Decontamination Co). Nos 617, 620 and 622 have been identified. In spite of the similarity of titles, these are definitely medical units and not smoke troops like decontamination and road-decontamination battalions.

14. Armee-Sanitätspark (Army Medical Park). Numbered in series 501-700. Both officers and other ranks wear dark blue with the Arabic number of the park.

The following figures show the tactical signs for medical units:--

Basic sign=

Motorized army medical regiment.

Ambulance battalion.

Motorized war hospital regiment.

XII VETERINARY UNITS (Veterinär-Einheiten)

Carmine is the distinguishing color of veterinary units. For division units see Order of Battle of the German Army. In addition, the following GHQ veterinary units may be encountered.

1. Heeres-or Armee-Pferdelazarett (GHQ or Army Veterinary Hospital). Numbered in series 501-700.

2. Pferde-Transportkolonne (mot.) (motorized Horse Transport Column). Numbered in the same series.

3. Armee-Pferdepark (Army Horse Park). Numbered in the same series. One is assigned to each army (excluding Panzer armies).

4. Armee-Veterinärpark (Army Veterinary Park). Numbering and allocation as for paragraph 3 above. The personnel of both types, officers as well as other ranks, wear carmine piping with the Arabic number of the park.

The following figures show the tactical signs for veterinary units:--

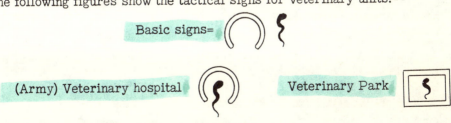

Basic signs=

(Army) Veterinary hospital

Veterinary Park

XIII MILITARY POLICE UNITS (Feldgendarmerie-Einheiten)

Military police units wear orange piping and carry no number. They wear, however, on the left upper arm the Nazi eagle and swastika surrounded by an oak-wreath, and on the lower arm a brown band inscribed with the word "Feldgendarmerie" in silver.

1. Feldgendarmerie-Abteilung (Military Police Bn). One is allotted to each army or Panzer army. The following units of this type have been identified: 501, 520, 521, 531, 541, 551, 571, 582, 591, 682, 683, 690, 697.

2. Feldgendarmerie-Trupp (Military Police Detachment). Detachments of military police allocated to the military administration of an occupied country are believed to carry the number of the Kommandantur to which they are attached. See section (XVI).

3. ·Verkehrsregelung -Bataillon (Traffic Control Bn). Seven units of this type, carrying numbers in series 751-760, have been identified to date. A battalion or a company may be allocated for as long as necessary to an army on the move.

4. Geheime Feldpolizei, G.F.P. (Field Secuirty Police). Gruppen (groups) of the G.F.P. may be assigned impartially to army or GAF organizations. There is normally one Gruppe at the disposal of each army, and one or more attached to the military administration of each occupied country. Series 501-800.

The following figures show the tactical sign for military police units:--

Basic sign=

Motorized military police battalion

XIV LOCAL DEFENSE UNITS (Landesschützen-Einheiten)

Local defense units wear white piping with the Latin "L", followed by an Arabic number in the case of Landesschützen regimental staffs and battalions. Various other types of unit fall under the same heading in the German classification, although they are not specifically described as Landesschützen and lack the distinghishing "L".

1. Landesschützen-Regiment (Landesschützen Regt Staff). This is a regimental Hq controlling a varying number of battalions. Some are qualified z.b.V. and sometimes include various attached units. In the case of two-figure numbers the first, and in the case of three-figure numbers the first two figures give the Wehrkreis of origin (e.g., Lds. Schtz. Rgt. 115 comes from Wkr. XI).

2. Landesschützen-Bataillon (Landesschützen Bn.). Battalions vary in strength from two to six companies. Some are qualified "z.b.V." and have various attached units. Within Germany they are employed for guard duties at PW camps and vulnerable points. In occupied territories they provide the main support for the military administration. On L of C they may be used to guard dumps, parks, etc. Some 400 battalions have been identified, numbered according to the Wehrkreis of origin as follows:--

Wkr.	Series	Wkr.	Series
I	201-250	IX	601-650
II	251-300	X	651-700
III	301-350	XI	701-750
IV	351-400	XII	751-800
V	401-450	XIII	801-850
VI	451-500	XVII	851-900
VII	501-550	XVIII	901-950
VIII	551-600	Various	951-1001

The GAF also has Landesschützen units. These, however, may be distinguished from army Landesschützen, since they wear double numbers, Roman for the Luftgau of origin and Arabic for the particular unit.

3. Wachregiment (Guard Regt). Two regiments of this type have been identified, namely Wachrgt. Clüwer (named after its commander) and Wachrgt. Paris (probably the 745th Inf Regt of the 712th Inf Div). The latter unit, though formed from Landesschützen personnel, now forms part of the infantry series.

4. Wachbataillon (Guard Bn). There are two main types, namely Heimatwachbtl. and Wachbatl. serving with the armies in the field, with different war establishments and numbered in two series, 1-500 and 501-800. The former type includes bridge guard battalions (Nos 58, 99, 122 and 143 identified) and cyclist guard battalions (No 326 identified). The units of the latter type are assigned to armies to provide guards for army parks, etc. (16 identified to date).

5. Grenzwacht (Frontier Guard). In peace time, the regular units stationed in the frontier districts were reinforced by a frontier guard organization, with the following chain of command:

    Grenzschutz-Abschnittskommando (Sector Command= Regt Hq)
    Grenzschutz-Unterabschnitt (Sub-sector= Bn Hq)
    Grenzwacht-Kompanie (Frontier Guard Co)

Each sector has a signals co, one or more fixed bns of arty and other units. On mobilization, the sector commands were renamed regiments and numbered on the same principle as the Landesschützen regiments (paragraph 1 above). It is probable that they have since been renamed Landesschützen regiments (e.g., 122d Lds. Schtz. Regt. is probably for former 122d Frontier Guard Regt, from Wkr. XII, renamed).

Some Landesschützen units have been reported to wear light green piping, the color of mountain rifle and rifle (Jäger) units. The reason for this is not known.

The tactical signs for Landesschützen units are the same as those for the comparable infantry units, with the addition of the letter L.

143

XV CONSTRUCTION UNITS (Bau-Einheiten)

Light brown is the distinguishing color of construction units, but railway construction battalions wear black piping, as do bridge-building battalions (with the possible exception of those carrying numbers below 501) and fortress construction battalions. The following types may be encountered:

1. Oberbaustab (High Construction Staff). Equivalent in status to a brigade staff. Numbered in series 1-20.

2. Kommandeur der Bautruppen (CO Construction Troops): Regimental commander and staff. Two series, 1-50 and 101-150 (about 20 identified).

3. Baubataillon, Bau-Btl. (Construction Bn). Series 1-500 (about 100 identified, of which the majority carry numbers below 300), excluding bridge building, fortress and railway construction battalions which are numbered concurrently.

4. Brückenbau-Bataillon, Br.Bau-Bt. (Bridge Building Bn). Series 1-500 (to date, 15 identified) and 501-800 (about 20 identified). The battalions in the higher series regularly operate with the armies in the field, and are reckoned as engineers in all respects. The lower series is more likely to be used on the L of C.

5. Festungsbau-Bataillon, Fest.Bau-Btl. (Fortress Construction Bn). Some 15 have been identified, carrying numbers between 19 and 242 inclusive. They operate under the direction of fortress engineer staffs (paragraph 2, Section VII).

6. Strassenbau-Bataillon, Str.Bau-Btl. (Road Construction Bn). Series 501-700 (shared with field army bridge building battalions) about 30 have been identified, including seven Radfahr- (cyclist) battalions (in series 501-510, intended to accompany spearhead formations). They may be qualified as leichte or schwere (i.e., light or heavy), but it is not known how the two varieties differ from each other.

7. Eisenbahn-Baubataillon, Eisb.Bau-Btl. (Railway Construction Bn). Nos 83, 111, 116, 511 and 512 have been identified. It is believed their function is to provide less specialized labor than that of the construction companies described in paragraph 3 Section VII.

8. Marine-Baubataillon, Mar.Bau-Bt. (Naval Construction Bn): Nos 311, 312 and 323 in the main series are described thus. They are presumably intended to carry out construction works for the German Navy, though their personnel are provided by the Army. (The coast defense units belong to the German Navy).

9. Kriegsgefangenen-Bau- und Arbeits-Bataillon (PW Construction and Labor Bn). Series 1-50 (half a dozen identified to date). The German cadre personnel acts as guards to PW employed within Germany or on the L of C.

10. Landesbau-Bataillon (Agricultural Bn). A series 1-6 has recently been identified. They are presumably intended to assist in the agricultural exploitataion of the Ukraine.

The following figures show the tactical signs for construction units:--

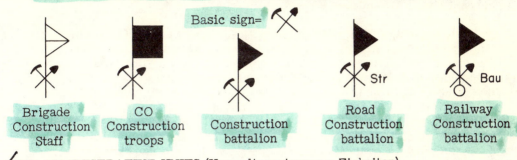

Basic sign=

| Brigade Construction Staff | CO Construction troops | Construction battalion | Road Construction battalion | Railway Construction battalion |

XVI ADMINISTRATIVE UNITS (Verwaltungstruppen-Einheiten)

This category includes a variety of units, and no single distinghishing color can be specified for it. For particulars of corps and divisional units see Order of Battle of the German Army. In the following list units have been grouped for convenience approximately according to their functions and to their place in the German war establishment.

1. Administration of supplies

Units in this group are largely staffed by officials (Beamten) who wear dark green piping. Officers wear the color of their original arm of the service.

a. Bäckerei-Kompanie, Gross-Bäckerei-Kompanie (Bakery Co, Large Bakery Co). Allotted random numbers in series 501-700.

b. Schlächterei-Einheiten (Animal Slaughter Units). These vary in size, description and range of numbering as follows:--

Abteilung (Battalion). Nos 201 and 619 identified.
Kompanie (Company). Nos 503, 556, 582, 622, 635, and 641 identified.
Zug (Platoon): Nos 571, 592, 602, 605, 613, 615, 626, 636, 675 and 697
   identified.

The companies are allotted to armies. Principles for the allocation of battalions and platoons are not available.

c. Eisenbahn-Küchenwagen-Abteilung (Railway Kitchen-car Detachment) Nos 1 and 2 have been identified.

d. Heeres-Betreuungsabteilung (Army Welfare Bn): Series 1-6 identified.

e. Armee-Verpflegungsamt, A.Vpfl.Amt. or A.V.A. (Army Ration Supply Depot). There are several of these available for each army in the field, carrying numbers selected from the series 501-800.

f. Heeres-Verpflegungsamt, H.V.A. (GHQ Ration Supply Depot): Numbered concurrently with those under e above.

g. Feldpostamt, F.P.A. (Field Post Office). Army and GHQ field post offices carry numbers selected from the series 501 and upwards. In addition to its proper number, each post office (including corps and division offices) uses, for all open correspondence, a Kenn-Nummer (Code number) selected at random from the series 1-999: thus, K 943 might be the code number for 571st Army FPO. It is therefore necessary to exercise particular care in studying identifications of FPOs.

h. Armee-Briefstelle (Army Postal Station): Numbered in the same series as establishments in g above, these are branches of the army FPO for the collection and delivery of the field post.

i. Armee-Bekleidungsamt (Army Clothing Depot). Numbering same as for Armee-Verpflegungsämte in e above.

2. Administration of ordnance stores, etc.

Officers wear the color of their original arm. Enlisted personnel light blue piping. All except serial 10 are distinguished by Latin "FZ" on shoulder straps.

a. Feldzeugkommando (Ordnance Command). One or two in each Wehrkreis in Germany (the Gothic letters "FZ" followed by a Roman numeral give the identification), and some in occupied countries (e.g. Belgium and Northern France). The officer appointed to this post has the status of a brigade commander. In the zone of operations there is no comparable post.

b. Oberfeldzeugstab (Higher Ordnance Staff). Series 1 and upwards. The commander has the status or a regimental commander.

c. Feldzeugstab (Ordnance Staff). Series 1-50 (a dozen identified). Equivalent in status to battalion Hq.

d. Feldzeugbataillon (Ordnance Bn). Series 1-50 (half a dozen identified).

e. Zentral-Ersatzteillager, Z.E.L. (Central Spare Parts Depot). Series 1-200.

f. Munitions-Verwaltungskompanie, Mun. Verw.Kp. (Am Adm Co). Series 501 and upwards.

g. Betriebsstoffs-Verwaltungskompanie, Betr.Verw.Kp. (Gas and Oil Adm Co). Series 971-980.

3. Administration of occupied territory

Other ranks belonging to units of the following types wear white piping, with the Latin letter "K" followed by the Arabic number of their unit.

a. Oberfeldkommandantur, O.F.K. (Higher Field Hq). Hq of this type in the zone of operations come under Army L of C Commander, or CG Army Group L of C Area. In occupied territory outside the zone of operations they come under the general officer in command of the military administration, and in such cases they are distinguished by the addition of (V)-- for Verwaltung--to their title. Nos 365, 372, 379 and 393 were formed in Poland from the staffs of divisions disbanded in 1940, and continue to carry the same numbers. All other identified units carry numbers in series 501 and upwards.

b. Subordinate field Hq. The following Hq carry numbers in the same series, in which the lowest number yet identified is 178 and the highest 928. According to their special description or the rank of the officer in command their relative importance may be deduced, but there is no system discoverable in the allocation of numbers to them:

> Feldkommandantur (Field Hq). Approximately equivalent to an area command of a Wehrkreis (See Part B). The term may also be used, loosely, to describe one of the following special types.

> Ortskommandantur (Town Hq). Town major's command in a small town.

> Stadkommandantur (City Hq). Town major's command in a city or large town.

> Kreiskommandantur (Rural Hq). Town major's command in a rural district.

About 150 examples, in all, have been identified to date, the majority of which carry numbers above 500.

4. Administration of PW Camps

The following types of PW camp staffs all carry numbers in a single series 1-400. Personnel wear the color of their original arm. It should be noted that a PW camp located in a Wehrkreis also carries (and in all open correspondence uses) the Roman numeral of the Wehrkreis followed by a letter of the alphabet (e.g., Stalag XXI A).

a. Frontstalag (Forward PW Camp). Twenty-five identified.

b. Dulag (PW Transit Camp). Twenty identified.

c. Oflag (Camp for Officer PW). Series 1-100 (10 identified).

d. Stalag (Camp for enlisted PW). Series 301-400 (40 identified).

XVII GAF ANTIAIRCRAFT UNITS

A list of identified units is given in Order of Battle of the German Army.

1. System of Numbering

All units carry numbers in series 1-1,000. In some cases, one number is carried by two or more units of different types. The following are the principal groups in the main series.

a. Nos. 1-70. Regiments consisting of Hq, I and II Battalions, each of three heavy and two light gun batteries , III Battalion of three searchlight batteries, and a personnel replacement battalion carrying the regimental number without qualification.

b. Nos 71-99. Light battalions each of three light batteries (there are also a number of independent regimental staffs carrying numbers in this series).

Most of the units in the above two groups existed in peace time.

c. Nos 100-997. Units formed on or after mobilization are allotted numbers on no deducible system. They include regiments, regimental staffs,and independent battalions (heavy, mixed, light or searchlight). Army AAA batteries receive numbers in the same series. Marine (Naval) batteries are numbered in a separate series, as are transport, balloon barrage and plotting units (which belong to the same branch of the GAF). The term Reserve prefixed to units in this group indicates that they have a special war organization (with a lower allocation of MT). It does not mean that the units in question were necessarily formed on mobilization.

2. Employment

The tactical unit is the battalion (Abteilung) and not the regiment. In action battalions (whether regimental or independent) rarely operate under a regimental staff of the same number.

AAA serving with the armies in the field is fully motorized. Units intended to cooperate with the spearhead of the attack are equipped for cross-country operation. Command is exercised through the chain corps—division—regiment—battalion. There is no fixed allotment of units to higher formations, but the following range has been noted:—

To AAA corps (Flakkorps): Two to four AA divisions.

To AAA division (Flakdivision): Two to five regiments.
To AAA regiment (Flak-Regiment): Three to five battalions.

In general, the AAA corps controls the area of an army group, and the AAA division the area of an army. Allotment of units varies according to the estimated needs but an army corps commonly has an AAA battalion attached to it during operations, and a light or mixed battalion will often be found attached to a Panzer division. An infantry division is not likely to be allotted more than an AAA battery.

3. Control

GAF AAA organizations and units operating with the army are subordinated operationally to the army unit concerned, and administratively to the nearest GAF ground organization staff (Luftgaustab). The function of AAA in the field is the defense of the zone of the armies. In practice, this is not confined to the protection of troop columns and concentrations, supply dumps and L of C—on the contrary, mobile AAA units regularly operate in the spearhead of the attack, being employed not only for defense against air attack but against land targets (tanks, pill-boxes and other strong points, etc.). For this purpose the 88mm (3.46 in) gun, with which the heavy battery is normally equipped, has proved conspicuously successful.

XVIII OTHER GAF UNITS

The following are the principal types of unit likely to be found cooperating with army units in fighting on land.

1. Parachute troops (Fallschirmtruppen). The formations and units concerned are as follows: —

XI Fliegerkorps (XI Air Corps). Controlling all air-borne operations.
7th Fliegerdivision (7th Air Div). Containing units marked with an asterisk below.
Fallschirmjäger-Regiment (Parachute Rifle Regt). Nos 1-3* and 5 have been identified.
F.S.-Artillerie-Regiment (Parachute Arty Regt). No 1* identified.
F.S.-Panzerjäger-Abteilung((Parachute AT Bn). Unnumbered*.
F.S.-M.G. Btl. (Parachute MG Bn). Unnumbered*.
F.S.-Nachrichtenkompanie (Parachute Sig Co). No. 7*.
F.S.-Fla.Btl. (Parachute AAA MG Bn). Unnumbered.
F.S.-Pionier-Btl. (Parachute Engineer Bn). Unnumbered.
F.S.-Sanitats-Kompanie (Parachute Medical Co). Unnumbered.
Sturm-Regiment (Glider Regt). No 1 identified.

2. Army cooperation reconnaissance units. Army cooperation Staffeln (squadrons of nine aircraft) are described as H. Staffelin if designed for tacti-

cal reconnaissance and F. Staffeln in the case of long range reconnaissance units. The addition of Pz. indicates that a Staffel is trained to cooperate with Panzer units. The H Staffeln are operationally independent sub-units of Gruppen (groups), of which the following have been identified: 10-14, 21-23, 31-33 and 41. Each Gruppe may contain up to seven Staffeln. On Order of Battle the Staffel is shown thus: 3 (H) 13 or 2 (H) 23 Pz. Long-range Staffeln are shown thus: 3 (F) 33.

3. Army cooperation signal units. Luftnachrichten-Abteilung (Heer) motorisiert, abbreviated L.N. Abt. (H) mot. (Air Signal Bn (Army) (Mtz). Numbered in series 1 and upwards, and allocated on the basis of one to each army.

In addition, GAF construction supply or transport units may be encountered. These can readily be distinguished because, like GAF Landesschutzen units (see paragraph 2, Section XIV), they carry a double number, Arabic (for the particular unit) and Roman (for the Luftgau or GAF administrative district in which it was formed).

The tactical signs for the units in paragraphs 2 and 3 above and for GAF AAA units, are given in the following figures:--

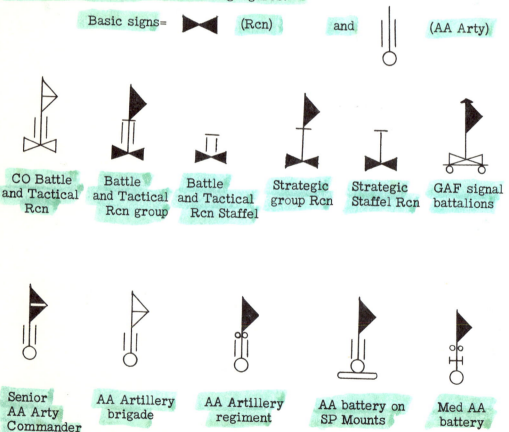

Basic signs= ▶◀ (Rcn)   and   ‖‖ (AA Arty)

CO Battle and Tactical Rcn   Battle and Tactical Rcn group   Battle and Tactical Rcn Staffel   Strategic group Rcn   Strategic Staffel Rcn   GAF signal battalions

Senior AA Arty Commander   AA Artillery brigade   AA Artillery regiment   AA battery on SP Mounts   Med AA battery

150

PART E--INDEXES OF SENIOR OFFICERS

CONTENTS

PART E

I INTRODUCTION

1. In this part are included lists of senior officers, arranged alphabetically by rank down to **Major General** inclusive; of known General Staff Officers (Staff College graduates)--i.e., officers from Captain to Colonel inclusive who wear the uniform of the General Staff Corps and have the qualification i.G. = im Generalstabe added to their title of rank--arranged alphabetically regardless of rank; of known commanders of units (providing an index to the officers shown in Part C); and of senior officers of the German Air Force, whose titles of rank are indistinguishable, except in the case of full generals, from those of Army officers.

2. Lists of senior officers of the S.S and Police are given in Part F, sections VI and VII, below. It has not proved practicable to include a consolidated alphabetical index of all the officers mentioned, and it has been found necessary to exclude colonels from the present edition. It is hoped that a list of colonels and a consolidated index may be issued subsequently.

3. The classified lists are preceded by a series of brief notes on German surnames, titles and ranks, which are liable to provide stumbling blocks for all except specialists in their study.

II GERMAN SURNAMES

Note: In the name John Henry Ducrot, John Henry are Christian names while Ducrot is a family name or surname.

1. The most confusing form of German surname is that in which a person has two surnames, of which he habitually uses only one, since there is no general rule to indicate which of the two names is generally used. For example, Field Marshal von Lewinski genannt von Manstein (literally, von Lewinski called von Manstein) is customarily known as von Manstein, and he is listed among the field marshals under the letter M. However, Lt General von Hartlieb genannt Walsporn is normally known as von Hartlieb, and he is therefore listed under the letter H.

2. In some cases of double surnames, where the term genannt is not employed, the von (equivalent to de in French surnames) is customarily transposed; for example, General Geyr von Schweppenburg, formerly German Military Attache in London, is normally referred to as von Geyr. In general, where two surnames are connected by und (and), the first of the two is used: thus, Lt General von Rothkirch und Panthen is usually called von Rothkirch. Hyphenated names are often but not invariably used in full.

3. Christian names are seldom if ever used in signatures. Officers sign orders with family name and rank only. It is therefore difficult, at times, to discover an officer's Christian name or initials (neither of which is shown in any official document, except in the original registration, or when two men of the

same name and rank must be distinguished from each other), so that in a few cases in the following lists there is a possibility of confusion between officers having the same surname.

4. Academic degrees, such as Dr. or Dr. Ing., are regularly shown before the surname both in official documents and in signatures, and are therefore included in the following lists.

III GERMAN TITLES

1. Persons with hereditary titles are more frequently found in Germany than in Great Britain, because German titles do not pass only from eldest son to eldest son, or to the nearest male blood relation (as in the United Kingdom), but from the father to all his sons. They in turn transmit the title to their sons (except in certain princely families in which the title Prinz is borne solely by the head of the family). The titles most commonly used are listed below.

2. Graf (Count) corresponds approximately to Earl. As with other titles, it is usually followed by von, though in referring to a Count the prefix is often omitted; thus, Lt General Graf von Sponeck is normally described as Graf Sponeck.

3. Freiherr, abbreviated Frhr. (Baron) corresponds approximately to the lowest degree of the British peerage. The title Baron, which also occurs, is of non-German origin. In conversation a Freiherr is generally referred to as Baron, the prefix von being omitted; thus, Colonel General Frhr v. Weichs may be described as Baron Weichs.

4. Ritter (Knight) corresponds in some cases to Baronet and in others to Knight. A Ritter whose title is hereditary usually owns a Rittergut or Knight's estate and takes his name from it. In other cases, the title is derived from a grant made to an officer for heroism in action or for distinguished service to the state. In Bavaria, until 1919, the Military Order of Max Joseph carried with it a patent of Knighthood which was not hereditary--hence the title of Field Marshal Ritter von Leeb whose son, killed in action in Poland in 1939, was Lieutenant Leeb.

5. Edler (Noble) approximately equivalent to Baronet. The titles Ritter and Edler are, in most cases, of Bavarian or Austrian origin.

6. The prefix von corresponds most closely to the English suffix Esquire (in the strict sense), denoting the right to bear arms.

IV GERMAN MILITARY RANK

1. In the following table the approximate American equivalent is given for each German rank. It should be noted, however, that the appointments held by officers of any given rank may vary widely in status, and no appointment carries or presupposes specific rank: for example:--

A Generalmajor may command an infantry regiment a division or on occasions, an army corps.

An infantry regiment may be commanded by a Generalmajor, an Oberst, an Oberstleutnant or, on occasions, a Major.

A "First General Staff Officer" (Ia) (our G-3) may be a Hauptmann, Major, Oberstleutnant or Oberst.

Abbreviation	In full	American Equivalent
Genfeldm., Gen. Feldm.	Generalfeldmarschall	No corresponding grade (Field Marshal)
Genobst., Gen. Obst.	Generaloberst	No corresponding grade (Col Gen)
Gen. (d. Inf., d.Geb.Tr., d. Kav., d.Pz.Tr., d.Art., d.Pion., d.Na.Tr.; d.Flieg., d.Flak, d.Luftna.Tr.)	General (der Infanterie --Gebirgstruppen-- Kavallerie--Panzer- truppen--Artillerie-- Pioniere -- Nach- richtentruppen; der Flieger -- Flakartil- lerie -- Luftnach- richtentruppen).	General of (Infantry, Mountain Troops, Cavalry, Panzer Troops, Artillery, Engineers, Signal Troops; Air, AAA, Air Signal Troops
Genlt., Gen. Lt.	Generalleutnant	Lt General
Genmaj., Gen. Maj.	Generalmajor	Maj General
None	None	Brigadier General
Obst.	Oberst	Colonel
Oberstlt., Obst. Lt.	Oberstleutnant	Lt Colonel
Maj.	Major	Major
Hptm.	Hauptmann	Captain
Rittm.	Rittmeister	Captain (Cavalry)
Oblt., Ob. Lt.	Oberleutnant	Lieutenant
Lt., Ltn.	Leutnant	Second Lieutenant
Fhj.	Fahnenjunker	None

2. In the German Army, acting or temporary rank is not granted--hence the variety in rank to be found among officers holding similar commands. But two qualifications of rank may occur:--

Ernennung (approximately the equivalent of brevet rank): An Oberstleutnant may be ernannt Oberst, or an Oberst ernannt Generalmajor, in order to obtain the higher rank sooner than his seniority in the lower rank would permit (promotion is normally strictly according to seniority up to the rank of Genlt. inclusive. Such officers receive the pay of the higher rank, but do not obtain a specific seniority (Rangdienstalter, abbreviated R.D.A.) until their actual promotion.

Charakterisierung (honorary rank): An officer may be charakterisiert to a higher rank (e.g., Major to Oberstleutnant). Such officers do not receive the pay of the higher rank until their actual promotion, but they obtain a specific seniority in a separate charakterisiert list. The qualification is regularly shown in titles of rank: e.g., char. Oberst.

3. Officers are listed separately, according to their status, as follows:--

Regular officers on the active list.--An aktiv officer is distinguished by the title of his rank without qualification: e.g., Oberst.

Regular officers on the supplementary list.--During the period of maximum expansion of the German Army (1934-1939), large numbers of additional officers were required, particularly for administrative appointments. To meet this special demand, an Ergänzungs (supplementary) list was formed on which ex-officers were recommissioned after undergoing suitable courses. An Ergänzungs officer is distinguished by the addition of (Erg.) or (E) to the title of his rank: e.g., Oberst (Erg.). Officers on this list take precedence immediately after those holding the same rank on the active list.

Reserve officers.--Retired officers from the active or Ergänzungs list may be transferred to the reserve list, to which suitable candidates may also be commissioned directly. Commissions on this list correspond to some extent, in peace time, to commissions in the Organized Reserve Corps. A reserve officer takes precedence immediately after Ergänzungs officers of the same rank, and is distinguished by the addition of der Reserve, d.Res. or d.R. to the title of his rank: e.g., Oberst d.R.

Landwehr officers.--Reserve officers may be transferred to the Landwehr list because of age or relative unfitness. Such officers are distinguished by the addition of der Landwehr, d.Landw. or d.L. to the title of rank: e.g., Major d.L.

Over age officers.--Officers who have passed the age limit for their rank and classification, but remain fit and willing to serve, are transferred to the zur Verfügung (i.e., available) list and are distinguished by the addition of z.V. to the title of rank: e.g. Maj. d. R.z.V.

Unemployable retired officers.--Retired officers who are no longer fit or suitable for military service of any kind are described as ausser Dienst (out of service) or a.D.: e.g., Oberst a.D.

Officers on the emergency list.--For the duration of the war, emergency commissions (auf Kriegsdauer, abbreviated a.K.) are granted to suitable candidates. Such commissions rank immediately below those on the aktiv list.

V OFFICERS OF THE ARMY MEDICAL AND VETERINARY SERVICES

1. The names of officers of the German Army Medical and Veterinary Services are not included in the following lists. The ranks in these services of the German Army, with the appointments normally held, are as follows:--

Medical Officers	Ranking as	Normal appointment
Generaloberstabsarzt.	General	Chief Inspector of Army Medical Services or Surgeon General.
Generalstabsarzt	Generalleutnant	Chief Med O of an army group or army
Generalarzt	Generalmajor	Chief Med O of a corps or Wehrkreis
Oberstarzt	Oberst	Chief Med O of a division
Oberfeldarzt	Oberstleutnant	Chief Med O of a regiment, station, hospital or/medical battalion
Oberstabsarzt	Major	Senior Med O of a battalion, or Comdr of a medical company
Stabsarzt	Hauptmann	In a hospital, medical
Oberarzt	Oberleutnant	unit, etc., or attached
Assistenzarzt	Leutnant	to a combat unit
Feldunterarzt	--	

Veterinary Officers	Ranking as	Normal appointment
Generaloberstabs- veterinär	General	Chief Inspector of Army Veterinary Service
Generalstabs- veterinär	Generalleutnant	Chief Vet O of an army group or army
Generalveterinär	Generalmajor	Chief Vet O of a corps or Wehrkreis
Oberstveterinär	Oberst	Chief Vet O of a division, CO
Oberfeldveterinär	Oberstleutnant	of a veterinary hospital
Oberstabsveterinär	Major	Senior Med O of a battalion or regt, CO of a veterinary company

Stabsveterinär	Hauptmann ⎫	In a veterinary unit or at-
Oberveterinär	Oberleutnant ⎬	tached to a veterinary unit
Veterinär	Leutnant ⎭	

VI SOME COMMON ABBREVIATIONS

1. The following list contains the commonest abbreviations of name, style and appointment. It should be used in conjunction with the list of abbreviations of ranks in Section IV.*

Abbreviation	Meaning	American equivalent
Abt. Chef	Abteilungschef	Head of a section or department.
a.D.	ausser Dienst	Retired. See ¶3, Section IV.
AHA	Allgemeines Heeresamt	General Army Office. War Department.
a.K.	auf Kriegsdauer	Emergency Commission.
Bfh.	Befehlshaber	Commander, usually of an army or larger unit.
char.	charakterisiert	Characterized or Designated Rank.
ch. (d. Genstb.)	Chef (des General-stabes)	C of S
Ch H Rü u. BdE	Chef der Heeres-rüstung und Befehl-shaber des Ersatz-heeres.	Chief of Materiel and Equipment Division and Head of the Replacement Training Army**
d.B.	des Beurlaubten-standes	Holder of Reserve or Landwehr Commission.
d.G.	des Generalstabes	Of the General Staff.
d.L., d.R.	der Landwehr, der Reserve.	Of the Landwehr or of the Reserve.
Dipl.	Diplomierter	Graduate.
Dr.	Doktor	Doctor (Degree of any branch of learning)
Erg., E	Ergänzungs	Supplementary.

*It should be noted that the Germans sometimes do and do not use periods with their military abbreviations. Americans, of course, use no periods with military abbreviations.

**See Part A.

157

ern.	ernannt	Named.
Frhr.	Freiherr	Baron.
Fü.	Führer	Leader or Commander
gen.	genannt	Named.
Gen. Qu	Generalquartier-meister	G-4.
Genstb. d. H.	Generalstab des Heeres	General Staff of the Army
höh.	höherer	Higher or senior.
Ia	(pronounced "einss ah")	G-3.
i.G.	im Generalstabe	In the General Staff.
Ing.	Ingenieur	Technical engineer.
Insp., Inspiz.	Inspekteur, In-spizient	Inspector
Kdr.	Kommandeur	CO or commander.
Kdt.	Kommandant	CO or commandant.
Kom. Gen.	Kommandierender General	Commanding General
Landw., L.	Landwehr	Landwehr. (units containing personnel from 35 to 45 years of age).
Leit.	Leiter	Leader or Chief.
Lw.	Luftwaffe	German Air Force (GAF).
Ob. Bfh.	Oberbefehlshaber	Commander-in-Chief.
Ob. d. H.	Oberbefehlshaber des Heeres.	Chief of Staff of the Army.
Offz.	**Offizier**	Officer
O.K.H.	Oberkommando des Heeres.	Army GHQ, or War Department.
O.K.W.	Oberkommando der Wehrmacht.	GHQ of the Armed Forces (No American equivalent).
OQü	Oberquartier-meister	Deputy Chief of Staff.
PA	Heeres-Personalamt	Army Personnel Office (G-1).
R.D.A.	Rangdienstalter	Senior (in rank).
Res., R.	Reserve	Reserve.
R.L.M. u.Ob.d.L.	Reichsluftfahrt-minister und Ober-befehlshaber der Luftwaffe.	Secretary of Air and C in C of of the Air Force (Goering)
Ru	Rüstungs-	Equipment, armament.
stv.	stellvertretender	Representative, deputy, assis-tant.
Uffz.	Unteroffizier	NCO
v.	von	Of or from.
(V)	(Verwaltung)	Administration.
WaA	Heeres-Waffenamt	Ordnance Office or Office of Chief of Ordnance.

WeWi	Wehrwirtschaft	Military Economy (The economics of Germany).
z.b.V.	zu besonderer Verwendung	For special employment. Special duty or assignment.
z.V.	zur Verfügung	Available (for duty).

VII ROSTERS OF GERMAN COMMANDERS AND STAFF OFFICERS

1. Rank: FIELD MARSHAL (Generalfeldmarschall)

Name (age)	Appointment (date)	Seniority	Origin	Arm
v. BOCK, Fedor (61)	Army Group B (1/IV/42)	19/VII/40		Inf
v. BRAUCHITSCH, Walthur (60)	(Retired)	19/VII/40	Silesia	Arty
KEITEL, Wilhelm (59)	Chief of O.K.W.	19/VII/40		Arty
v. KLUGE, Günther (59)	Army Group Center (8/IV/42)	19/VII/40		Arty
v. KLÜCHLER, Georg (61)	Army Group North (1/V/42)	19/VII/40		Arty
Ritter v. LEEB, Wilhelm (65)	(Retired)	19/VII/40	Bavaria	Arty
LIST, Wilhelm (62)	Army Group A (11/V/42)	19/VII/40	Württemberg	Inf
v. LEWINSKI gen. v. MANSTEIN, Fritz (54)	Eleventh Army (15/V/42)	III/42		Inf
ROMMEL, Erwin (51)	Panzer Army of Africa (22/VI/42)	22/VI/42	Württemberg	Tks
v. RUNDSTEDT, Gerd (66)	Army Group West (15/V/42)	19/VII/40		Inf
v. WITZLEBEN, Erwin (60)		19/VII/40	Silesia	Inf

2. Rank: COLONEL GENERAL (Generaloberst)

BLASKOWITZ, Johannes (58)	First Army (1/V/42)	1/X/39	Baden	Inf
BUSCH, Ernst (57)	Sixteenth Army (1/III/42)	19/VII/40	Westphalia	Inf
DIETL, Eduard (52)	Army of Lapland (31/V/42)	5/VI/42	Bavaria	Mtn Trs
DOLLMANN, Friedrich (60)	Seventh Army (1/V/42)	19/VII/40	Bavaria	Arty
v. FALKENHORST, Nikolaus (57)	Army of Norway (1/V/42)	19/VII/40	Silesia	Inf
FROMM, Fritz (53)	Ch H Rü u. BdE*	19/VII/40		Arty

*See ¶ I Section VI

GUDERIAN, Heinz (54)		19/VII/40		Tks
HAASE, Curt (60)	Fifteenth Army (1/III/42)	19/VII/40	Württem-berg	Inf
HALDER, Franz (58)	Chief of General Staff of German Army (1/V/42)	19/VII/40	Bavaria	Arty
HOEPPNER, Erich (55)	Fourth Panzer Army (1/X/41)	19/VII/40		Cav
HOTH, Hermann (58)	Seventeenth Army (12/II/42)	19/VII/40		Inf
v. KLEIST, Ewald (61)	First Panzer Army (1/V/42)	19/VII/40		Cav
MODEL, Walter (50)	Ninth Army (7/III/42)	1/II/42		Tks
REINHARDT, Georg-Hans (55)	Third Panzer Army (1/V/42)	1/III/42	Saxony	Tks
RUOFF, Richard (57)	Fourth Army (18/III/42)	1/IV/42	Württem-berg	Inf
SCHMIDT, Rudolf (56)	Second Panzer Army (1/IV/42)	1/III/42		Tks
STRAUSS, Adolf (62)		19/VII/40		Inf
Frhr. v. WEICHS, Maximilian (60)		19/VII/40	Bavaria	Cav

3. Rank: GENERAL

ANGELIS, Maximilian		1/III/42	Austria	Arty
v. ARNIM, Jürgen (52)	A Corps ?	1/X/41	Silesia	Tks
BADER, Paul (56)	LXV Corps Command (15/V/42).	1/VII/41		Arty
BEHLENDORFF (53)		1/X/41		Arty
BIELER, Bruno (53)	XXXXII Inf Corps (15/XI/41).	1/X/41		Inf
BOCK (60)	Wkr. XX (27/XI/41)	1/XII/40		Inf
v. BÖCKMANN, Herbert (54)	L Inf Corps (3/III/42)	1/IV/42	Baden	Inf
BÖHME, Franz (56)	XVIII Mtn Corps (1/II/42)	1/VIII/40	Austria	Inf
v. BOETTICHER, Friedrich (60)		1/IV/40	Saxony	Arty
v. BOTH (58)		1/VI/40		Inf
BRAND, Fritz (54)	A Corps (4/IX/41)	1/VIII/40		Arty
BRANDT, Georg (65)	XXXIII Corps Command (15/III/42).			Cav
BRENNECKE, Kurt (51)	C of S Army Group North (1/VIII/41).	1/II/42		Inf
Graf v. BROCKDORFF-AHLEFELDT, Walter (55).	II Inf Corps (15/III/42)	1/VIII/40		Inf
v. der CHEVALLERIE, Kurt (50)	LIX Inf Corps (1/V/42)	/42		Inf

CLÖSSNER, Erich (55)	LIII Inf Corps (15/IV/42)	1/I/42	Hessen	Inf
v. COCHENHAUSEN, Friedrich (62).	Wkr. XIII (1/I/42)	1/XII/40		Arty
CRÖWELL, Ludwig (50)	(Prisoner of War)	1/XII/40		Tks
Frhr. v. DALWIGK zu LICHTENFELS (61).	Wkr. III (15/IX/41)	1/XII/40		Inf
EBERT, Karl (64)			Bavaria	Arty
ERFURTH, Waldemar (62)	Mil. Mission, Finland (1/IV/40)	1/IV/40		Inf
FAHRMBACHER, Wilhelm (53)		1/XI/40	Bavaria	Arty
v. FALKENHAUSEN, Alexander (63)	C G Belgium and Northern France (15/IV/42)		Silesia	Inf
FEIGE, Hans (61)				Inf
FELBER, Hans (53)	XIII Inf Corps (15/XI/41)	1/VIII/40		Inf
FELLGIEBEL, Erich (55)	Chief Sig O	1/VIII/40		Sig C
FESSMANN, Ernst (60)		30/IX/37	Bavaria	Tks
FEURSTEIN, Valentin (56)	LXX Corps Command (20/IV/42)	1/IX/41	Austria	Mtn
FISCHER v. WEIKERSTHAL, Walter (51)	A Corps ?	1/XII/41	Württemberg	Inf Tr
FÖHRENBACH, Max (68)	Wkr. II (15/V/42)	1/IX/40		Arty
FÖRSTER, Otto (57)	VI Inf Corps (11/IX/41)	1/IV/38		Pion
FRETTER-PICO, Maximilian (51)	A Corps (20/III/42)	1/VI/42	Baden	Arty
FRIDERICI, Erich (56)	L of C Area Army Group South (1/I/42)	1/IV/39	Saxony	Inf
GALLENCAMP, Curt (52)		1/IV/42		Arty
GEIB, Theodor (56)	Director General of Supply (1939)	1/XII/41	Bavaria	Arty
GERCKE, Rudolf (57)	Director of Army Transport (1/VIII/41)	1/IV/42		Inf
GEYER, Hermann (59)	IX Inf Corps (15/XI/41)	1/VIII/36	Württemberg	Inf
Frhr. GEYR v. SCHWEPPENBURG, Leo (56).	XXIV Pz Corps (26/VII/41)	1/IV/40	Württemberg	Tks
Frhr. v. GIENANTH (63)	C. G. Gen. Govt. (15/III/42)	1/IV/36		Cav
GLOKKE, Gerhard (57)	Wkr. VI (15/V/41)	1/XII/40		Inf
GRAESSNER (50)		1/VI/42		Inf
v. GREIFF, Kurt (65)	XXXXV Corps Command (13/XI/41)	27/VIII/38	Württemberg	Inf
GRÜN, Otto (59)	Insp of Arty (8/V/42)		Bavaria	Arty
HALM, Hans (62)	Wkr VIII (17/V/41)			Inf
v. HANNEKEN (51)	Mil Economics Dept (20/I/42)	1/XII/41		Inf
HANSEN, Christian (56)	X Inf Corps (1/III/42)	1/VI/40		Arty

HANSEN, Erik (53)	LIV Inf Corps (15/IX/41)	1/VIII/40		Cav
HARPE, Josef (52)	XXXIX Pz Corps (1/VI/42).	1/VI/42		Tks
HARTMANN, Otto (57)		1/IV/40	Bavaria	Arty
HEINRICI, Gotthard (55)	A Corps (24/IX/41)	1/VI/40		Inf
HEITZ, Walter (63)	VIII Inf Corps (1/III/41)	1/IV/37		Arty
HOLLIDT (52)		1/II/42	Hessen	Inf
JACOB, Alfred (58)	Insp General of Engineers and Fortifications (1939).	1/VI/40	Bavaria	Pion
JODL, Alfred (51)	C of S O.K.W. (15/V/42).	1/VII/40	Bavaria	Arty
KAEMPFE, Rudolf (58)	XXXV Corps Command (1/IV/42).	1/VII/41		Arty
KAUPISCH, Leonard (63)	A Corps (1/II/42)			Arty
KEITEL (55)	Army Personnel Office, O.K.H.	1/IV/41		Inf
KEMPF, Werner (55)	XXXXVIII Pz Corps (1/VI/42).	1/IV/41		Tks
KIENITZ, Werner (57)	XVII Inf Corps (12/IX/41)	1/IV/38		Inf
KIRCHNER, Friedrich (57)	XXXXI Pz Corps (1/XI/41)	1/II/42	Saxony	Tks
KLEFFEL, Philipp (54)	I Inf Corps (3/III/42)	1/III/42		Inf
KOCH, Friedrich (62)				
KOCH-ERPACH, Rudolf (55)	A Corps ?	1/XII/42	Bavaria	Cav
KÖSTRING, Ernst (65)		1/IX/40		Cav
KONRAD, Rudolf (50)	XXXXIX Mtn Corps (1/I/42).	1/III/42	Bavaria	Mtn
v. KORTZLEISCH, Joachim (51)	XI Inf Corps (1/I/42)	1/VIII/40		Inf
KÜBLER, Ludwig (52)		1/VIII/40	Bavaria	Inf
KUNTZE, Walter (58)	Deputy C in C , Southeast (15/IV/42).	1/III/38		Pion
KUNTZEN, Adolf (53)	LVII Pz Corps (17/VII/41)	1/IV/41		Tks
Frhr. v. LANGERMANN u. ERLENCAMP, Willibald (52).	LVI Pz Corps (19/IV/42)	1/VI/42	Baden	Inf
LEEB, Emil (60)	Army Ordnance (1/V/42).	1/IV/39	Bavaria	Arty
LEMELSEN (54)	XXXXVII Pz Corps (20/IV/42).	1/VIII/40		Tks
LIEBMANN, Curt (61)	(Retired)	1/IV/35		Inf
LINDEMANN, Georg (58)	Eighteenth Army (18/III/42)	1/XI/40		Cav
LUCH, Herbert (55)		1/X/41	Bavaria	Arty
LÜDKE, Erich (59)	XXXI Corps Command and C G Denmark (1/V/42).	1/XII/40		Inf
LUTZ, Oswald (65)	Liaison Staff, S Ukraine (1/I/42).	1/X/35	Bavaria	Tks
v. MACKENSEN, Eberhard (53)	III Pz Corps (15/V/42).	1/VIII/40		Cav

Name	Assignment	Date	Region	Branch
MATERNA, Friedrich (56)	XXVIII Inf Corps (4/IX/41)	1/XI/40	Austria	Inf
MATTENKLOTT, Frantz, (57)		1/X/41	Silesia	Inf
METZ, Hermann (63)	A Corps (1/IV/42)	/41		Inf
MUFF, Wolfgang (61)	Wkr. XI (15/IX/41)	1/XII/40	Württemberg	Inf
MÜLLER, Eugen (50)	Q M G, GHQ (1/I/42)	1/VI/42	Bavaria	Arty
v. OBSTFELDER, Hans (55)	XXIX Inf Corps (1/IX/41)	1/VII/40	Thuringia	Inf
OLBRICHT, Friedrich (54)	General Army Branch, O.K.H. (15/X/41)	1/VI/40	Saxony	Inf
OSSWALD, Erwin (59)	Wkr. V (1/II/42)	1/XII/40	Württemberg	Inf
Dr. OTT (52)	Inspector of Infantry, O.K.H. (2/X/41)	1/X/41		Inf
OTTO, Paul (60)		1/XII/40		Inf
PAULUS, Friedrich (52)	Sixth Army (1/V/42)	/42	Baden	Tks
PETRI, Hans (64)				Inf
PETZEL, Walter (58)	Wkr. XXI (1/IV/42)	1/X/39		Arty
v. POGRELL, Günther (62)	XXXVII Corps Command (1/XI/41)	1/X/36		Cav
Ritter v. PRAGER, Karl (66)		1/IX/40	Bavaria	Inf
Dr. phil. h.c.v. RABENAU, Friedrich (57)	Records Branch, O,K.H. (1/I/42)	1/IX/40		Arty
RASCHICK, Walther (59)	Wkr. X (15/IV/42)	1/IV/39		Inf
REINECKE, Hermann (54)	A dept., O.K.W. (27/III/42)	1/VI/42		Inf
REINHARD, Hans (53)	LI Inf Corps (6/II/42)	1/XI/40	Saxony	Inf
v. ROQUES, Karl (62)	L of C Area, Army Group North (1/III/42)	/41		Inf
v. SALMUTH, Hans (53)		1/VIII/40		Inf
SCHAAL, Ferdinand (52)		1/X/41	Baden	Tks
SCHALLER-KALIDE, Hubert (59)	Wkr. XVIII (22/III/41)	1/XII/40		Inf
v. SCHENCKENDORFF, Max (65)	L of C Area, Army Group Center (1/IV/42)	1/XII/40		Inf
SCHMIDT, Hans (65)	A Corps (28/IV/42)	/42	Württemberg	Inf
SCHNIEWINDT, Rudolf (63)	Wkr. IX (1/IV/40)	1/IX/40		Inf
SCHÖRNER, Ferdinand (48)	Norway Mountain Corps (1/V/42)	1/VI/42	Bavaria	Mtn Trs
SCHROTH, Walter (56)	XII Inf Corps (28/II/42)	1/II/38		Inf
SCHUBERT, Albrecht (56)	XXIII Inf Corps (22/IX/41)	1/VI/40	Silesia	Inf

SCHWANDNER, Max-imilian (60)	A Corps (22/II/41)	1/XII/40	Bavaria	Inf
v. SCHWEDDER, Viktor (57)	IV Inf Corps (1/III/42)	1/II/38		Inf
v. SEYDLITZ-KURZ-BACH, Walter (53)	A Corps (1/IV/42)	1/VI/42		Arty
v. SODENSTERN, Georg (52)	C G S, Army Group South (25/IX/41).	1/VIII/40		Inf
STEPPUHN, Albrecht (62)	Wkr. XII (1/I/41)	27/VIII/39		Inf
STRAUBE, Erich (54)		1/VI/42	Silesia	Inf
STRECCIUS, Alfred (63)	Wkr. XVII (1/V/42)			Inf
STRECKER, (56)		1/IV/42		Inf
v. STÜLPNAGEL, Heinrich (55)		1/IV/39		Inf
v. STÜLPNAGEL, Otto (63)	C G Occupied France (15/IV/42)	1/I/32		Inf
STUMME, Georg (56)	XXXX Pz Corps (15/IV/42)	1/VI/40		Tks
THOMAS, Georg (52)	Mil Economics Branch, O.K.W. (1/V/42)	1/VIII/40		Inf
ULEX, Wilhelm (61)		1/X/36		Arty
VEIEL, Rudolf (58)		1/IV/42	Würt-temberg	Tks
v. VIEBAHN, Max (54)	CGS, Army Group West (?)	1/III/41		Inf
VIEROW, Erwin (52)	LV Inf Corps (1/XII/41)	1/I/41		Inf
v. VIETINGHOFF gen. SCHEEL, Heinrich (55).	XXXXVI Pz Corps (21/IV/41).	1/VI/40		Tks
VOGL, Oskar (61)	Head of Armistice Commission (1/XII/41).	/41	Bavaria	Arty
v. VOLLARD-BOCK-ELBERG (67)		1/X/33		Arty
WACHENFELD, Edmund (63)	Wkr. VII (1/X/41)			Arty
WÄGER, Alfred (58)	XXVII Inf Corps (18/VI/41)	1/XI/38	Bavaria	Inf
WEISENBERGER, Karl (51)		1/IV/41	Bavaria	Inf
WEYER, Peter (62)	Wkr. I (1/VIII/41)	1/XII/40		Arty
v. WIETERSHEIM, Gustav (58)	XIV Pz Corps (1/I/42)	1/II/38		Inf
WIKTORIN, Mauriz (58)	A Corps (?)	1/XI/40	Austria	Inf
WITTHÖFT (55)		1/III/42	Thuring-ia	Inf
WODRIG, Albert (59)	XXVI Inf Corps (1/X/41)	1/X/39		Arty
WÖLLWARTH, Erich (70)	Wkr. IV (1/V/42)	1/IX/40	Würt-temberg	Inf
Zorn, Hans (51)		1/VI/42	Bavaria	Inf

4. Rank: LIEUTENANT GENERAL (Generalleutnant)

Name (age)	Command (date)	Seniority	Origin	Arm
ANDREAS (56)	208th Inf Div (1/V/42)	1/IV/41		Inf
v. APELL (56)		1/VI/38		Inf
AULEB (53)		1/XII/40	Hessen	Inf
BALTZER (55)	217th Inf Div (27/III/42)	1/X/39		Inf
BARCKHAUSEN, Franz (59)	Mil. Economics Depot, Occupied France (2/III/42)	1/III/38		Arty
v. BASSE, Hans (52)		1/IV/42		Inf
BAYER	181st Inf Div (1/III/42)	1/X/40		Inf
BEHSCHNITT, Walter (56)	15th Inf Div (1/VIII/41)	1/IX/40	Silesia	Inf
v. BERG, Ludwig (60)	Insp of Recruiting, Koblenz, Wkr. XII (1939)	1/XI/40	Baden	Arty
BERLIN (52)	Artillery School, Jüterbog, Wkr. III (15/VIII/41)	1/III/42	Baden	Arty
BERNARD, Kurt (55)		1/X/39	Silesia	Tks
BERTRAM, Georg (57)	Judge Advocate's Dept (1939)	1/VIII/39		Cav
BEUTTEL (55)	Cmdt of Lemberg (17/III/42)	1/III/41		Inf
BIELFIELD (53)	Cmdt of Posen, Wkr. XII (8/III/42)	1/II/42		Inf
BLÜMM, Oskar (57)	An Inf Div (1/XII/41)	1/IV/40	Bavaria	Inf
BOCK v. WÜLFINGEN, Ferdinand (58).	Insp of Recruiting Berlin, Wkr. III (1/XI/41)	1/IV/38		Arty
v. BOEHM-BEZING, Diether (61)	A Corps (1/IX/40)	1/IV/35		Cav
BOETTCHER (56)		1/XI/39		Inf
BÖTTCHER, Karl (52)		1/III/42	Silesia	Arty
BOHNSTEDT, Wilhelm (52)	21st Inf Div (20/IV/42)	1/IV/42		Inf
BOLTZE, Arthur (63)	Star of Training Command (1/XI/41)		Saxony	Arty
Frhr. v. BOTZHEIM, Erich (71)			Bavaria	Arty
BRAND, Albrecht (54)	311th Div (1/VI/40)	1/X/39	Silesia	Arty
BRAUNER, Josef	C of S, Gen. Govt. (1/VII/41)	1/III/41	Austria	Inf
BREMER (56)	580 L of C Area (1/V/42)	1/X/38		Arty
v. BRODOWSKI, Fritz (56)	Field Reinforcement Div Staff B (1/XI/41)	1/II/41		Cav

Name (age)	Command (date)	Seniority	Origin	Arm
BUCHS (56)	Neustettin Fortifications, Wkr. II (1939)	1/X/39		Inf
BUHLE (48)	Head of a Section, O.K.H. (1939)	1/IV/42	Württemberg	Inf
BURCKHARDT (52)		1/III/42		SigC
BUSCHMANN (54)		1/XI/41		Arty
CARP, Georg (55)	Insp of Recruiting Kattowitz, Wkr. VIII (1/IV/41)	1/VI/41	Hessen	Arty
de L'HOME de COURBIERE, Rene (55)	213th "Sicherungs" Div (1/I/42)	1/VI/40		Inf
DEHMEL (54)		1/VI/41	Silesia	Pion
DENECKE, Erich (50)	Landwehr Comdr Darmstadt, Wkr. XII (1939)	1/XII/39	Saxony	Inf
DENNERLEIN Max (56)	290th Inf Div (1/V/40)	1/III/40	Bavaria	Pion
DETMERING (55)	Insp of Recruiting, Frankfurt/Main, Wkr. IX (1939)	1/VI/41	Bavaria	Inf
DIPPOLD, Benignus (52)		1/X/41	Bavaria	Inf
DITTMAR (52)	Chief Engineer, Army Group West (20/VI/41)	1/IV/42		Pion
DOEHLA, Heinrich (61)			Bavaria	Inf
DROGAND (59)	Inspector of Welfare, O.K.W. (15/IX/41)	1/VII/41		Inf
EBERHARDT (51)	60th Mtz Div (5/11/42)	1/II/41		Cav
ECKSTEIN)52)		1/VI/42		Pion
ENDRES, Theodore (65)	212th Inf Div (17/VI/41)	3/IX/31	Bavaria	Arty
ENGELBRECHT, Erwin (50)	163d Inf Div (1/I/42)	1/XI/40	Silesia	Cav
v. FABER du Faur, Moritz (56)	Comdt of Bordeaux (1/I/42)	1/IV/39	Württemberg	Cav
FELDT, Kurt (53)		1/II/42		Cav
FETT, Albert (69)	An Inf Div (10/IV/42)			Inf
FISCHER, Herbert (59)	172d Training Div (1/IV/40)	1/I/36	Württemberg	Inf
v. FÖRSTER, Sigismund (54)	Staff of L of C Command, Army Group South (15/X/41)	1/IV/38	Thuringia	Inf
FOLTTMANN (54)	164th Inf Div (20/XI/41)	1/II/41	Silesia	Inf
FRANKE, Hermann (63)	162d Inf Div (13/II/42)			Inf
FRIEDRICH, Rudolf (52)	114th Arty Comd (1/X/41)	1/IV/42	Saxony	Arty
Frhr. v. GABLENZ, Eccard (50).	7th Inf Div (1/I/42)	1/VIII/40		Inf

Name	Unit	Date	Region	Branch
GERCKE, Hubert (60)				Inf
GERHARDT, Paul (61)	421st Div z.b.V. (1/I/42)	1/II/41		Inf
GILBERT, Martin (53)	An Inf Div (1/I/42	1/I/42	Saxony	Inf
v. GIMBORN (61)				Inf
van GINKEL, Oskar (59)	Insp of Recruiting, Munich, Wkr. VII (1/XI/41)		Bavaria	Arty
GOETTKE (57)	O.K.H.	1/XI/41	Silesia	Arty
GOLLWITZER, Friedrich (52)	88th Inf Div (1/I/42)	1/X/41	Bavaria	Inf
GRAF, Karl (59)	330th Inf Div (1/V/42)		Bavaria	Inf
v. GREIFFENBERG, Hans (48)		1/IV/42		Inf
GROPPE, Theodor (59)		1/XI/39		Arty
Frhr. GROTE, Waldemar (64)	218th Inf Div (21/I/42)	1/XI/39		Cav
GÜNTZEL (53)	113th Inf Div 1/VI/41	1/X/41		Arty
GUNZELMANN, Emil (55)	Insp of Recruiting, Graz, Wkr. XVIII (1939)	1/X/41	Bavaria	Inf
HAARDE (53)	25th Pz Div (20/II/42	1/X/41		Tks
HAASE, Conrad (53)	An Inf Div (1/I/42)	1/I/42	Saxony	Inf
HAENICKE, Siegfried	61st Inf Div Wkr. VI (10/III/42)			Inf
v. dem HAGEN, Heinrich (68)	Cmdt of PW Camps			Inf
HAMMER, Carl (58)	75th Inf Div (1/I/42)	1/XI/40	Hessen	Inf
v. HARTLIEB gen. WALSPORN, Maximilian (58)		1/IV/39	Württemberg	Tks
v. HASE, Paul (56)	Cmdt of Berlin Wkr. III (1/VIII/41)	1/IV/40		Inf
HEBERLEIN, Hans (53)	Training Area (1/IX/41)	1/IV/41	Bavaria	Inf
v. HEINECCIUS (60)	Cmdt of Hamburg, Wkr. X (21/IV/41)	1/II/41	Thuringia	Inf
HEINEMANN, Erich (60)				Arty
HELD (60)	Div No 147, Wkr. VII (15/III/42)			Inf
HELL (55)	An Inf Div (15/V/41)	1/VII/40		Arty
HELLMICH, Heinz (50)	An Inf Div (22/VIII/41)	1/IX/41		Inf
HEMMERICH (60)	Head of Topographical Section, O.K.H. (1939)	1/XII/41		Inf
HENGEN, Fritz (55)	Insp of Recruiting Chemnitz, Wkr. IV (15/V/41)	1/II/41	Bavaria	Arty

Name	Position	Date	Region	Branch
HENRICI, Sigfrid (54)	25th Mot Div (23/X/41)	1/VI/41	Hessen	Arty
HERZOG, Kurt (54)	29th Inf Div (1/XI/41)	1/II/41	Saxony	Inf
HEUNERT (54)	XXXVI Corps Command (1/IV/42)	1/X/40		Cav
HILPERT, Karl (53)		1/XI/40	Bavaria	Inf
Dr. HINGHOFER, Walter		1/VII/41	Austria	Inf
v. HÖBERTH, Eugen	Cmdt of Cracow (17/III/42)		Austria	Cav
HÖFL, Hugo (63)	206th Inf Div (15/XII/41)	1/VII/41	Bavaria	Inf
HOEGNER, Hermann (57)	1 Supply Group (15/IX/41)	1/II/41		H-DrT
v. HÖSSLIN, Wilhelm (63)	Div No 188, Wkr. XVIII (1/X/41)		Bavaria	Inf
HOPFF, Hermann (66)				Pion
HORN, Max (53)	214th Inf Div (1/IV/42)	1/X/41	Saxony	Inf
HUBE, Hans (52)	16th Pz Div (1/III/42)	1/IV/42	Anhalt	Inf
Dr. HUBICKI, Alfred (55)	9 Pz Div (1/IV/42)	1/VIII/40	Austria	Tks
HÜTTMANN (62)	Div No 165 Wkr. V (23/III/42)			Inf
JAENECKE, Erwin (50)	Asst. QMG, Army Group West (8/VIII/41)	1/XI/41		Pion
JAHN (50)		1/XI/40	Thuringia	Arty
KARL, Franz (53)		1/III/41	Bavaria	Inf
KAUFFMANN (51)	256th Inf Div (1/VIII/41)	1/IV/41		Inf
KEINER, Walter (51)	62d Inf Div (19/VIII/41)	1/IX/40		Arty
v. KEMPSKI, Hans (57)	199th Inf Div (1/II/42)	1/II/41		Inf
KERN, Emil (60)	Chief Engineer Fourth Army 1/X/41	1/X/41	Austria	
Edler v. KIESLING auf KIESLINGSTEIN, Bruno (64)	Insp of Recruiting Regensburg, Wkr. XIII (1939)	1/XI/41	Bavaria	Inf
v. KLEIST (55)		1/IV/41		Cav
KLUTMANN (62)	Div No 156 Wkr. VI (12/III/41)	1/IV/42		Inf
v. dem KNESEBECK (65)	Insp of Recruiting Münster, Wkr. VI (1939)	1/II/41		Cav
KNIESS, Baptist (56)	Landwehr Comd Heilbronn, Wkr. V (1939)	1/VII/40	Bavaria	Inf

Name	Unit/Command	Date	Region	Branch
v. KNOBELSDORFF (54)	19th Pz Div (1/XI/41)	1/XII/40		Inf
KÖRNER, Willy (61)	223d Inf Div (1/V/40	1/XI/39	Saxony	Inf
KOHL, Otto		1/IX/41		Inf
KRAMPF, Heinrich (53)		1/XII/41	Bavaria	Inf
KRATZERT, Hans (58)	303d Higher Arty Comd (1/X/41)	1/I/38	Saxony	Arty
KRIEBEL, Kurt (53)	Military Academy, Dresden, Wkr. IV (1/II/41)	1/VIII/40	Bavaria	Inf
KRISCHER, Fredrich (51)		1/XII/41	Austria	Arty
KÜHLENTHAL, Erich (61)		1/X/33		Arty
KÜHNE, Fritz (58)		1/IV/35	Silesia	Inf
KURZ	Insp of Recruiting, Danzig, Wkr. XX (1/VI/41)	1/III/42		Inf
LAUX, Paul (54)	126th Inf Div (28/IV/42)	1/I/41	Saxony	Inf
LECHNER, Adolf (57)	112th Arty Comd (1/III/41)	1/III/42	Bavaria	Arty
LEHMANN, Joseph (54)	82d Inf Div (20/XII/41)	1/VI/41	Bavaria	Inf
LEISTER (54)		1/I/41		Arty
v. der LEYEN, Ludwig (56)		1/VI/38		Inf
LEYKAUF, Hans (57)	Military Economics, Wkr.VIII (1/I/40)	1/II/41	Saxony	Inf
LICHEL, Walter (56)	123d Inf Div (1/X/41)	1/II/40		Inf
LIEBER, Hans (59)				Arty
v. LOEPER (54)	31st Inf Div (10/X/41)	1/IX/40		Inf
LÖWENECK, Ludwig (54)		1/II/41	Bavaria	SigC
LOHMANN, Hans (59)		1/II/41		Arty
LÜTERS, Rudolf (58)		1/X/38	Hessen	Inf
MACHOLZ (52)	An Inf Div (29/I/42)	1/VI/42		Inf
MADERHOLZ, Karl (56)	An Inf Div (1/X/40)	1/X/41	Bavaria	Inf
MARCKS, Erich (51)	A Light Div (8/VII/41)	1/III/41		Arty
MEHNERT, Karl (54)	Cmdt of Dresden, Wkr. IV (17/III/41)	1/XI/40	Saxony	Sig C
MEYER-BUERDORF, Heinrich (53)	131st Inf Div (15/XI/41)	1/IX/41		Arty
MEYER-RABINGEN, Hermann (53)	197th Inf Div (6/V/42)	1/XI/41		Inf
MIETH (55)	112th Inf Div (1/XII/41)	1/III/40		Inf
Ritter v. MITTELBERGER, Hilmer (63)		1/I/32	Bavaria	Inf
MOSER, Willi (54)	299th Inf Div (1/I/42)	1/VIII/41		Arty
MOYSES, Karl (58)	Insp of Recruiting, Köslin, Wkr. II (1939)	1/II/41	Austria	Pion
MÜHLMANN, Max (53)	Arty Comd	1/IX/41	Saxony	Arty

Name	Assignment	Date	Region	Arm
MÜLLER, Erich (52)		1/VI/42		Cav
MÜLLER, Kurt	An Inf Div (3/IV/42)			
MÜLLER, Ludwig	Feldkdtr. 458 (15/IV/40)			
MÜLLER-GEBHARD, Alfred (53)		1/I/42	Saxony	Inf
Dr. habil. MUNDT (55)		1/IX/40		Inf
NAGY, Emmerich (58)	LXXI Corps Comd (1/III/42)	1/VI/39	Austria	Inf
NAUMANN (52)		1/IV/42		Tks
NEHRING, Walter (50)		1/II/42		Tks
NEULING, Ferdinand (56)	239th Inf Div (1/I/42)	1/XII/40	Saxony	Inf
NEUMANN, Friedrich-Wilhelm		1/II/42		Inf
NEUMANN-NEURODE, Karl (62)	Mil District B, Occupied France (7/III/42)		Silesia	Inf
v. OBERNITZ, Justin (57)	293d Inf Div (1/XII/41)	1/VI/40		Cav
OSTERKAMP (49)	Army Administration Branch, O.K.H. (1/IV/41)	1/IV/41		Arty
OSTERROHT (61)	Insp of Recruiting Magdeburg, Wkr. XI (7/II/40)	1/II/41		Inf
OTTENBACHER, Otto (54)		1/III/41	Württemberg	Inf
v. OVEN, Karl (53)	56 Inf Div (25/III/42)	1/VII/41		Inf
PELLENGAHR, Richard (59)		1/VI/40	Westphalia	Arty
PELTZ, Joachim (58)		1/IV/41	Saxony	Inf
Frhr. v. PERFALL, Gustav	Inspector of Recruiting Nürnberg, Wkr. XIII (24/IX/41)	1/VIII/39	Bavaria	Cav
PFEFFER, Max (56)	297th Inf Div (12/XII/41)	1/VIII/38		Arty
PFEIFFER, Georg (52)	94th Inf Div (21/VIII/41)	1/VI/42		Arty
PFLUGBEIL, Johann (59)	221st Inf Div (1/V/41)	1/X/39	Saxony	Inf
PFLUGRADT (52)	An Inf Div (13/IV/41)	1/IV/42		Inf
PILZ		1/II/42		Inf
PINCKVOSS (56)	Insp of Recruiting, Kassel, Wkr. IX (1939)	1/II/42		Inf
Edler Herr u. Frhr. v. PLOTHO, Wolfgang (62)	285th "Sicherungs" Div	10/IV/42		Inf
POETTER, Adolf (58)	410th Div z.b.V. (20/IX/41)			Inf

PRETORIUS, Robert (59)	Inspector of Recruiting, Dresden, Wkr. IV, (22/IV/42)	1/II/38	Silesia	Arty
PRAGER, Karl (53)		1/II//42	Bavaria	Arty
v. PRONDZYNSKI (60)	Insp of Recruiting, Prague (26/X/41)	1/IV/42		Arty
v. PUTTKAMER, Alfred (57)	An Army L of C Area (3/IV/42)	1/VIII/39		MT
Ritter v. RADLMAJER, Ludwig (55)		1/VII/40	Bavaria	Tks
Recke (52)	An Inf Div (1/I/42)	1/VI/42		Inf
v. REICHE (57)	Insp of Recruiting, Oppeln, Wkr. VIII (1939)	1/IV/38		Cav
Dr. RENDULIC, Lothar (54)	An Inf Div (1/I/42)	1/XII/41	Austria	Inf
RENNER, Theodor (55)	211th Inf Div (25/X/41)	1/VII/40	Saxony	Inf
RENZ, Maximilian (58)	An Inf Div (8/XI/41)	31/X/38	Bavaria	Cav
RICHTER (53)	205th Inf Div (1/V/40)	1/X/39	Baden	Inf
RIEBESAM, Ludwig (54)	Insp of Recruiting, Linz, Wkr. XVII (1939)	1/VI/41	Austria	Inf
v. RINTELEN, Enno (51)	MA Rome (1/I/42)	1/VI/41		Inf
Frhr. ROEDER v. DIERSBURG, Kurt (56)	Insp of Recruiting, Cologne Wkr. VI (30/I/40)	1/II/41	Baden	Arty
ROETTIG (52)		1/VI/41		Inf
ROSENBUSCH (52)	Chief Engineer, Army of Norway (1/VIII/41)	1/IV/42	Silesia	Pion
Frhr. v. ROTBERG (66)	A Mil. District Occupied France (1/III/42)	/42		Inf
v. ROTHKIRCH u. PANTHEN, Friedrich-Wilhelm (58)	Chief Liaison O with Roumanian Army (1/I/42)	1/VIII/40	Hessen	Cav
Graf. v. ROTHKIRCH u. TRACH, Edwin (53)		1/III/42		Cav
RÜHLE v. LILIENSTERN, Alexander (61)	Insp of Recruiting, Königsberg, Wkr. I (1939)	1/II/41		Inf
RUSSWURM, Josef (54)	Army Sig School, Halle, Wkr. IV (1939)	1/IX/40	Württemberg	Sig C
RUSSWURM, Wilhelm (54)		1/IX/40	Württemberg	Sig C
SACHS (56)	An Inf Div (1/II/42)	1/I/40		Pion
SANNE (52)	100th Light Div (1/IV/42)	1/IV/42	Hessen	Inf
SATOW (54)	Insp of Recruiting, Frankfurt/Oder,	1/XI/41	Baden	Cav

Wkr. III (11/III/40)

Name	Position		Region	Branch
Ritter v. SAUER, Otto (66)			Bavaria	Inf
Frhr. v. SCHACKY auf SCHÖNFELD, Sigmund (55)	An Inf Div (14/V/41)	1/VIII/40	Bavaria	
Dr. v. SCHAEWEN (54)	Chief Engineer, Wkr. III (1939)	1/II/41		Pion
SCHAMBURG, Ernst (61)	Cmdt of Paris (1/II/42)	1/II/38		Inf
v. SCHAUROTH, Athos (56)	Insp of Recruiting, Breslau, Wkr. VIII (14/VIII/41)	1/IV/38		Inf
SCHEDE, Wolfgang (54)	Fortress Cmdt, Allenstein Wkr. I (1939)	1/VII/40	Baden	Inf
v. SCHELL, Adolf (48)	Insp of Army Motorization (17/I/42)	1/IV/42		MT
SCHELLBACH, Oskar	An Army L of C Area (11/IV/42)			Arty
SCHELLERT (54)	253d Inf Div (1/IV/42)	1/I/41		Inf
SCHIMPF (54)	Chief Fortress Engineer, Wkr. VI (1939)	1/XII/40	Württemberg	Pion
SCHINDLER, Maximilian (61)	Insp of Armaments, Gen. Govt. (1/XI/40)	1/II/34	Bavaria	Inf
SCHLENTHER (61)		1/II/38		Inf
SCHLIEPER (50)	Mil. Mission to Slovakia (15/IV/42)	1/XI/41		Arty
SCHMETZER, Rudolf (58)	Chief Fortress Engineer, Wkr. V (1939)	1/II/41	Bavaria	Pion
SCHMID-DANKWARD Walter (54)		1/XII/40	Thuringia	Arty
SCHMIDT-LOGAN, Wolfgang (58)			Württemberg	Arty
SCHONHÄRL, Hans (63)		1/XII/40	Bavaria	Inf
SCHREIBER (64)	Cmdt of Hannover, Wkr. XI (1/I/42)		Hessen	Inf
SCHROECK (53)		1/VI/41		Inf
SCHUBERT, Artur (66)			Saxony	Arty
SCHÜNEMANN, Otto (58)		1/VIII/37	Hessen	Inf
SCHWANTES, Günther (60)		1/VI/38	Silesia	Cav
SCHWARZNECKER (57)	Insp of Recruiting, Vienna, Wkr. XVII (10/XI/41)	1/II/38		Inf
v. SCHWERIN, Otto (60)	431st Div z.b.V. (1/X/41)			Cav
v. SCOTTI (54)		1/II/41		Arty
SEIFERT, Ernst (57)		1/VIII/38		Inf

Name	Unit	Date	Region	Branch
SIEBERT, Friedrich (53)	44th Inf Div (17/XII/41)	1/IV/41	Bavaria	Inf
SINNHUBER (54)	28th Light Div (1/XII/41)	1/IV/41		Arty
SINTZENICH, Rudolf (52)	132d Inf Div (3/X/40)	1/XII/41	Bavaria	Inf
SIXT v. ARNIM, Hans Heinrich (52)	95th Inf Div (9/XII/41)	1/III/40		Inf
v. SOMMERFELD, Hans (53)	526th Div (1/V/40)	1/IX/41		Inf
SORSCHE, Konrad (58)	50th Inf Div (1/V/40)	1/III/38	Silesia	Arty
SPANG, **Karl** (55)	Lower Rhine Fortifications (1/V/40)	1/IV/40	Württemberg	Arty
Dr. SPEICH, Richard (57)	539th Div (22/VI/41)			Pion
Graf. v. SPONECK (52)		1/II/40		Inf
SPONHEIMOER, Otto (55)	An Inf Div (10/IX/41)	1/VII/41	Bavaria	Inf
STAPF, Otto (51)		1/II/41	Bavaria	Inf
STEMMERMANN, Wilhelm (53)	296th Inf Div 1/V/40)	1/VIII/41	Baden	Arty
STENGEL, Hans (61)	Landwehr Comd Chemnitz, Wkr. IV (1939)	1/IV/41	Saxony	Cav
STEPHANUS	Div No 187, Wkr. XVII (5/IV/40)			Inf
STEVER (53)		1/VI/41		Cav
STIELER v. HEYDEKAMPF (60)	Insp of Armaments, Wkr. III (11/III/42)	1/II/41		Inf
STIMMEL (55)	An Inf Div (30/III/40)	1/VI/41	Baden	Inf
STOEWER, Paul (52)	An Inf Div (1/VI/41)	1/II/42		Inf
STRACK, Heinrich (54)	Cmdt of Danzig, Wkr. XX (25/IX/41)	1/IX/41		Inf
STUD (52)	Head of a Dept, Army Ordnance Branch 10/VI/41)	1/II/40		Arty
v. STUDNITZ, Bogislav (55)	87th Inf Div (29/I/42)	1/VIII/40	Thuringia	Cav
STÜMPFL, Heinrich (58)	Comdt of Vienna, Wkr. **XVII** (23/IV/42)	1/VI/40	Austria	Inf
STUMPFF, Horst (54)	20 Pz Div (3/X/41)	1/II/41		Tks
SUTTNER (55)		1/IV/40	Württemberg	Inf
TARBUK v. SENSENHORST, Karl	540th Div (1/V/42)		Austria	Inf
v. TETTAU, Hans (52)	24th Inf Div (1/VIII/40)	1/III/42	Saxony	Inf
THEISEN, Edgar (53)	262d Inf Div (4/III/42)	1/X/39		Inf
v. TIEDEMANN, Karl (63)	207th "Sicherungs" Div (22/IV/42)	1/XI/39		Inf
TIEMANN (53)	93d Inf Div (1/I/42)	1/X/39		Pion
v. TIPPELSKIRCH, Kurt (50)	30th Inf Div (3/XII/41)	1/VI/40		Inf

Name	Assignment	Date	Region	Branch
TITTEL, Hermann (52)	169th Inf Div (20/I/42)	1/IX/41		Arty
TSCHERNING, Otto (60)	Insp of Recruiting, Stuttgart, Wkr. V (16/IX/41)	1/IV/36	Württemberg	Arty
v. UTHMANN, Bruno (51)	MA Stockholm (1/I/42)	1/IX/41		Inf
VOLK, Erich (58)	Insp of Recruiting, Eger, Wkr. XIII (6/VIII/40)	1/II/41	Thuringia	Cav
v. VOSS, Hans	Psychological Tests Dept O.K.W. (1939)			Inf
v. WACHTER, Fredrich-Karl (52)	267th Inf Div (1/X/41)	1/IV/42	Hessen	Inf
WAGNER, August (57)		1/VIII/40	Bavaria	Tks
WAGNER, Eduard (48)	Staff of Seventh Army (20/V/41)	1/IV/42	Bavaria	Arty
Frhr. v. WALDENFELS, Wilhelm (58)	Insp of Recruiting, Innsbruck, Wkr. XVIII (17/III/41)	1/II/41	Saxony	Inf
v. WALDOW (60)	539th Frontier Guard Div Prat (23/III/41)			Inf
WANGER, Rudolf (53)	An Inf Div (1/III/41)	1/II/42	Bavaria	Inf
WARLIMONT, Walter (48)	Head of Operations Section, O.K.W. (20/IV/42)	1/IV/42		Arty
v, WEDDERKOP, Magnus (60)	Insp of Recruiting, Hamburg, Wkr. X (22/IV/42)	1/II/41		Inf
WEINGART, Erich (54)	Insp of H-DrT (1939)	1/VIII/40	Bavaria	H-DrT
WETZEL (54)	255th Inf Div (1/V/40)	1/XII/40		Inf
WILCK, Hermann (57)	708th Inf Div (1/III/42)	/42	Thuringia	Inf
WILLICH, Fritz (60)			Württemberg	Inf
Frhr. v. WILMOWSKY, Friedrich (60)	Insp of Recruiting, Potsdam, Wkr. III (1939)	1/VIII/35		Cav
WINDECK (52)		1/IV/42		Inf
WINTZER, Heinz (51)	Insp of Armaments, Wkr.I (1939)	1/X/41		Arty
WITKE, Walter (53)	170th Inf Div (15/IV/40)	1/VIII/41		Inf
WOLLMANN (51)		1/VI/40		Pion
WOYTASCH, Kurt (60)		1/VIII/41		Inf
Frhr.v.WREDE, Theodor (53)	An Inf Div (9/III/42)	1/III/41		Cav
ZEHLER, Albert (54)		1/XII/41	Bavaria	Arty
v.ZEPELIN,Ferdinand (55)	Insp of Recruiting, Hannover, Wkr. XI (15/IX/39).	1/VI/41		Inf
ZICKWOLFF (53)	227th Inf Div (1/V/40)	1/X/41	Wurttemberg	Inf
ZIMMERMANN, Georg (62)				Inf
v.ZÜLOW, Alexander (52)	C of S Wkr.II (28/X/40)	1/X/41	Silesia	Inf

ZUKERTORT Johannes (56)		1/II/4 1 Saxony	Arty
ZWENGAUER Karl (59)	Mil.Economics Dept Wkr. III(15/IX/39)	1/II/41 Bavaria	Arty

5. Rank: MAJOR GENERAL (Generalmajor)

Name (age)	Command (date)	Seniority	Origin	Arm
ABT (50)	CSO, IX Inf Corps (1939)	1/IV/42		SigC
ADAM, Wilhelm (60)	Insp of Transport Trs (31/III/40)	1/II/31		H-DrT
ADOLPH (65)	Cmdt of Dniepropetrovsk (25/II/42)			Inf
AGRICOLA, Kurt (53)	Landwehr Comd Oppeln, Wkr. VIII (1939)	1/I/38	Saxony	Inf
ALLMENDINGER, Karl (49)	An Inf Div (9/VIII/41)	1/VIII/40	Württemberg	Inf
v. ALTEN, Viktor (54)		1/II/41		Inf
Dr. ALTRICHTER, Friedrich (51)	58th Inf Div (28/IV/42)	1/IV/41		Inf
v. ALTROCK, Wilhelm (52)	379th Area Comd (17/III/42)	1/IV/40	Saxony	Inf
v. AMANN (60)	Cmdt of Breslau, Wkr. VIII (11/III/40)			Inf
v. AMMON, Carl (60)	Insp of Recruiting Stettin Wkr. II (16/IX/41)			Cav
ANGER (53)		1/X/39		Arty
ANGERN, Günther (50)	11th Pz Div (1/IX/41)	1/IX/41		Cav
ANSAT (50)	102d Inf Div (1/XI/41)	1/VIII/40		Arty
v. APELL, Wilhelm (49)	22d Pz Div (12/IV/42)	1/IV/41		Inf
ARNOLD (52)	Insp of Munitions, SE Area (1939)	1/VI/41		Inf
Baron v. ASCHEBERG, Percy (60)	Wesel, Wkr. VI (admin) (1939)	1/VI/42		SigC
ASCHENBRANDT, Henrich (57)	Area Comd, NE Esthonia (22/IV/42)	1/XII/41	Bavaria	Arty
AUER, Franz (63)			Bavaria	Arty
BAARTH (51)	Remount School, Beeskow Wkr. III (1939)	1/IV/42		Cav
BADINSKI, Kurt (48)	An Inf Div (12/III/42)	/42		Inf
BAESSLER, Erich (50)	*JR 399 (170th Inf Div) (6/X/41)	1/I/42		Inf
BAESSLER, Hans (48)	C of S, XI Corps (1/XI/41)	1/II/42	Silesia	Tks
BAIER, Albrecht (48)	An Inf Div (1/II/42)	1/II/42		Arty
BALTZER, Martin (51)	CSO, XII Inf Corps (1939)	1/IV/41	Saxony	Sigs
BALTZER, Robert (51)		1/IV/41		SigC
Dr. BAMBERG (53)	Cmdt of Riga (1/X/41)	1/II/41	Saxony	Inf
BAMLER, Rudolf (47)	CGS, Army of Norway (1/VI/42)	1/IV/42		Arty

*Note: The Germans use capital J and capital I interchangeably.
For example: Infantry Regiments may be designated JR or IR.

BARENDS (60)	Neustrelitz, Wkr. II (admin) (1939)	1/VI/41		Inf
BARTON, Gottfried	Cavalry School, Sch- losshof, Wkr. XVII (1939)	1/II/42	Austria	Cav
v. BASSE, Max (57)	Staff of VIII Inf Corps (1939)	1/IV/42		Inf
BAUER, Franz				
BAUMGARTNER, Richard		1/XII/39	Austria	Pion
Dipl. Wirtsch. BECHT (47)	OKW (1939)	1/IV/42		Arty
Frhr. v. MAUCHEN- HEIM gen. BECHTOLSHEIM, Gustav (52)	707th Inf Div (30/I/42)	**1/VIII/41**	**Bavaria**	**Inf**
BECKER, Fritz		1/IV/42		Inf
v. BEEREN (50)	JR 193 (69th Inf Div) (5/V/42)	1/II/42		Inf
v. BEHR (52)	Div No 173, Wkr. XIII (15/III/42)	1/XI/40		Inf
BEHRENS, Wilhelm (50)	An Inf Regt (1/I/42)	1/I/42		Inf
BEININGER		1/VIII/41		
v. BERG		1/III/38	Baden	Arty
BERGEN, Johann (51)	An Inf Regt (27/VII/41)	1/X/41	Bavaria	Inf
BERKA (61)	Neisse, Wkr. IV (admin) (1939)	1/III/41		Inf
BERNHARD, Friedrich Gustav (52)		1/VIII/40		SigC
v. BERNUTH, Julius (45)	C of S Third Panzer Army (20/IV/42)	1/IV/42	Hessen	Tks
v. BESSEL	Landwehr Training O Karlsruhe, Wkr. V. (1939)	1/VI/41		Inf
Dr. BEYER (51)	An Inf Regt (15/IX/41)	1/II/42		Inf
BIERMANN (65)	O.K.H. (31/III/42)	1/IV/41		Pion
BILHARZ, Eugen (54)	2 Supply Group (15/IX/41)	1/II/41	Saxony	Inf
v. BISMARCK, Kurt (60)	Potsdam II, Wkr. III (admin) (15/IX/41)	1/IV/41		Inf
v. BLOCK, Lothar (50)	Psychological Tests Dept, Wkr. XX (1939)	1/II/42		Inf
BLUMENTRITT (49)	97th Light Div (11/XII/41)	/41	Thuringia	Inf
BOEGE, Ehrenfried (48)	An Inf Regt (8/I/42)	1/IV/42	Silesia	Inf
BOEHRINGER, Gustav (50)	Head of a Section, O.K.H. (1939)	1/II/42	Württemberg	Pion
BÖMERS, Hans (48)		1/IV/42		Arty

Name	Position	Date	Region	Branch
BOESSER (62)		1/IV/42		Arty
BÖTTGER, Karl (51)	Head of a Section, O.K.W. (1939)	1/IV/41	Saxony	Inf
Frhr. v. BOINEBURG LENGSFELD, Wilhelm (53)	23d Pz Div (21/V/41	1/X/41		Cav
v. BOLTENSTERN, Walter (51)	29th Mot Div (1/IX/41)	1/VIII/40		Inf
BORDIHN (53)	Insp of Fortress Engineers, Wkr. IV (1939)	1/XI/40		Pion
BOROWSKI (60)	Landwehr Training O, Elbing, Wkr. XX (1939)	1/IV/41		Arty
BOYSEN, Wolf (58)	Field Reinforcement Div Staff C (16/VIII/41)	1/VIII/39		Inf
BRABÄNDER (51)	416th Div z.b.V. (1/II/42)	1/XI/41		Inf
BRANDENBERGER, Erich (49)	8th Pz Div (1/VIII/41)	1/VIII/40	Bavaria	Arty
BRAUMÜLLER, Hans (58)	Psychological Tests Dept. Wkr. IX (10/IV/42)	1/VI/41		Arty
BREITH, Friedrich (49)		1/IV/42	Bavaria	Arty
BREITH, Hermann (49)	3d Pz Div (1/II/42)	1/VIII/41		Tks
BRENKEN (61)	Koblenz, Wkr. XII (admin)	1/VI/42		Cav
BRUNS (51)		1/IV/42		Pion
BRUNS, Walter	MA, Madrid (1/IX/41)	1/IV/42		Inf
v. BÜLOW, Cord (50)	Cavalry School Krampnitz Wkr. (1939)	1/II/42		Cav
BULOWIUS, Karl (51)	Chief Fortress Engineer, Wkr. X (1939)	1/IV/42		Pion
v. BÜNAU, Rudolf		1/IX/40	Württemberg	Inf
BURDACH, Karl (48)	Head of a Section O.K.H. (1939)	1/VI/41	Saxony	Arty
BUSCHENHAGEN, Erie	CGS Army of Lapland 1/IV/42	1/VIII/41		Inf
BUTZE (50)	340th Inf Div (1/III/42)	1/XI/41		Inf
CANTZLER, Oskar (51)	Chief Engineer, Army Group South (10/II/42)	1/VIII/40	Bavaria	Pion
Dipl. Ing. CASTORF, Helmut (51)		1/II/42	Thuringia	Inf
v. CLAER, Bernhard (53)	J.R. 4 (32d Inf Div (1939)	1/IV/42		Inf
CONRADI, Siegfried (53)		1/I/40	Saxony	Arty
CRAMOLINI (60)	Leipzig III, Wkr. IV (admin) (15/III/42)	1/VI/41		Cav
CRATO (60)	Düsseldorf, Wkr. VI (admin) (1939)	1/VI/42		Arty
CURTZE, Heinrich (65)	Field Reinforcement Div Staff A (1/X/41)	1/II/32	Bavaria	Arty
DAHLMANN (51)	Chief Supply O, Wkr. I (1939)	1/VII/40		Inf

DANHAUSER, Paul (49)	An Inf Regt (23/II/42)	1/IV/42	Bavaria	Inf
Edler v. DANIELS, Alexander (51)	J.R. 18 (6th Inf Div) (1939)	1/I/42		Inf
DEBOI (48)		1/IV/42	Bavaria	Inf
DEHNER, Ernst (52)	An Inf Div (23/X/41)	1/X/40	Bavaria	Inf
DEINDL, Otto (51)	L of C Area, Africa Pz Army (1/VI/42)	1/II/42	Bavaria	Tks
DEMOLL (60)	Ludwigshafen, Wkr. XII (admin) (1939)	1/VI/41		Arty
v. DETTEN, Gustav	Psychological Tests Dept Wkr. V (1939)	1/XI/41		
DETTLING (51)		1/XI/41	Württemberg	Inf
DICKMANN (61)	Dortmund I, Wkr. VI (admin) (1939)	1/VI/42		Inf
Baron DIGEON v. MONTETON, Albrecht (50)		1/IV/42		Cav
DIHM, Friedrich (61)	Chief Supply O, Wkr. VII (1939)	1/X/40	Bavaria	Arty
v. DIRINGSHOFEN		1/VIII/41		Cav
v. DOHREN (56)	Landwehr Training O, Wiesbaden, Wkr. XII (1939)	1/VII/41		Inf
Burggraf u. Graf z. DOHNASCHLOBITTEN, Heinrich (60)	C of S XXXVI Corps (22/VIII/41)	1/VI/42		Cav
Dipl. Ing. v. DONAT (50)	Eisb. Pi. Regt 3 (1941)	1/XI/41		Pion
DOSTLER, Anton (50)	57th Inf Div (1/I/42)	1/IX/41	Bavaria	Inf
v. DRABICH-WAECHTER Viktor (50)	Head of a Dept, Army Personnel Office (1/XII/41)	1/VIII/40		**Inf**
DREES	Head of a Dept, Army Ordnance (1/I/40)	1/VII/41		Arty
DROBNIG (54)		1/VII/41		Arty
DÜMLEIN, Friedrich(66)	Staff of Wkr. VII(1/VIII/41)		Bavaria	Inf
DÜVERT, Walther (50)		1/I/41		Arty
EBELING, Curt (50)		1/IV/42		Arty
EBELING, Fritz (54)		1/VI/41		Inf
EBERBACH, Hans (46)	A Pz Brig (10/I/42)	1/III/42	Württemberg	Tks
EBERLE, Rene (50)		1/IV/41	Austria	Inf
EBNER, Karl (56)		1/IV/39	Austria	Arty
ECKARDT, Eduard	Army Welfare Dept, Wkr III (1/I/40)	1/IV/41		Inf
EDELMANN, Karl (50)	J.R. 103 (4th Inf Div) (13/XII/39)	1/XI/41	Saxony	Inf
EGLSEER, Karl	4th Mtn Div (1/I/42)	1/IV/41	Austria	Inf
EHRENBERG, Hans (52)	409th Div z.b.V. (15/XII/40)	1/VIII/40	Saxony	Inf
EHRIG, Richard (58)	Staff of Wkr. IV (1939)	1/VI/41	Saxony	Inf

Name	Command	Date	Region	Branch
v. EISENHART-ROTHE, Hans-Georg (51)		1/IV/42		Cav
v. ERDMANNSDORF, Werner (50)	18th Mot Div (1/IV/42)	1/IV/42	Saxony	Inf
ERTEL, Theodor (68)	Chief Supply O, Wkr.VII (1/IX/41)	1/IX/41	Bavaria	Arty
Frhr. v. ESEBECK, Hans-Karl (50)		1/IV/41		Cav
v. FABRICE, Eberhard (50)	383d Inf Div (20/II/42)	1/III/42		Inf
Frhr. v. FALKENSTEIN, Erich (62)	Chief Supply O, Wkr. VII (1939)	1/IV/41		Inf
FAULENBACH (49)		1/IV/42		Inf
FEHN, Franz (58)	Landwehr Training O, Bayreuth, Wkr. XIII (1939)	1/VI/41	Bavaria	Cav
FEHN, Gustav (50)		1/VIII/40		Inf
FISCHER, Karl (59)	Staff of Wkr. VII (1939)	1/III/42		Arty
FISCHER, Wolfgang (51)	10th Pz Div (1/I/42)	1/VIII/41		Inf
FISCHER, Hermann (47)	J.R. 340 (196th Inf Div (1/IX/41)	1/IV/42	Thuringia	Inf
FISCHER, Karl		1/IV/42		Inf
FOERTSCH, Hermann (47)	C of S Twelfth Army (1/II/42)	1/II/42		Inf
FORST, Werner (47)	146th Arty Comd (1/I/42)	1/III/42		Arty
FORTNER, Johann (58)	718th Inf Div (1/I/42)	1/VI/41	Bavaria	Inf
Dr. FRANEK, Friedrich	196th Inf Div (1/III/42)	1/IV/42	Austria	Inf
FREMEREY (51)		1/VI/41		Cav
FRIEDRICHS, Walter (57)	Landwehr Comd, Munich, Wkr. VII (1939)	1/X/37	Bavaria	Inf
FRIEMEL, Georg (51)	(Prisoner of War)	1/II/41		Inf
FRIESSNER, Johannes (50)	Insp of Army Training (8/XII/41)	1/VIII/40	Saxony	Inf
FUCIK, Karl		1/VII/41	Austria	Inf
Ritter v. FÜCHTBAUER, Heinrich (62)	Feldkdtr. 568 (29/XII/41)	1/IX/41	Bavaria	Inf
FÜRST, Friedrich (52)	14th Mot Div (1/II/42)	1/X/40	Bavaria	Inf
Frhr. v. FUNCK, Hans (47)	7th Pz Div (1/III/42)	1/I/41		Cav
GAUL, Hans (65)	Comd P W Area G. (30/I/42)		Bavaria	Inf
GAUSE (48)	CGS Panzer Army Africa (2/II/42)	1/VI/41		Pion
GEBAUER, Artur		1/VI/42	Austria	Inf
GENÉE, Paul (61)				MT
GENTHE, Friedrich (69)	A P W Camp (22/IV/42)		Saxony	Cav
GERKE, Ernst (51)	C of S Army Group South (18/X/41)	1/II/41	Saxony	Sigc

v. GERMAR (63)	Stolp, Wkr. II (admin) (10/IV/40)	1/III/41		Inf
GIEHRACH (59)	Staff of Wkr, XVII (1939)	1/VIII/41		Arty
Frhr. v.u.zu GILSA, Werner (52)	216th Inf Div (1/I/42)	1/II/41		Inf
GIMMLER (52)	Head of Section, Army Ordnance (1/I/40)	1/IV/41		SigC
Dr. h.c. GLAISE, v. HORSTENAU, Edmund	Mil. Mission to Croatia (14/IV/42)		Austria	
GLODKOWSKI, Erich(61)	Insp of Recruiting, Essen, Wkr. VI (21/IV/41)	1/IV/41		Inf
v. GOECKEL, Hans (53)	Ohrdruf Training Area, Wkr. IX (1939)	1/II/41	Thuringia	Inf
v. GOELDEL (52)	Judge Advocate's Dept. (1939)	1/II/41		Inf
GOERITZ (50)		1/XII/41	Baden	Inf
GOESCHEN (53)	Cmdt of Bamberg, Wkr. XIII (12/III/40)	1/VIII/41		Cav
GOLLNICK (50)	36th Mot Div (15/XI/41)	1/VI/41		Inf
GRÄSER, Fritz Hubert (54)	An Inf Regt (27/VII/40)	1/X/41		Inf
v. GRAEVENITZ, Hans (48)	Head of a Section, O.K.W. (10/X/41)	1/II/42	Württemberg	Inf
GRASE, Martin (50)	An Inf Regt (23/X/41)	1/X/41		Inf
GRASSER, Anton(50)	J.R. 119 (25th Mot Div) (14/V/42)	1/IV/42		Inf
GREINER, Heinz (46)	J.R. 499 (268th Inf Div) (15/XII/41)	1/III/42	Bavaria	Inf
GROENEVELD (61)			Baden	Inf
GROSCHUPF (60)	Potsdam I, Wkr. III (admin) (1939)	1/IV/40		Arty
GROSSMANN (49)	An Inf Regt (10/IX/41)	1/X/41		Inf
GÜMBEL (50)	J.R. 118 (36th Mot Div) (9/XI/41)	1/II/42		Inf
v. GUNDELL, Walther (50)	Camp Cmdt, GHQ (1/X/41)	1/XII/41		Inf
GUHR (69)			Sileisa	Inf
GULLMANN, Otto (55)	Cmdt of Münster, Wkr.VI (1939)	1/II/41	Bavaria	Inf
HABENICHT (51)	Field Reinforcement Div Staff E (1/IX/41)	1/VI/41	Hessen	Inf
HACCIUS, Ernst (48)	Staff of Wkr. X (1939)	1/IV/42		Inf
HAECKEL, Ernst (51)	263d Inf Div (18/IV/42)	1/X/40	Bavaria	Inf
HAGL, August (53)		1/XII/40	Bavaria	Inf
HAHM (47)	An Inf Regt (24/XI/41)	1/IV/42	Silesia	Inf
HAMANN, Adolf	J.R. 327 (239th Inf Div) (4/VIII/41)	1/VI/42		Inf
HARTMANN, Walter (50)	Cmdt of Budweis, Protectorate (1/IV/40)	1/X/41	Saxony	Arty

v. HARTMANN (51)	71st Inf Div (15/X/41)	1/I/41		Inf
HASSE, Ulrich (47)		1/II/42		Inf
Ritter v. HAUENSCHILD (48)	24 Pz Div (11/V/42)	1/IV/42	Bavaria	Tks
HAUFFE (49)	Head of Mil. Mission to Roumania (28/X/41)	1/VI/40		Inf
HAUPT (60)	C of S, Wkr. III (1/III/41)	1/III/41		Inf
HAVERCAMP, Wilheim (50)		1/VIII/41	Bavaria	Inf
HEDERICH, Hans (62)	Chief Supply O, Wkr. II (1939)	1/IV/41		Arty
HEDERICH, Willy (62)	Feldkdtr. 520 (30/I/42)	1/II/42		Arty
v. HEINZ (56)				Inf
HELLWIG, Georg		1/VI/42		Pion
Ritter v. HENGL	2 Mtn Div 1/II/42)	1/IV/42	Bavaria	Inf
Dipl. Ing. HERNEKAMP, Karl (47)	105 Arty Comd (1/III/42)	1/VI/42		Arty
HERR, Traugott (48)	13th Mtz Inf Brig (13th Pz Div) (15/IV/42)	1/IV/42		Inf
HERRLEIN, Friedrich	Inf Gen, O.K.H. (22/II/42)	1/I/42		Inf
HEUSINGER (47)		1/X/41		Inf
HEYL, Friedrich (60)	Munich II, Wkr. VII (admin) (1939)	1/X/41	Bavaria	Arty
HIEPE, Hellmuth (50)	A.R. 17 (17th Inf Div (1939)	1/II/42		Arty
HILDEMANN (51)		1/XI/41		Pion
Dipl. Ing. HILLERT, Walter	Head of a Section, O.K.H. (1939)	1/I/42		Inf
v. HINDENBURG, Oskar (57)				Cav
HOCKER (49)		1/IV/42		Inf
HÖCKER, Erich (59)	Landwehr Training O, Oppeln 2, Wkr. VIII (1939)	1/VI/41		Inf
HOFERT, Johannes (57)	Munich I, Wkr. VII (admin) (3/X/41)			Arty
HOHNE, Gustav (50)	8th Light Div (1/I/42)	1/VIII/40		Inf
Ritter v. HORAUF, Franz (63)	Cmdt of Litzmannstadt, Wkr. XXI (1/XII/40)		Bavaria	Inf
Dr. HORMANN, Maximilian (49)		1/IV/42	Bavaria	SigC
HOERNLEIN, Walter (48)	J.R. "Grossdeutschland" (1/IV/42)	1/IV/42		Inf
HOFFMANN, Kurt (50)	342d Inf Div (1/III/42)	1/II/42		Inf
HOFFMANN, Max		1/I/42		SigC
HOFFMANN, Paul		1/VI/41		
HOFFMANN, Paul	Allenstein, Wkr. I (admin) (1939)	1/VI/42		Inf
HOFMANN, Erich	Staff of Wkr. XVIII (1939)	1/IX/41	Austria	

Name	Assignment	Date	Region	Branch
HOFMANN, Rudolf (46)		1/IV/42	Bavaria	Inf
Frhr. v. HOFMANN (50)		1/VI/42		Inf
Dr. Ing. Ritter v. HORSTIG gen. d'AUBIGNY v. ENGEL-BRUNNER (48)		1/III/42		Arty
HOSSBACH, Friedrich (47)		1/III/42	Hessen	Inf
Dr. HOTZY, Otto	J.E.R. 239 (1/IX/41)	1/IV/42	Austria	Inf
HÜBNER, Kurt (50)	Cmdt of Sofia (11/I/42)	1/IV/42	Bavaria	Cav
HUHNER, Werner (51)		1/IX/41		Inf
HÜHNLEIN, Friedrich (68)	277 Div (29/VIII/41)		Bavaria	Inf
Dipl. Ing. HÜNERMANN, Rudolf (48)	Staff of Armistic Commission (15/XII/40)	1/IV/42		Arty
IHSSEN (55)	Chief Supply O, Wkr. III (15/IX/41)	1/X/40		Arty
JACOBI		1/XII/41		
JACOBI, Alfred (57)	Feldkdtr. 549 (25/X/41)	1/VII/41		Inf
JAHR, Max (52)	Chief Engineer, Seventeenth Army (1/II/41)	1/XII/40		Pion
JANSEN (60)		1/XI/41		Sig C
JANSSEN, Adolf Wilhelm (64)				Cav
JASCHKE, Erich (50)	J. R. 90 (20th Mtz Div) (1/I/42)	1/X/41		Inf
JATZOW (61)	Schwerin, Wkr. II (admin) (1939)	1/X/41		Inf
JORDAN, Hans (49)	An Inf Regt (1/I/42)	1/X/41	Anhalt	Inf
JORDAN, Gerhard (47)	Chief Engineer, Panzer Army of Africa (1/X/41)	1/IV/42	Hessen	Pion
JUPPE, Hans (50)	C of S, Sig C, O.K.W. (1/I/42)	1/VIII/40		Sig C
KALDRACK, Otto (61)				Inf
v. KALM, Otto (51)		1/II/41	Hessen	Arty
KAMECKE (51)	J.R. 124 (72d Inf Div) (31/V/40)	1/XI/41		Inf
KASPAR, Johann (63)	C of S, Wkr. VII (23/IX/41)		Bavaria	Cav
KEIM (61)	Cmdt of Liege (1/I/42)		Hessen	Inf
KERSTEN	C of S, X Inf Corps (1939)	1/X/40	Saxony	Sig C
KESSEL, Hans (51)	Cmdt Maierhofen, Wkr. XIII (25/I/40)	1/VIII/41		Inf
Ritter v. KIEFFER, Friedrich (61)	Cmdt of Munich, Wkr. VII (17/III/41)	1/II/32	Bavaria	Inf
KIRCHHEIM, Heinrich (58)	Staff of Africa Panzer Army (15/V/42)	27/VIII/39		Inf
KITTEL, Heinrich (49)		1/I/42	Bavaria	Inf
KLEEMANN, Werner (49)	90th Light Div (5/VI/42)	1/XI/41	Baden	Cav
KLEIST (56)		27/VIII/39		Arty
Dr. KLEPP, Ernst		1/IV/42	Austria	Inf

Name	Position	Date	Region	Branch
KLINGBELL, Erich (60	Insp of GHQ Labor Units (28/III/41)			Pion
Ing. KLISZCZ, Otto	Staff of VI Inf Corps (1939)	1/IX/41	Austria	Pion
KOBUS	War Establishments Committee (Material) (1939)	1/IV/40		Inf
KOCH, Hellmuth	Landwehr Training O, Glatz, Wkr. VIII (1939)	1/VIII/41		Arty
Dipl. Ing. KOCH, Walter (50)		1/IV/42		Arty
KÖCHLING, Friedrich (49)	An Inf Regt (1/II/42)	1/IV/42		Inf
KOEHLER, Carl-Erich (48)	General Staff	1/IV/42		Cav
KOHL, Gustav (54)	Cmdt of Linz, Wkr. XVII (5/IV/40)	1/II/41	Bavaria	Inf
KOREUBER (52)	Zossen Training Area, Wkr. III (1/V/41)	1/I/41		Tks
KORTE, Heinz (50)	102d Arty Cmdr (1/X/41)	1/IV/42	Hessen	Arty
KOSSACK, Walter (59)		1/VI/42		Arty
KRÄTZER, Franz	J.R. 359 (181st Inf Div)	1/VI/42	Austria	Inf
KRAISS (51)	An Inf Div (12/III/42)	1/II/41	Württemberg	Inf
KRAUSE, Walter (50)	Lehr-Regt 900 (1/VII/41)	1/I/42		Inf
v. DEWITZ gen. v. KREBS	137th Inf Div (18/IV/42)	1/VIII/41		Inf
KRECH, Franz (51)	Insp of Munitions, W. Area (1939)	1/IV/42		Inf
v. KRENZKI, Kurt (55)	Feldkdtr. 808 (23/II/42)	1/VIII/36		Inf
KREYSING, Hans (51)		1/VII/40	Oldenburg	Inf
Ritter v. KRIEBEL		1/II/41		
KRIEGER, Hans (49)		1/VI/42		Inf
v. KROPFF (54)		1/III/39		Inf
KRÜGER, Walter (51)	1st Pz Div (17/II/42)	1/IV/41	Saxony	Cav
KRUSE, Hermann		1/II/41		Arty
KÜHLWEIN (49)	45th Inf Div (27/II/41)	1/IV/42		Inf
KÜHN, Friedrich (52)	14th Pz Div (22/V/42)	1/VII/40		Tks
v. KUMMER	Comdt of Weimar, Wkr. IX (1/IX/41)	1/IX/41		
KUNZE, Friedrich (61)		1/IV/40		Arty
v. KURNATOWSKI (61)		1/II/42		Inf
v. KUROWSKI, Eberhard (46)		1/VI/42		Inf
LAHODE, Kurt (53)		1/X/39	Saxony	Inf
LANDGRAF, Franz (53)	4th Pz Brig (1/XII/41)	1/IX/40	Bavaria	Tks
LANZ, Hubert (45)	1st Mtn Div (1/I/42)	1/XII/40	Württemberg	Inf
LECHNER, Heinrich		1/VII/41	Austria	Inf
Frhr. v. LEDEBUR (61)				Inf
LEMKE (52)		1/VIII/41		Inf

Name	Position/Unit	Date	Region	Branch
LENDLE (50)	Chief A Tk O Wkr. V (1939)	1/IV/42	Württemberg	Tks
v. LENSKI, Arno (50)	School for Mobile Trs, Krampitz, Wkr. (11/II/42)	1/VI/42		Tks
LETTOW (50)		1/IV/42		Inf
LEUZE, Walter (50)	J.R. 687 (336th Inf Div) (1/IX/41)	1/IV/42	Bavaria	Cav
v. LEYSER (51)	32th Inf Div (24/IX/41)	1/II/41		Inf
LEYTHAEUSER, Hermann (56)	Elsenborn Training Area, Wkr. VI (1939)	1/IV/40	Bavaria	Cav
LICHT (50)	S.R. 40 (17th Pz Div) (15/X/41)	1/II/42		Inf
LIEB (51)	J.R. 27 (12th Inf Div)(1939)	1/VI/41	Württemberg	Inf
LIEGMANN, Wilhelm (52)		1/VI/41	Saxony	Inf
v. der LINDE (50)	Chief A TK O Wkr. IV (1939)	1/III/42		Cav
LINDEMANN, Frtiz (49)	An Inf Div (6/V/42)	42		Arty
LINDENAU (60)	Cmdt of Flensburg, Wkr. X (1/IV/40)	1/VIII/41		Inf
LINDIG, Max (52)	Head of a Section, O.K.H. (1939)	1/12/40		Arty
LINKENBACH (52)		1/VIII/41		Cav
LINN		1/I/40		Inf
v. der LOCHAU, Axel (58)		1/VII/41		Inf
LOEHNING (52)		1/IV/40		Inf
LONTSCHAR, Adalbert	Cmdt of Belgrade (10/IV/42)	1/VII/41	Austria	Inf
LORENZ, Hans (60)	Staff of Wkr. V. (1939)	1/IV/41		Inf
LUCHT, Walter (59)	336th Inf Div (1/III/42)	1/X/40		Arty
LUER, Hilmar (58)	Liegnitz, Wkr. VIII (admin)(10/IV/42)	1/VIII/41		Inf
Frhr. v. LUTZOW, Kurt-Jürgen (49)	12 Inf Div (1/III/42)	1/I/42		Inf
MACK (50)	20th Mtz Inf Brig (20 Pz Div) (23/II/42)	1/IV/42		Pion
MAERCKER				Inf
v. MAJEWSKI (52)		1/IV/40		Pion
Ritter v. MANN, Edler v.	Garrison Cmdt, Bucharest (9/X/41)	1/IV/42	Bavaria	Inf
TIECHLER, Ferdinand (50)				
MANTELL (61)		1/X/40		Arty
MARCINKIEWICZ, August		1/XII/41	Austria	Pion
MARKGRAF, Emil		1/IX/41	Austria	Inf
MARSEILLE, Siegfried (54)	Bremen I, Wkr. X (admin) (1/I/42)	1/VII/41		Inf
MARTINEK, Robert	7th MTn Div (1/IV/42)	1/VI/41	Austria	Arty
MATTERSTOCK, Otto (52)	Cmdt of Würzburg, Wkr. XIII (1939)	1/VI/41	Bavaria	Inf

MATZKY, Gerhard (49)	MIS (1/I/42)	1/IV/41		Inf
Dr. Dr.-Ing. MAYER, Johannes (47)	An Inf Regt (19/IX/41)	1/IV/42		Inf
MEDEM (49)	2 Engineer School (1939)	1/IX/41		Pion
MEINHOLD (51)		1/IV/42		Inf
Dr. MEISE, Wilhelm (50)		1/IX/40	Bavaria	Pion
MEISSNER, Hans (57)	C of S, Wkr. XII (9/X/40)		Saxony	**SigC**
MEISSNER, Robert		1/IV/41	Austria	Inf
MELTZER, Rudolf (50)		1/IV/42		SigC
MERTENS (68)	Oflag IIC **(Officers PW Camp) (19/IX/41)**	1/IX/41		Inf
METSCHER, Karl	A.E.R. 7 (1/XI/41)	1/VI/42		Arty
MEYER, Carl Ludwig		1/IV/42		
MEYER, Heinrich	Cmdt of Mainz, Wkr. XII (22/IV/40)			Tks
MIERZINSKY (61)	Feldkdtr. 245 (1/X/41)	1/II/42		Inf
MIKULICZ, Adalbert		1/IX/41	Austria	Inf
MITTERMAIER, Wilhelm (52)		1/IX/40		Inf
Ritter v. MOLO, Louis (60)	An Inf Div (13/III/41)		Württemberg	Inf
MORITZ		1/XII/41		Cav
MOST	Landwehr Comd, Weinsberg, Wkr. V (1939)		Württemberg	Inf
MÜLLER, Angelo (49)		1/IV/42	Bavaria	Arty
MÜLLER, Richard (49)	Chief Engineer, V Inf Corps (1939)	1/III/42		Pion
MÜLLER, Vizenz (47)		1/II/42	Württemberg	Pion
MUMMENTHEY (54)		1/IV/37		Inf
MYLO, Walter (61)	Fulda, Wkr. IX (admin) (31/III/40)	1/I/42		Inf
NAKE, Albin		1/IV/42	Austria	Inf
Frhr. v. NEUBRONN u. EISENBURG, Alexander (62)		1/XII/40		Inf
NEUMAYR, Franz (51)	Cmdt of Augsburg, Wkr. VII (1939)	1/IV/42	Bavaria	Inf
NICHTERLEIN (60)	Gottingen, Wkr. XI (admin) (10/III/40)	1/IV/41		Inf
NIEDENFÜHR, Günther (53)				Arty
NOACK (60)	Div No 156, Wkr. VI (14/III/42)			Inf
NOLTE, Hans Erich (60)	Div z.b.V., Bialystok (1/XII/41)	1/X/40		Cav
v. NOSTITZ-WALLWITZ, Gerhard (56)		1/XII/41		Inf

Name	Position	Date	Region	Branch
OBERHAUSSER, Eugen (52)	C of S, Army Group Center (1/I/42)	1/XI/40	Bavaria	SigC
OCHSNER, Harrmann (49)	Head of a Section O.K.H. (1/X/39)	1/IV/42	Bavaria	Smoke Trs
OELSNER, (53)	Wandern Training Area, Wkr. III (1939)	1/II/41		Inf
v. OESTERREICH (60)		1/III/41		Inf
OFFENBÄCHER, Konrad (51)	Dollersheim Training Area, Wkr. XVII (1939)	1/VI/41	Hessen	Inf
OHNACKER (50)	Chief Supply O, Army Group West (10/IX/41)	1/IV/42		
v. ONDARZA, Herbert (63)	O.K.H.	1/X/40	Mecklen- burg	Arty
OPPENDLÄNDER (50)		1/XI/41	Württem- berg	Inf
ORTNER, Bruno	69th Inf Div (1/X/41)	1/IV/41	Austria	Inf
OTT, Eugen (54)	Ambassador to Japan (since 1938)	1/X/37	Württem- berg	Arty
OTTO (54)	Eifel Fortifications (1/V/40)	1/VIII/38	Baden	Pion
PACHMAYR	Army Mechanics School (1/IX/41)	1/IX/41		Arty
PAUER, Ernst		1/IX/41	Austria	Arty
Frhr. v. PECHMANN, Albrecht (62)	Feldkdtr. 598 (1/IX/41)	1/IX/41	Bavaria	Arty
PETERSEN, Matthias	Cmdt of Kaiserslautern Wkr. XII (1/X/41)	1/II/42		Inf
PETERSEN, Wilhelm (50)		1/IV/42		Pion
PETSCH (54)	710th Inf Div (15/IX/41)	1/VI/41		Inf
PETTER (61)	Cmdt of Frankfurt/Main, Wkr. IX (16/I/40)			Inf
PFLAUM, Karl (52)	258th Inf Div (9/X/41)	1/X/40		Inf
PFLIEGER (52)		1/X/40		Arty
PHILIPP, Lothar	6th Mtn Div (1/IV/42)	1/IV/40	Austria	Inf
Dipl. Ing. PHILIPPS		1/X/41	Saxony	Tks
v. PITREICH, August	Staff of CG, Protectorate (16/VII/41)		Austria	
PLAMBOCK (61)	Lötzen Fortifications, Wkr. I (1/X/41)	1/IV/41		Arty
PLEWIG, Willy (61)	Salzbrunn, Wkr. VIII (ad- min) (1/II/42)	1/IV/41		Inf
POEL, Gerhard (56)	Remount School, Wkr. V (1939)	1/VII/41		Cav
v. POHL (67)				Arty
POPPE (49)	J.R. 39 (26 Inf Div) (1939)	1/IV/42	Thuringia	Inf
v. PRIEM (58)		1/I/42		Inf
v. PRITTWITZ u. GAF- FRON, Max (66)	Cmdt of Lemberg (17/III/42)	1/IX/41	Silesia	Inf

Name	Assignment	Date	Region	Branch
Dr. PRÜGEL, Karl (65)	Cmdt of Zagreb (22/IV/42)		Bavaria	SigC
v. PUTTKAMER (60)	Insp of Recruiting, Schwerin, Wkr. II (11/III/40)			Inf
RAAB, Matthias		1/IV/42	Austria	Arty
RABSILBER, Friedrich (62)	Osnabruck, Wkr. XI (admin) (1939)	1/IV/41		Inf
v. RAESFELD, Werner (50)	Transport Office, Essen, Wkr. VI (1939)	1/VI/42	Silesia	Inf
RÄSSLER, Rudolf (57)	Landwehr Training Off, Aachen, Wkr. VI (1939)	1/VI/42	Saxony	Cav
RAITHEL, (47)		1/IV/42	Bavaria	Arty
Frhr. RAITZ v. FRENTZ, Maximilian (61)	Staff of Wkr. VI (1939)	1/VI/41		Arty
v. RANDOW, Heinz (49)	24 Mtz Inf Brig (24 Pz Div) (1/III/42)	1/IV/42		Cav
RATHKE (53)		1/X/39		Arty
RAUCH, Erwin (53)	An Inf Div (1/I/42)	1/VIII/41		Inf
RAUS, Erhard	A Mtz Inf Brig (17/X/41)	1/IX/41	Austria	Inf
v. RAVENSTEIN, Johann	Prisoner of War			Inf
RECKNAGEL, Hermann (49)	An Inf Regt (8/VIII/40)	1/III/42	Hessen	Inf
v. REIBNITZ (53)		1/VII/40		Inf
REICHER, Franz	Staff of Wkr. XVII (14/XII/41)		Austria	Inf
REICHERT, Josef (50)	Div No 177 Wkr. XVII (1/X/41)	1/IX/41	Bavaria	Inf
REINHARDT, Fritz (51)		1/IV/41	Saxony	Inf
RIBBENTROP, Friedrich (61)	A.E.R. 168 (1/VII/41)	1/IV/41	Saxony	Arty
RICHERT (50)		1/IV/42		Inf
RICHTER, Werner (49)		1/III/41	Saxony	Inf
RIEGER, Leopold (51)	Chief Supply O, Wkr. XIII (1939)	1/VI/41	Saxony	Arty
RINGEL, Julius	5th Mtn Div (1/I/42)	1/VI/40	Austria	Inf
RITTAU (50)	129th Inf Div (12/XI/41)	1/VIII/40		Inf
RITTER, Rene		1/IV/42	Austria	Inf
RITTWEGER (55)	Cmdt of Karlsruhe, Wkr. V (1/X/41)	1/II/42		Inf
RODENBURG (47)		1/IV/42	Baden	Inf
RODEWALD (55)	Staff of First Army (1/VII/40)			H-DrT
ROESINGER, Otto (51)		1/IV/42	Bavaria	Pion
ROSLER, Eberhard	An Inf Regt (21/X/41)	1/IV/41	Württem- berg	Inf
ROHDE, Hans (49)	MA, Ankara (1/V/42)	1/I/42		Inf
Frhr. v. ROMAN, Rudolf (48)	35th Inf Div (1/IV/42)	1/IX/41	Bavaria	Arty
ROSSUM (52)		1/XII/40		Inf

Name	Position	Date	Region	Branch
Dipl. Ing. RÜDIGER		1/VI/41		Arty
RÜGAMER, Ferdinand	Insp of Munitions, Wkr. XIII (1939)	1/VII/41	Austria	Arty
RÜGGENMANN, Alfons (50)	Head of a Section O.K.H. (1939)	1/IV/42		**H-DrT**
RUNGE, Wilhelm (51)	Insp of Engineer Equipment, Wkr. I (1939)	1/VI/41		Pion
RUPP (50)		1/III/42		Inf
RUPPERT, Hans Eberhard (50)		1/VI/42		**H-DrT**
RUPPRECHT, Wilhelm (51)	An Inf Div (15/VI/41)	1/XI/40	Bavaria	Inf
SAGERER		1/VII/41	Bavaria	Inf
SALITTER, Fritz	A Training Area (3/IV/42)	1/IV/41		Arty
SANDER (50)		1/XI/41		Arty
v. SAUCKEN, Dietrich (48)	A Pz Div (1/I/42)	1/I/42		Cav
SAUVANT (50)	A Training Area (1939)	1/III/4 2		Inf
SCHADE		1/VII/41		Inf
SCHAEFER (49)		1/IV/42	Silesia	Inf
SCHAEFFER	Cmdt of Kassel, Wkr. IX (1939)	1/II/41		Inf
SCHARTOW (51)	429th Div z.b.V. (19/II/42)	1/III/41		Inf
SCHAUM (51)		1/X/41		Pion
SCHAUWECKER (60)	Insp of Recruiting, Schleswig-Holstein, Wkr. X (1939)			SigC
v. SCHEELE, Hans Karl (50)		1/X/41		Inf
SCHEFOLD (54)	Feldkdtr. 510 (20/VIII/41)		Württemberg	Arty
SCHELLER, Walther (50)	Head of a Section, O.K.W.	1/X/41	Hessen	Inf
SCHELLER (64)	Königsberg II, Wkr. I (admin) (1939)	1/VI/42		Arty
SCHELLMANN (60)		1/IV/41		Inf
SCHERBENING (51)	Psychological Tests Dept, Wkr. VI (1939)	1/IX/41		Inf
SCHERER, Theodor (52)	An Inf Div (1/IV/42)	1/XI/40	Bavaria	Inf
v. SCHICKFUS u. NEUDORFF, Erich (61)		1/II/32		Inf
SCHILLING, Walter (47)		1/VI/42		Cav
SCHIRMER, Georg (51)		1/I/41		Inf
Frhr. v. SCHLEINITZ, Siegmund (52)	9th Inf Div (19/VII/41)	1/XII/40		Inf
Frhr. v. SCHLEINITZ, Joachim (50)	Judge Advocate's Dept, (1939)	1/IV/42		Inf
SCHLEMMER, Ernst (52)		1/XII/40	Bavaria	Inf
Dipl. Ing. SCHLEMMER, Hans (47)	An Inf Div (27/IV/42)	1/III/42	Bavaria	Arty
SCHLÖMER, Helmutt (49)	7 Mtz Inf Brig (7 Pz. Div) (1/III/42)	1/IV/42		Inf

Graf v. SCHMETTOW (50)	CG Channel Islands (1/VI/42)	1/IV/42	Silesia	Cav
SCHMIDT, Arthur (47)		1/VI/42		Inf
SCHMIDT, Curt (51)		1/II/41		Inf
SCHMIDT, Friedrich (50)	J.R. 72 (46th Inf Div)(1939)	1/III/42		Inf
SCHMIDT, Gustav (48)		1/IV/42		Inf
SCHMIDT, Otto		1/X/41		
SCHMIDT, Otto (50)	J.R. 35 (12th Inf Div) (29/VI/40)	1/I/42		Inf
SCHMIDT-KOLBOW (62)	Div No 158 (from Wkr. VIII) Wkr.V (25/XI/40)			Arty
SCHMITT, Artur	Prisoner of War	1/II/41		Inf
SCHMUNDT, Rudolf (54)	Chief Adjutant to Hitler (1/IV/42)	1/X/41		Inf
SCHNECKENBURGER (50)	Head of a Section, O.K.H. (1939)	1/VII/40	Württem-berg	Inf
v. SCHNEIDEMESSER, Gustav (50)		1/VI/42		Inf
SCHNEIDER, Friedrich	Berlin VIII, Wkr. III (admin) (1939)	1/IV/41		Inf
SCHNEIDER, Otto		1/XII/41		
SCHNEIDER (58)	Chief Fortress Engineer, Wkr. XI (3/III/41)	1/IV/40		Pion
SCHÖNBERG, Wilhelm (68)				Arty
SCHÖNFELDER, Fritz (51)	Chief Engineer, Wkr. XVII (1939)	1/IV/41	Saxony	Pion
SCHÖNHERR, Otto		1/IX/41	Austria	Inf
SCHOPPER (49)		1/VII/41		Arty
SCHRADER (52)	C of S, Army Group West (2/VIII/41)	1/VII/40		SigC
SCHREIBER, Alfred (50)		1/VI/42		Inf
SCHRÖDER (59)	Army Welfare Dept, Wkr. XX (12/IX/41)			Pion
v. SCHROETER (51)		1/I/42		Cav
Dipl.-Ing. SCHROETTER (49)		1/IV/42		Tks
SCHUBERT, Rudolf (51)	C of S Twelfth Army (21/I/42)	1/IV/41		SigC
v. SCHULER, Rüdiger (51)	Adjutant, Sixth Army (1/I/42)	1/IX/41		Inf
SCHUNCK, Theodor (52)		1/VI/41		Arty
SCHUSTER, Friedrich (60)		1/I/42	Bavaria	Inf
SCHWARTZ (51)	Head of a Section, Army Personnel Branch (1939)	1/VIII/41		H-DrT
v. SCHWERIN, Richard (47)	An Inf Regt (27/X/39)	1/VI/42		Inf
SCULTETUS, Bruno (60)		1/XII/41		Inf
SCULTETUS, Herbert (61)		1/XII/41		Inf
SEEGER (51)	292d Inf Div (1/X/41)	1/IX/41	Württemberg	Inf

SEHMSDORF, Hans (54)	3 Supply Group (15/IX/41)	1/II/41		Inf
v. SENGER u. ETTERLIN, Fridolin (50)	Liaison with Italian Armistice Commission (1/V/42)	1/IX/41	Baden	Cav
SEUFFERT, Franz (52)	Field Reinforcement Div Staff D (1/IX/41)	1/XII/40	Bavaria	Inf
SEYFFARDT (48)	J.R. 111 (35th Inf Div)(28/I/42)	1/VI/42		Inf
v. SICHART, Werner (60)	Kiel, Wkr. X (admin) (1/I/42)	1/IX/41	Saxony	Inf
SIEGLIN, Kurt (57)	Area Comd, Piaseczno (15/II/41)		Württemberg	Inf
SINZINGER, Adolf	An Inf Regt (1/IV/42)	1/IV/42	Austria	Inf
SIRY, Max (50)	An Inf Div (18/VI/42)	1/VIII/41	Bavaria	Arty
SIXT, Friedrich (47)	C of S, XXXXIV Corps (1/V/40)	1/VI/42	Bavaria	Arty
SODAN (60)		1/XII/40		Cav
SOHN (58)	Chief Supply O, Wkr. XVII (15/IX/41)	1/IX/41		Arty
STAHL (52)		1/XII/40		Tks
STAHR, Wolfgang (50)	II Armorer Schooll (15/X/41)	1/IV/42	Saxony	Inf
STEINBACH, Paul (52)	Chief Supply O, Wkr. XX (15/IX/41)	1/X/41	Bavaria	Arty
STEINBAUER, Gerhard (52)		1/X/40	Bavaria	Arty
STEMPEL, Richard (52)	183d Inf Div (1/I/42)	1/IV/41	Saxony	Inf
STENZEL, Richard		1/IV/42	Austria	Arty
STEUDNER (61)	Staff of Wkr. II (1/XII/41)			Arty
Graf v. STILLFRIED u. RATTONITZ, Waldemar (65)	Staff of Training Command (3/IV/42)			Inf
Dipl. Ing. v. STOCKHAUSEN (47)		1/IV/41	Hessen	Inf
v. STOCKHAUSEN (70)	Feldkdtr. 816 (1/IX/41)	1/IX/41		
STRACK, Karl (50)	J.R. 253 (34th Inf Div) (13/VII/40)	1/II/42		Inf
STREICH, Hans (50)		1/II/41		Tks
STUBENRAUCH, Wilhelm (56)		1/VI/41	Saxony	Cav
v. STULPNAGEL, Siegfried (50)	NCO School, Frankenstein, Wkr. VIII (1939)	1/VI/42		Inf
STUMM, Berthold (50)		1/VI/42		Inf
v. STUMPFELD (56)	Landwehr Training O, Hamburg, Wkr. X (1939)	1/X/40		Arty
SZELINSKI (50)	J.R. 38 (8th L Div) (25/XI/41)	1/II/42		Inf
TARBUK, Johann	Nikolsburg, Wkr. XVII (admin) (1939)	1/VIII/41	Austria	Inf
TESCHNER (69)			Baden	Inf
THÄTER, Maximilian (63)	Würzburg, Wkr. XIII (admin) (1939)	1/XII/41	Bavaria	Inf

THAMS	Brdy-Wald Training Area (1939)	1/III/41		Inf
THEISS, Rudolf		1/IX/41	Austria	Tks
THOFERN, Wilhelm	A Training Area (17/X/41)	1/VIII/39		Inf
THOMA, Heinrich (51)	An Inf Regt (4/XI/41)	1/IX/41	Bavaria	Inf
Ritter v. THOMA, Wilhelm (50)	17th Pz Div (1/I/42)	1/VIII/40	Bavaria	Tks
THOMAS (53)	2 Engineer School, Dessau-Rosslau, Wkr. XI (1939)	1/XI/40		Pion
THOMASCHKI (47)		1/III/42		Arty
Frhr. v. THÜNGEN, Karl (48)		1/XII/41	Bavaria	Cav
TOUSSAINT, Rudolf (50)	CG, Protectorate (1/I/42)	1/X/41	Bavaria	Inf
TRAUCH, Rudolf (49)	Head of a Section, O.K.H. (1940)	1/X/41	Bavaria	H-DrT
TRAUT, Hans (47)	An Inf Regt (23/I/42)	1/IV/42		Inf
v. TRESCKOW, Joachin (48)		1/VI/42		Inf
TRIERENBERG (51)	C of S, Wkr. VI (1/V/40)	1/VIII/41		Inf
v. TSCHAMMER u. OSTEN, Eckart (54)	Landwehr Training O, Dortmund, Wkr. VI (1939)	1/XII/40		Inf
Frhr. v. UCKERMANN, Horst (50)	Div No 160 in Denmark (1/V/42)	1/II/42		Inf
v. UNRUH, Walther (64)	L of C Area, Fourth Army (17/III/42)			
v. VAERST, Gustav (49)	15th Pz Div (15/V/41)	1/IX/41	Hessen	Cav
VASSOLL (58)	An Arty Regt (16/IX/41)	1/VI/42		Arty
VATERRODT	Cmdt of Strasbourg (8/IV/41)	1/III/41		Inf
VEITH, Richard (51)		1/VIII/40	Bavaria	Inf
VÖLCKERS, Paul (51)	78th Inf Div (1/V/42)	1/I/41		Inf
VOIT, Paul (65)	C of S, Wkr. XIII (24/IX/41)	1/IV/38	Bavaria	Inf
VOSS, Erich	Staff of Wkr. VIII (13/IV/41)	1/VI/42		SigC
WAGNER, Georg (61)	Halberstadt, Wkr. XI (admin) (1939)	1/IV/41		Inf
WANDEL (51)	An Inf Div (7/XII/41)	1/IV/41	Silesia	Arty
WARNICKE (60)	Staff of Wkr. I (1939)	1/VIII/41		H-drT
WEGENER, Wilhelm (47)	An Inf Regt (19/I/42)	1/VI/42		Inf
WEIDINGER, Wilhelm (52)	Insp of Army AAA (28/III/42)	1/X/40		Arty
WEIDLING (50)		1/II/42		Arty
WEISS, Walter (51)	An Inf Regt (17/IX/41)	1/IX/40		Inf
WEISS, Wilhelm	IR 138 (2d Mtn Div) (15/IX/40)	1/X/41	Austria	Inf
WENING, Ernst (57)	Landwehr Training O, Innsbruck, Wkr. XVIII (1939)	1/VI/41	Bavaria	Cav

Frhr. v. WERTHERN, Georg Thilo (50)		1/VI/42		Arty
WESSEL, Walter (49)		1/II/42		Inf
v. WICKEDE, Emil (49)	J.R. 4(32d Inf Div) (27/VIII/40)	1/VI/42		Inf
WILL, Otto (50)	Insp of Railway Troops, O.K.H. (1/I/42)	1/XII/40	Bavaria	Pion
WINKLER, Hermann (53)	Psychological Tests Dept Wkr. II (1939).	1/VII/41	Saxony	Inf
WINTER, Paul (48)	Head of a Section, O.K.H. (1939)	1/XI/41	Bavaria	Arty
WINTERGERST, Karl (49)		1/IV/42	Bavaria	Arty
WIRTZ (50)	Chief Engineer, VII Inf Corps (1939)	1/IV/42		Pion
v. WITZLEBEN, Hermann (50)		1/VI/42		Cav
WÖHLER (48)	C of S of an Army (19/I/41)	1/I/42		Inf
WOLFF		1/II/41		Inf
WOLFF, Ludwig (49)	22d Inf Div (1/I/42)	1/IX/42	Saxony	Inf
WOLFSBERGER, Franz	C G Latvia (1/XII/41)	1/VII/41	Austria	Inf
WOLPERT, Johann (52)	Cmdt of Nürnberg, Wkr. XIII (10/III/40).	1/IX/41	Bavaria	Inf
WOSCH (51)		1/III/41		Inf
ZAHN, Alois (51)		1/VIII/41	Württem- berg	Inf
v. ZANGEN, Gustav (50)	An Inf Div (26/I/42)	1/II/42		Inf
v. ZANTHIER (51)	J.R. 349 (181st Inf Div) (1/XI/41).	1/X/41		Inf
ZEDNICEK, Franz		1/IV/42	Austria	Pion
ZEITZ, Erich (54)	Staff of Fourth Army (31/I/41)	1/II/41	Bavaria	Cav
ZELLNER, Emil	C of S, Wkr. XVII (9/XII/41)	1/IV/41	Austria	Inf
ZIEGLER, Heinz (48)	C of S, XLII Inf Corps (1/V/40)	1/II/42		Arty
ZUKERTORT, Karl (52)	Head of Section, Army Ordnance Branch (1939)	1/IV/40	Saxony	MT
ZUNEHMER				Inf
ZUTAVERN (49)		1/VI/42	Baden	Arty

6. GENERAL STAFF OFFICERS

Rank	Name	Rank	Name
Obst.	ADAM, Kurt	Obstlt.	v. BOGEN u.
Maj.	v.AHLEFELD		SCHONSTEDT
Maj.	Frhr.v. ALBEDYLL	Obst.	BÖHME
Hptm.	v. AMSBERG, Rik.	Maj.	BONTE
Hptm.	ANNUS,S	Obst.	BORK
Obstlt.	ASSMANN	Maj.	BOTH
		Maj.	BRANDSTÄDTER
Obstlt.	BABEL, Ottomar	Maj.	BRANDT, Heinz
Obstlt.	BACKHAUS	Hptm.	BRAUN, Kurt
Obstlt.	BADER	Maj.	BREITHAUPT
Obst.	BAENTSCH, Alfred	Maj.	Baron v. BROCK-
Hptm.	v.BAER		DORFF,
Hptm.	BANG, Gunter		Friedrich
Maj.	BARCHEWITZ	Maj.	v. BRUNN
Hptm.	BAUMANN	Maj.	BRUSCHKE
Obst.	BAUR	Obst.	BUCHER
Obstlt.	BAYERLEIN	Maj.	v. BÜNAU
Maj.	BEHLE	Obstlt.	BÜRKER
Maj.	BEICHELE	Obstlt.	v. BUTTLAR
Obstlt.	BEIGEL	Obstlt.	CLAUSIUS
Maj.	v. BELOW, Nicolaus	Maj.	CLAUSS
		Maj.	v. COELIN
Maj.	BERGER	Obst.	v. COLLANI
Maj.	BERGER, Klaus	Maj.	COLLASIUS
Hptm.	Frhr.v.BERLICHINGEN-	Maj.	CONRAD
	JAGSTHAUSEN	Maj.	v. CRIEGERN
Maj.	BERLIN		Fritz
Maj.	BERLING	Maj.	CROME
Maj.	v. BERNSTORFF	Maj.	DANKE
		Obstlt.	Ritter u. Edler v.
Hptm.	BEUCK		DAWANS
Obst.	BEUTLER, Otto	Hptm.	DEHLE, Otto
Hptm.	BIELITZ	Maj.	DEINHARDT
Obstlt.	BLAUROCK	Hptm.	v.DERSCHAU,
Hptm.	BLEICKEN Otto Hein-		Christoph Fried-
	rich		rich
Maj.	BLOCH v. BLOTTNITZ,	Obst.	DEUTELMOSER
	Johann Gottlob	Maj.	DEYHLE, Willy
Maj.	BLÜMKE	Maj.	DIERMAYER
Maj.	v. BLUMRÖDER	Obst.	DIESENER, Paul
Obst.	BOECKH-BEHRENS	Maj.	DIETL
Hptm.	BOEHLES	Maj.	DINGLER
Hptm.	BOEHM, Eberhard	Maj.	DISSELL, Gerhard
Maj.	v. BOELTZIG, Hans Die-	Hptm.	v. DOBSCHÜTZ
	trich	Hptm.	DOEPNER

Obst.	DOERR, Hans
Maj.	DONKE
Obst.	DORN, Hellmuth
Maj.	v. DRABICH-WAECHTER
Maj.	DRESCHER
Rittm.	DREWS, Werner
Hptm.	DUENSING
Maj.	v. DÜRLING
Obst.	EHRIG, Werner
Maj.	EHLERT Hans
Maj.	EICHLER
Maj.	EINBECK
Maj.	v. EINEM
Maj.	ELCHEPP
Obstlt.	Frhr. v. ELBERFEDLDT
Maj.	ENGELHORN
Hptm.	EPPENDORFF
Hptm.	ERHARDT, Kurt
Obstlt.	EMMERICH, Albert
Obst.	FAECKENSTEDT, Ernst Felix
Maj.	FÄHNDRICK
Maj.	FAUNER
Obst.	FELLER, Gustav
Maj.	Frh. v. FINCK
Obst.	FLECK, Hans
Obst.	FORSTER
Obstlt.	FRANZ
Obst.	FREGE
Maj.	Baron FREYTAG v. LORINGHOVEN, Wessel
Obstlt.	FRIEBE
Maj.	FROVERT
Obstlt.	GÄDE, Heinz
Maj.	GEBAUER
Obstlt.	v. GELDERN-CRISPENDORF, Joachim
Obst.	GERLACH, Erwin
Maj.	GIESE, Karl
Obstlt.	GITTNER, Hans
Obst.	GLASL, Anton
Maj.	v. GOLDAMMER
Maj.	Ritter v. GOSS
Obst.	GOTH
Maj.	v. CRAEVENITZ
Maj.	GREME
Obst.	GRIMMEISS
Obstlt.	GROBLER
Maj.	v. der GROEBEN, Peter
Obstlt.	v. GROLMANN, Helmuth
Maj.	GROME
Hptm.	GRONEMANN-SCHÖN-BORN
Hptm.	GUNDELACH
Obst.	v. GYLDENFELDT
Hptm.	v. HAACKE
Obstlt.	HAAS
Maj.	HAINRICH
Maj.	HAMBERGER
Hptm.	Frhr.v.HAMMERSTEIN-GESMOLD
Obst.	v. HANSTEIN Hans
Obstlt.	v. HARBOU
Hptm.	v. HARLING
Obst.	HAUCK
Maj.	HAUSER
Hptm.	HAYESSEN
Obstlt.	HEIDER
Obst.	HEIDKÄMPER
Obst.	HEIM, Ferdinand
Maj.	HEINRICH
Obst.	HEISTERMANN v. ZIEHLBERG, Gustav
Obstlt.	v. HEITERER-SCHALIER
Maj.	HELBIG
Maj.	HERBER
Obstlt.	HERBERG, Friedrich
Hptm.	HERRE
Obst.	HERRMANN, Paul
Hptm.	HERZOG
Obst	HERRMANN, Paul
Hptm	HERZOG
Obstlt.	HESSE
Hptm.	HESSE
Hptm.	HEYSE
Obst.	HILDEBRANDT, Hans Georg
Hptm.	HILGERT
Hptm.	HINRICH, Otto
Hptm.	v. HOBE, Cord
Maj.	HOEFS
Obstlt.	HÖLTER
Hptm.	HÜBNER
Obst.	v. HÜNERSDORFF
Maj	HUHS
Obstlt.	IRKENS

Obstlt.	JACOBI, GEORG	Obstlt.	KÜHNE, Gerhard
Maj.	Dr. JACOBI	Maj.	KUHNEMANN
Maj.	JAIS, Franz	Obst.	KULLMER, Artur
Obst.	JANK	Hptm.	KUTZBACH, Friedrich
Hptm.	V.JENA, Egbert	Maj.	LAEGLEER
Maj.	JESSEL	Obst.	LAHOUSEN, Erwin
Obst.	JODL	Hptm.	LANGE
Maj.	JOHN	Obst.	LANGE, Wolfgang
Obstlt.	KAHLEN	Obstlt.	LANGHAEUSER
Obst.	v. KAUFMANN	**Maj.**	**LAMPE, Fritz**
Hptm.	v. KESSEL, Guido	Maj.	LEUTHEUSSEN
Maj.	Ritter u. Edler v.	Hptm.	LIEBE
	KIENLE	Obst.	Frhr. v. LIEBEN-
Obst.	KINZEL		STEIN, Kurt
Obstlt.	Gf. v. KIRCHBACH, Hans Hugo	Hptm.	LIESE
Hptm.	KLARHOEFER	Maj.	LIESNER
Maj.	KLEINSCHMIT	Hptm.	v. LINDEQUIST, Olaf
Maj.	v. KLEIST	Hptm.	LINKE, Ernst
Maj.	Graf v. KIELMANSERGG	Obstlt.	v. LINSTOW
Maj.	KLIMKE	Obstlt.	LÖHR, Erich
Hptm	Graf v. KLINCKOWSTROEM,	Obst.	LONGIN, Anton
	Karl Heinrich	Maj.	LORENZ
Hptm	v. KLUGE	Maj.	LORT
Obst.	KNESCH	Obst.	v. LOSSBERG, Bernard
Hptm-	v. der KNESEBECK	Obst.	v. LUDWIGER
Obstlt.	KNOLL	Hptm.	LÜHL
Maj.	KNÜPPEL, Wilhelm	Obstlt.	LYNCKER, Julius
Obst.	KOCH	Obstlt.	MAAS
Maj.	KOEHN	Maj.	Frhr.v.MALTZAHN
Obstlt.	v. KÖLLER	Maj.	MARKERT
Maj.	KÖNIG	Obst.	v.MELLENTHIN,
Obstlt.	Dr. KOERBLER		Horst
Hptm.	KÖRDEL	Obstlt.	v.MELLENTHIN,
Obst	KOERNER, Karl Theodor		**Friedrich Wilhelm**
Maj.	KÖRNER, Gottfried	Maj.	Baron MENGDEN v.
Maj.	KÖSTLIN		ALTENWOGA
Hptm	KOLLER-KRAUS	Obstlt.	MENSING
Obst.	KOPECKY, Karl	Obst.	MERIDIES, Walter
Maj.	KRANTZ, Hans Ulrich	Maj.	MERKEL
Obst.	KREMLING, Ludwig	Maj.	MERKER
Maj.	KRIEBEL, Rainer	Maj.	Ritter MERTZ v.
Obstlt.	v. KRIEGSHEIM		QUIRNHEIM
Obst.	v. KROSIGK	Maj.	METZ, Lothar
Hptm.	KRÜGER, Wolfgang	Obst.	METZ, Eduard
Hptm.	KRUSEMANN	Maj.	MEYER, Hans Ger-
Hptm.	KUBAN		hard
Obst.	KÜBLER, Josef	Maj.	MEYER-DETRING
Obst.	KÜHL, Claus	Hptm.	MICHALSKY
Hptm.	KÜHLEIN	Hptm.	MOLL, Dietrich

Hptm.	MOSER
Maj.	MÜLLER, Christian
Obst.	Dipl. Ing. MÜLLER, Gerhard
Obst.	MÜLLER, Ludwig
Maj.	MÜLLER
Hptm.	MÜLLER
Hptm.	MÜLLER, Hans
Hptm.	MÜLLER, Heinrich
Maj.	MÜLLER HILLEBRAND
Hptm.	Graf zu MÜNSTER, Eberhard.
Maj.	MURAU
Hptm.	MUSCHNER
Hptm.	NAGEL
Obst.	NÜRNBERG
Maj.	v. NATZMER, Oldwig
Hptm.	NECKELMANN
Maj.	NECKER
Hptm.	NEITZEL
Maj.	NIEMEYER
Maj.	NIKLAUS
Maj.	NOLTE
Obst.	OCHSNER, Wilhelm
Hptm.	OETJEN
Hptm.	OGILVIE
Maj.	OHRLOFF
Hptm.	ORLIK
Obstlt.	OSCHLIES
Rittm.	OSSWALD
Maj.	PANTOW, Heinz
Hptm.	PAUMGARTTEN
Obst.	PEMSEL, Max
Obstlt.	Dr. v. PETERSDORF, Fritz Julius
Hptm.	PETERSEN
Hptm.	v. PFISTER
Maj.	PETRL
Maj.	PFAFFEROTT
Maj.	PFLANZ
Maj.	PHILIPPE
Maj.	PICOT
Hptm.	PISTORIUS
Maj.	PITSCHMANN, Gerd
Hptm.	Edler v. d. PLANITZ, Ferdinand
Hptm.	v. PLATE Claus Henning

Rittm.	v. PLEHWE
Hptm.	PLÜCKNER
Obst.	POHLMANN
Maj.	PREUSSE
Obst.	PRIESS
Maj.	v. PRITTWITZ u. GAFFRON, Hans Eberhard
Obstlt.	v. PRITZBUER, Dietrich
Obst.	PRÜTER
Maj.	Graf v. PÜCKLER
Obst.	v. QUAST, August Viktor
Maj.	RADTKE
Maj.	RANCK, Werner
Obst.	RASP
Maj.	v. RAUCHHAUPT, Wilhelm
Obstlt.	REICHELT
Maj.	REINHARD, Walter
Hptm.	REISSINGER
Maj.	REISSINGER
Hptm.	v. RENVERS, Leopold
Maj.	RICHERT
Maj.	RICHTER
Obst.	Graf v. RITTBERG, Georg
Maj.	ROEDENBECK, Walter
Maj.	ROEDER, Wilhelm
Hptm.	ROESTEL.
Obst.	RÖHRICHT
Maj.	Ritter u. Edler v. ROSENTHAL
Obstlt.	ROSSMANN
Obst.	RÖTTIGER
Hptm.	v. RUBESCH
Maj.	RÜDEN, Heinz Friedrich
Hptm.	RÜMENAPP
Maj.	SAPAUSCHKE
Hptm.	SASS
Obstlt.	SAUBERZWEIG
Obstlt.	v. SCHAEWEN
Maj.	SCHAFER, Lothar
Obst.	SCHAFFITZEL
Obstlt.	SCHANZE, Ludwig

Hptm.	SCHELLER, Heinz Eberhard	Maj.	STEETS
Obstlt.	SCHERFF, Walter	Obstlt.	STEFFLER
Obstlt.	SCHEUERPFLUG	Obst.	STEINMETZ
Obst.	SCHIEL	Maj.	v STEINSDORFF
Hptm.	SCHIELE	Obstlt.	v. STEUBEN
Maj.	SCHILDKNECHT	Maj.	STIRIUS
Obst.	SCHIPP v. BRANITZ Joachim	Rittm.	v. STOCKHAUSEN, Hans August
Maj.	SCHIRNICK	Hptm.	STORP
Maj.	SCHLEUSENER	Obst.	Frhr. v. STRACHWITZ
Maj.	SCHLIEPER	Obst.	von le SUIRE
Obst.	SCHMIDT, Hans	Maj.	Frhr. v. SÜSSKIND-SCHWENDI
Obst.	SCHMIDT-RICHBERG		
Hptm.	SCHMIDT v. ALTENSTADT	Maj.	v. TEIN
Hptm.	SCHNEIDER	Maj.	v. TEMPELHOFF, Hans Georg
Obstlt.	SCHNIEWIND	Maj.	TESKE
Obstlt.	SCHOLL, Friedrich Wilhelm	Obst.	v. THADDEN
Obstlt.	SCHUCHARDT	Obstlt.	THEILACKER
Obst.	SCHULZ, Friedrich	Maj.	THEYSOHN
Obst.	SCHULZ, Otto	Obst.	THIELE, Fritz
Maj.	SCHUMANN	Hptm.	THILO
Maj.	SCHWANBECK	Obstlt.	v. TIPPELSKIRCH, Werner
Hptm.	SCHWANDNER	Maj.	TOPPE, Alfred
Maj.	SCUPIN	Obst.	TSCHIRDEWAHN
Hptm.	v. SEEBACH	Hptm.	TUMMELEY
Rittm.	SEELE	Hptm.	ÜBELHACK
Hptm.	SENGPIEL	Obstlt.	ULRICH, Justus
Obst.	SEULTETUS	Maj.	v. UNGER
Obst.	SERINI	Obstlt.	VOELTER
Hptm.	SIEDSCHLAG	Obst.	VOGEL, Emil
Obst.	SIEWERT, Curt	Hptm.	v. VOLLARD-BOCKELBERG
Hptm.	SIMONS, Ulrich	Obst.	v. VORMANN, Nikolaus
Maj.	SITTMANN	Maj.	VORWERCK
Hptm.	v. SOBBE	Hptm.	VOSS, Wilhelm
Maj.	SOSNA	Obst.	WAEGER, Kurt
Obst.	SOUCHAY	Maj.	WAGENER, Otto
Obst.	Dr. SPEIDEL, Hans	Hptm.	WAGNER, Gunter
Obst.	SPERL	Obst.	WAGNER, Herbert
Obst.	SPETH	Hptm.	Frhr. v. WANGENHEIM, Horst
Maj.	SPRENGER	Rittm.	Frhr. v. WANGENHEIM, Konrad
Maj.	STAATS	Maj.	v. WARBURG
Maj.	STAEDKE	Hptm.	WEBER, Josef
Maj.	STANGE	Hptm.	v. WEDEL
Maj.	STARKE, Robert		
Maj.	STAUBWASSER		

Obst.	WEINKNECHT
Obst.	v. WEISE, Hans
Hptm.	WEITZ
Hptm.	Frhr. v. WELCK
Obstlt.	v. WERDER
Obstlt.	WESTPHAL
Maj.	v WIDEKIND
Maj.	WIESE
Obstlt.	WILHELMI, Hans
Maj.	WILLEMER
Obst.	WINTER, August
Obst.	WISSMANN
Hptm.	WOITE
Obst.	WOLF, Friedrich
Obst.	WOLFF, Erich
Maj.	WOLFF, Werner
Hptm.	WOLFF
Maj.	WOITE
Maj.	v. WÜHLISCH, Georg
Obst.	WUTHMANN, Rolf
Obstlt.	v. WUTHENAU
Obst.	Ritter v. XYLANDER, Rudolf
Obst.	ZEITZLER
Maj.	ZELTMANN
Maj.	ZERBEL, Alfred
Hptm.	ZIEGELMANN
Maj.	ZIEGLER, Joachim
Maj.	v. ZIEGLER v. KLIPPHAUSEN
Maj.	ZIERVOGEL
Obstlt.	v. ZITZEWITZ
Maj.	ZOELLER

7. COMMANDERS OF UNITS

a. Army Groups

Rank	Name	Age	Army Group
Genfeldm.	v. BOCK, Fedor	61	B
Genfeldm.	v. KLUGE, Günther	59	Center
Genfeldm.	v. KÜCHLER, Georg	60	North
Genfeldm.	LIST, Wilhelm	61	A
Genfeldm.	v. RUNDSTEDT, Gerd	66	West

Average age: 61.

b. Armies and Panzer Armies

Rank	Name	Age	
Genobst.	BLASKOWITZ, Johannes	58	First
Genobst.	BUSCH, Ernst	57	Sixteenth
Genobst.	DIETL, Eduard	51	Lapland
Genobst.	DOLLMANN, Friedrich	60	Seventh
Genobst.	v. FALKENHORST, Nikolaus	56	Norway
Genobst.	HAASE, Curt	60	Fifteenth
Genobst.	HOEPNER, Erich	55	Fourth Pz
Genobst.	HOTH, Hermann	58	Seventeenth
Genobst.	v. KLEIST, Ewald	61	First Pz
Gen. d. Kav.	LINDEMANN, Georg	58	Eighteenth
Genfeldm.	(v.) (LEWINSKI gen) v. MAN-STEIN, Fritz Erich	54	Eleventh
Genobst.	MODEL, Walter	50	Ninth
Gen. d. Pz. Tr.	PAULUS, Friedrich	51	Sixth
Genobst.	REINHARDT, Georg Hans	55	Third Pz
Genfeldm.	ROMMEL, Erwin	51	Africa Pz
Genobst.	RUOFF, Richard	57	Fourth
Genobst.	SCHMIDT, Rudolf	56	Second Pz
Genobst.	Frhr. v. WEICHS, Maximilian	60	Second

Average age: 56.

c. Army Corps

Rank	Name	Age	Corps
Gen. d. Pz. Tr.	v. ARNIM, Jürgen	52	
Gen. d. Art.	BADER, Paul	56	LXV
Gen. d. Inf.	BIELER, Bruno	53	XXXXII
Gen. d. Inf.	v. BÖCKMANN, Herbert	54	L
Genlt.	v. BOEHM-BEZING, Diether	61	
Gen. d. Inf.	BOHME, Franz	56	XVIII
Gen. d. Art.	BRAND, Fritz	54	
Gen. d. Kav.	BRANDT, Georg	65	XXXIII

Gen. d. Inf.	Graf v. BROCKDORFF-AHLE-FELDT, Walter	55	II
Gen. d. Inf.	v. der CHEVALLERIE, Kurt	50	LIX
Gen. d. Inf.	CLOSSNER, Erich	55	LIII
Gen. d. Inf.	FELBER, Hans	53	XIII
Gen. d. Geb. Tr.	FEURSTEIN, Valentin	56	LXX
Gen. d. Inf.	FISCHER v. WEIKERSTHAL, Walter	51	
Gen. d. Pion.	FÖRSTER, Otto	57	VI
Gen. d. Art.	FRETTER-PICO, Maximilian	51	XXX
Gen. d. Inf.	GEYER, Hermann	59	IX
Gen. d. Pz. Tr.	Frhr. GEYR v. SCHWEPPEN-BURG, Leo	56	XXIV
Gen. d. Inf.	v. GRIEFF, Kurt	65	XXXXV
Gen. d. Art.	HANSEN, Christian	56	X
Gen. d. Kav.	HANSEN, Erik	53	LIV
Gen. d. Pz. Tr.	HARPE, Josef	52	XXXIX Pz
Geb. d. Inf.	HEINRICI, Gotthard	55	
Gen. d. Art.	HEITZ, Walter	63	VIII
Genlt.	HEUNERT	54	XXXVI
Gen. d. Art.	KAEMPFE, Rudolf	58	XXXV
Gen. d. Art.	KAUPISCH, Leonhard	63	
Gen. d. Pz. Tr.	KEMPF, Werner	55	XXXXVIII Pz
Gen. d. Inf.	KIENITZ, Werner	57	XVII
Gen. d. Pz. Tr.	KIRCHNER Friedrich	57	XXXXI Pz
Gen. d. Inf.	KLEFFEL, Philipp	54	I
Gen. d. Kav.	KOCH-ERPACH, Rudolf	55	
Gen. d. Geb. Tr.	KONRAD, Rudolf	50	XXXXIX Mtn
Gen. d. Inf.	v. KORTZFLEISCH, Joachin	51	XI
Gen. d. Pz. Tr.	KUNTZEN, Adolf	53	LVII Pz
Gen. d. Pz. Tr.	Frhr. v. LANGERMANN u. ERLENCAMP, Willibald	52	LVI Pz
Gen. d. Pz. Tr.	LEMELSEN	54	XXXXVII Pz
Gen. d. Inf.	LÜDKE, Erich	59	XXXI
Gen. d. Kav.	v. MACKENSEN, Everhard	53	III Pz
Gen. d. Inf.	MATERNA, Friedrich	56	XXVIII
Gen. d. Inf.	METZ, Hermann	63	
Genlt.	NAGY, Emmerich	60	LXXI
Genlt.	NEHRING, Walter	50	Africa Pz
Gen. d. Inf.	v. OBSTFELDER, Hans	55	XXIX
Gen. d. Kav.	v. POGRELL, Günther	62	XXXVII
Gen. d. Inf.	REINHARD, Hans	53	LI
Gen. d. Inf.	SCHMIDT, Hans	65	
Gen. d. Geb. Tr.	SCHÖRNER, Ferdinand	48	Norway Mtn
Gen. d. Inf.	SCHROTH, Walter	56	XII
Gen. d. Inf.	SCHUBERT, Albrecht	56	XXIII
Gen. d. Inf.	SCHWANDNER, Maximilian	60	

Gen. d. Inf.	v. SCHWEDLER, Viktor	57	IV
Gen. d. Pz. Tr.	STUMME, Georg	56	XXXX Pz
Gen. d. Inf.	VIEROW, Erwin	52	LV
Gen. d. Pz. Tr.	v. VIETINGHOFF gen. SCHEEL, Heinrich	55	XXXXVI Pz
Gen. d. Inf.	WÄGER, Alfred	58	XXVII
Gen. d. Inf.	v. WIETERSHEIM, Gustav	58	XIV Pz
Gen. d. Inf.	WIKTORIN, Mauriz	58	
Gen. d. Inf.	WODRIG, Albert	59	XXVI

Average age: 54.

d. Divisions

Rank	Name	Age	Div No
Genlt.	ANDREAS	57	208th Inf
Genmaj.	ALLMENDINGER, Karl	49	
Genmaj.	Dr. ALTRICHTER, Friedrich	51	58th Inf
Genmaj.	ANGERN Günther	50	11th Pz
Genmaj.	ANSAT	50	102d Inf
Genmaj.	v. APELL, Wilhelm	49	22d Pz
Genmaj.	BADINSKI, Kurt	48	
Genmaj.	BAIER, Albrecht	48	
Genlt.	BALTZER	55	217th Inf
*Genlt.	BAYER		181st Inf
Genmaj.	Frhr. v. MAUCHENHEIM gen. BECHTOLSHEIM, Gustav	52	707th Inf
Gen. d. Art.	BEHLENDORFF	53	34th Inf
Genmaj.	v. BEHR	53	173d
Genlt.	BEHSCHNITT, Walter	56	15th Inf
Genlt.	BLÜMM, Oskar	57	
Genmaj.	v. BISMARCK, Georg	49	21st Pz
Genmaj.	BLUMENTRITT	49	97th L
Genlt.	BOHNSTEDT, Wilhelm	52	21st Inf
Genmaj.	Frhr. v. BOINEBURG-LENGS-FELD, Wilhelm	53	23d Pz
Genmaj.	v. BOLTENSTERN, Walter	51	29th Mtz
Genmaj.	BOYSEN, Wolf	58	Fd. Reinf. C
Genmaj.	BRABÄNDER	51	416 z.b.V.
Genlt.	BRAND, Albrecht	54	31th
Genmaj.	BRANDENBERGER, Erich	49	8th Pz
Genmaj.	BREITH, Hermann	49	3d Pz
Genlt.	v. BRODOWSKI, Fritz	56	Fd. Reinf. B.
Genmaj.	BUTZE	50	340th Inf
Genlt.	de l'HOMME de COURBIERE, Rene	55	213th
Genmaj.	CURTZE, Heinrich	66	Fd. Reinf. A.
Genmaj.	DEHNER, Ernst	52	
Genlt.	DENNERLEIN, Max	56	290th Inf

Genmaj.	DOSTLER, Anton	50	57th Inf
Genlt.	EBERHARDT	51	60th Mtz
Genmaj.	EGLSEER, Karl	51	4th Mtn
Genmaj.	EHRENBERG, Hans	52	409th z.b.V.
Genlt.	ENDRES, Theodor	65	212th Inf
Genlt.	ENGELBRECHT, Erwin	50	163d Inf
Genmaj.	v. ERDMANNSDORF, Werner	50	18th Mtz
Genmaj.	v. FABRICE, Ebergard	50	383d Inf
Genlt.	FETT, Albrecht	69	
Genlt.	FISCHER, Herbert	59	172d
Genmaj.	FISCHER, Wolfgang	51	10th Pz
Genlt.	FOLTTMANN	54	164th Inf
Genmaj.	FORTNER, Johann	58	718th Inf
Genmaj.	Dr. FRANEK, Friedrich	51	196th Inf
Genlt.	FRANKE, Hermann	63	162d Inf
Genmaj.	FÜRST, Friedrich	52	14th Mtz
Genmaj.	Frhr. v. FUNCK, Hans	47	7th Pz
Genlt.	Frhr. v. GABLENZ, Eccard	50	7th Inf
Genlt.	GERHARDT, Paul	61	421 z.b.V.
Genlt.	GILBERT, Martin	53	
Genmaj.	Frhr. v.u.zu GILSA, Werner	52	216th Inf
Genmaj.	GOLLNICK	50	36th Mtz
Genlt.	GOLLWITZER, Friedrich	52	88th Inf
Genlt.	GRAF, Karl	59	330th Inf
Genlt.	Frhr. GROTE Waldemar	64	218th Inf
Genlt.	GÜNTZEL	53	113th Inf
Genlt.	HAARDE	53	25th Pz
Genlt.	HAASE, Conrad	53	
Genmaj.	HABENICHT	51	Fd. Reinf. E.
Genmaj.	HAECKEL, Ernst	51	263d Inf
Genlt.	HAENICKE, Siegfried	63	61st Inf
Genlt.	HAMMER, Karl	58	75th Inf
Genmaj.	v. HARTMANN	51	71st Inf
Genmaj.	Ritter v. HAUENSCHILD	48	24th Pz
Genlt.	HELD	61	147
Genlt.	HELL	55	
Genlt.	HELLMICH, Heinz	50	
*Genmaj.	Ritter v. HENGL		2d Mtn
Genlt.	HENRICI, Sigfrid	54	25th Mtz
Genlt.	HERZOG, Kurt	54	291st Inf
Genlt.	HÖFL, Hugo	63	206th Inf
Genmaj.	HÖHNE, Gustav	50	8th L
Genlt.	v. HÖSSLIN	63	188th
Genmaj.	HOFFMANN, Kurt	50	342d Inf
Genlt.	HORN, Max	53	214th Inf
Genlt.	HUBE, Hans	52	16th Pz
Genlt.	Dr. HUBICKI, Alfred	55	9th Pz
Genmaj.	HÜHNLEIN, Friedrich	68	277th

Genlt.	HÜTTMANN	63	165th
Genlt.	KAUFFMANN	51	256th Inf
Genlt.	KEINER, Walter	51	62d Inf
Genlt.	v. KEMPSKI, Hans	57	199th Inf
Genmaj.	KLEEMANN, Werner	49	90th L
Genlt.	v. KNOBELSDORFF	54	19th Pz
Genlt.	KÖRNER, Willy	61	223d Inf
Genmaj.	KRAISS	51	
*Genmaj.	v. DEWITZ gen. v. KREBS		137th Inf
Genmaj.	KRÜGER, Walter	51	1st Pz
Genmaj.	KÜHLWEIN	49	45th Inf
Genmaj.	KÜHN, Friedrich	52	14th Pz
Genmaj.	LANZ, Hubert	45	1st Mtn
Genlt.	LAUX, Paul	54	126th Inf
Genlt.	LEHMANN, Joseph	54	82d Inf
Genmaj.	v. LEYSER	51	32d Inf
Genlt.	LICHEL, Walter	56	123d Inf
Genmaj.	LINDEMANN, Fritz	49	
Genlt.	v. LOEPER	54	81st Inf
Genmaj.	LUCHT, Walter	59	336th Inf
Genmaj.	Frhr. v. LÜTZOW	49	12th Inf
Genlt.	MACHOLZ	52	
Genlt.	MADERHOLZ, Karl	56	
Genlt.	MARCKS, Erich	51	? L
*Genmaj.	MARTINEK, Robert		7th Mtn
Genlt.	MEYER-BUERDORF, Heinrich	53	131st Inf
Genlt.	MEYER-RABINGEN, Hermann	53	197th Inf
Genlt.	MIETH	55	112th Inf
Genmaj.	Ritter v. MOLO, Louis	60	
Genlt.	MOSER, Willi	54	299th Inf
Genlt.	NEULING, Ferdinand	56	239th Inf
Genmaj.	NOACK	60	156th Ers.
Genmaj.	NOLTE, Hans Erich	60	z.b.V. Bialy-stock
Genlt.	v. OBERNITZ, Justin	57	293d Inf
*Genmaj.	ORTNER, Bruno		69th Inf
Genlt.	v. OVEN, Karl	53	56th Inf
Genmaj.	PETSCH	54	710th Inf
Genlt.	PFEFFER, Max	56	297th Inf
Genlt.	PFEIFFER, Georg	52	94th Inf
Genmaj.	PFLAUM, Karl	52	258th Inf
Genlt.	PFLUGBEIL, Johann	59	221st
Genlt.	PFLUGRADT	52	
*Genmaj.	PHILIPP, Lothar		6th Mtn
Genlt.	Edler Herr u. Frhr. v. PLOTHO, Wolfgang	62	285th
Genlt.	POETTER, Adolf	58	410th z.b.V.
Genmaj.	RAUCH, Erwin	53	

Genlt.	RECKE	52	
Genmaj.	REICHERT, Josef	50	177th
Genlt.	Dr. RENDULIC, Lothar	54	
Genlt.	RENNER, Theodor	55	211th Inf
Genlt.	RENZ, Maximilian	58	
Genlt.	RICHTER	53	205th Inf
*Genmaj.	RINGEL, Julius		5th Mtn
Genmaj.	RITTAU	50	129th Inf
Genlt.	ROETTIG	52	
Genmaj.	Frhr. v. ROMAN, Rudolf	48	35th Inf
Genmaj.	RUPPRECHT, Wilhelm	51	
Genlt.	SACHS	56	
Genlt.	SANNE	52	100th L
Genmaj.	v. SAUCKEN, Dietrich	48	? Pz
Genlt.	Frhr. v. SCHACKY auf SCHÖN- FELD, Sigmund	55	
Genmaj.	SCHARTOW	51	429th z.b.V.
Genlt.	SCHELLERT	54	253d Inf
Genmaj.	SCHERER, Theodor	52	
Genmaj.	Frhr. v. SCHLEINITZ, Siegmund	52	9th Inf
Genmaj.	Dipl. Inf. SCHLEMMER, Hans	47	
Genmaj.	SCHMIDT-KOLBOW	62	158th Ers.
Genlt.	v. SCHWERIN, Otto	60	431 z.b.V.
Genmaj.	SEEGER	51	292d Inf
Genmaj.	SEUFFERT, Franz	52	Fd. Reinf. D.
Genlt.	SIEBERT, Friedrich	53	44th Inf
Genlt.	SINNHUBER	54	28th L
Genlt.	SINTZENICH, Rudolf	52	132d Inf
Genlt.	SIXT v. ARNIM, Hans Heinrich	52	95th Inf
Genlt.	v. SOMMERFELD, Hans	53	526th
Genlt.	SORSCHE, Konrad	58	50th Inf
Genlt.	Dr. SPEICH, Richard	57	539th
Genlt.	SPONHEIMER, Otto	55	
Genlt.	STEMMERMANN, Wilhelm	53	296th Inf
Genmaj.	STEMPEL, Richard	52	183d Inf
Genlt.	STEPHANIUS	59	187th
Genlt.	STIMMEL	55	
Genlt.	STOEWER, Paul	52	
Genlt.	v. STUDNITZ, Bogislav	55	87th Inf
Genlt.	STUMPFF, Horst	54	20th Pz
*Genlt.	TARBUK v. SENSENHORST, Karl		540th
Genlt.	v. TETTAU, Hans	53	24th Inf
Genlt.	THEISEN, Edgar	53	262d Inf
Genmaj.	Ritter v. THOMA, Wilhelm	50	17th Pz
Genlt.	v. TIEDEMANN, Karl	63	207th
Genlt.	TIEMANN	53	93d Inf
Genlt.	v. TIPPELSKIRCH, Kurt	50	30th Inf
Genlt.	TITTEL, Hermann	52	169th Inf
Genmaj.	Frhr. v. UCKERMANN, Horst	50	160th

Genmaj.	v. VAERST, Gustav	49	15th Pz
Genmaj.	VÖLCKERS, Paul	51	78th Inf
Genlt.	v. WACHTER, Friedrich Karl	52	267th Inf
Genmaj	WANDEL	51	
Genlt.	WANGER, Rudolf	53	
Genlt.	WETZEL	54	255th Inf
Genlt.	WILCK, Hermann	57	708th Inf
Genlt.	WITTKE, Walter	53	170th Inf
Genmaj.	WOLFF, Ludwig	49	22d Inf
Genlt.	Frhr. v. WREDE, Theodor	53	
Genmaj.	v. ZANGEN, Gustav	50	
Genlt.	ZICKWOLFF	53	227th Inf

Average age: 53

8. GERMAN AIR FORCE (GAF) OFFICERS.

Name (age)	Command or Appointment	Seniority	Origin

a. Rank: MARSHAL OF THE REICH (Reichsmarschall)

| GÖRING, Hermann (48) | C-in-C Air Force | 19/VII/40 | Bavaria |

b. Rank: FIELD MARSHAL (Generalfeldmarschall)

KESSELRING, Albert (56)	Second Air Fleet and C-in-C South	19/VII/40	Bavaria
MILCH, Erhard (49)	Inspector General, Air Force	19/VII/40	
SPERRLE, Hugo (57)	Third Air Fleet	19/VII/40	Württemberg

c. Rank: COLONEL GENERAL (Generaloberst)

JESCHONNEK, Hans (42)	C of S, Air Force	1/III/42	
KELLER, Alfred (58)	First Air Fleet	19/VII/40	
LÖHR, Alexander (56)	Fourth Air Fleet	/41	Austria
Dipl. Ing. Frhr. v. RICHTHOFEN, Wolfram.	VIII Air Corps	1/III/42	
STUMPFF, Hans Jürgen (52)	Fifth Air Fleet	19/VII/40	
WEISE, Hubert (56)	AA Command	19/VII/40	

d. Rank: GENERAL (General der Flieger, der Flakartillerie or der Luftnach-richtentruppen (General))

ANDRAE, Waldemar (51)	C G, Crete	1/VII/41	
BIENECK, Hellmuth (54)	Luftgau II	1/VII/41	
BODENSCHATZ, Karl (51)	C of S to Göring	1/VII/41	Bavaria
BOGATSCH, Rudolf (51)	Liaison with Army	1/VII/41	
CHRISTIANSEN, Friedrich (62)	C G Holland	1/I/39	
COELER, Joachim (42)	IX Air Corps	1/I/42	
DANCKELMANN (53)	C G, Serbia	1/IV/41	
DESSLOCH, Otto (52)	II A A Corps	1/I/42	Bavaria
DOERSTLING, Egon (52)	Supply Depot, R.L.M.	1/VI/42	Saxony
DRANSFELD, Eduard (58)	MT Depot, R. L. M.	1/X/40	
FELMY, Helmuth (56)	C G, Southern Greece	1/II/38	
FISCHER	Luftgaustab z.b.V.2	1/VI/42	

FÖRSTER, Hellmuth (52)	I Air Corps	1/V/41	
GEISSLER, Hans (50)	X Air Corps	19/VII/40	
GOSSRAU, Karl Siegfried (60)	Admin Dept, R. L.M.	1/IX/41	Württemberg
Ritter v. GREIM, Robert (49)	V Air Corps	19/VII/40	Bavaria
HAUBOLD, Alfred (53)	Luftgau III/IV	1/X/41	Saxony
HIRSCHAUER, Friedrich (58)	(AA) Luftgau XVII	1/VIII/39	Bavaria
KASTNER-KIRDORF, Gustav, (60)	Personnel Dept, R.L.M.	1/VII/41	
KITZINGER, Karl (56)	C G, Ukraine	1/X/39	
KLEPKE, Waldemar (59)	Insp of Reconnaissance and Photography	1/I/39	Silesia
KÜHL, Leonhard (56)	Director of Training, R.L.M.	1/IV/39	
LOERZER, Bruno (50)	II Air Corps	19/VII/40	
MARTINI, Hermann (50)	C of S, Air Force	20/IX/41	Saxony
MAYER, Wilhelm (55)	Luftgau SE	1/II/41	
MOHR	Luftgau I	1/IV/41	
PFLUGBEIL, Kurt (51)	IV Air Corps	1/II/42	Saxony
Ritter v. POHL, Erich	Air Attache, Rome, and Chief Liaison Officer with Italian Air Force.	1/II/42	Bavaria
QUADE, Erich (58)	Public Relations	1/IX/40	Hessen
RÜDEL, Günther (58)	(AA) Chief of Air Defense	1/X/37	Lorraine
RITTER, Hans (49)	Liaison with Navy	1/IV/42	
RUGGERA, Kamillo	(AA) Luftgau II	1/XII/40	Austria
SCHMIDT, August	(AA) Luftgau VI	1/VII/41	
SCHMIDT, Hugo		1/VII/41	
SCHWEICKHARD, Karl (59)		1/VI/38	Baden
v. SEIDEL, Hans Georg (50)	QMG, Air Force	1/I/42	
Ing. SIBURG, Hans (48)	Luftgau, Holland	1/IV/42	
SOMMÉ, Walter (54)	Luftgau, VIII	1/VI/42	
SPEIDEL, Wilhelm	Chief of Air Mission to Roumania	1/I/42	Württemberg
STUDENT, Kurt (51)	XI Air Corps	30/V/40	
v. der LIETH-THOMSEN Hermann (74).	R. L.M.	1/VIII/39	
VIERLING, Albert (55)	Luftgaustab z.b.V.4	1/VI/42	Bavaria
WABER	Luftgau, Kiev	1/III/42	Austria
Dr. WEISSMANN, Eugen (50)	(AA) Luftgau XII	1/VI/42	Württemberg
WENNINGER, Rudolf (51)		1/XI/40	Bavaria

WIMMER, Wilhelm (52)	Luftgau Belgium and N France	1/X/39	Bavaria
v. WITZENDORFF, Bodo (65)	R.L.M.	1/II/39	
WOLFF, Ludwig (55)	Luftgau XI	1/II/41	
ZANDER, Konrad (58)	?	1/IV/38	
ZENETTI, Emil (58)	Luftgau VII	1/II/41	Bavaria

e. Rank: LT GENERAL (Generalleutnant)

v. ARNAULD, de la PERRIÈRE		1/I/41	
BARLEN, Karl (50)		1/IV/41	
BRUCH, Hermann (58)	Air Comdr, N Norway	1/XI/40	
Frhr. v. BÜLOW, Hilmer	Military Science Dept, R.L.M.	1/IV/41	
CARLSEN		1/X/40	
CRANZ (53)	Training Command, Prague	1/XI/40	
DEINHARDT		1/I/42	
v. DÖRING, Kurt Bertrau (52)	Fighter Command Second Air Fleet	1/XI/41	
FAHRNERT, Friedrich (62)	Cadet College, Gatow (1939)	1/IV/40	Saxony
FEYERABEND, Walter (50)	AA Command, Norway	1/IV/41	
FIEBNIG		1/IV/42	
FRIEDENSBURG, Walter		1/XII/41	
FRÖLICH, Stephan (52)		1/I/42	Austria
GAUTIER	Insp of Armaments, Vienna	1/IV/41	
HAEHNELT, Wilhelm (66)		1/XII/40	
HANESSE (50)	German Air Force, Liaison Staff, Occupied France	1/IV/42	Hessen
HARMJANZ, Willi (50)	Luftgau, Norway	1/IV/41	
HEILINGBRUNNER, Friedrich (50)	Luftgau XIII	1/I/41	Bavaria
HERMANN	Cmdt of Pilsen	1/XI/40	
HOFFMANN v. WALDAU Otto (44)	Air Cmdr, North America	1/III/42	Silesia
KAMMHUBER, Josef	Night Fighter Div	1/XI/41	Bavaria
KARLEWSKI			
KESSLER (50)	Air Cmdr, Atlantic	1/IV/41	
KIEFFER, Maximilian (50)	Koluft of an Army Gp	1/VI/42	Bavaria
KOLB, Alexander (52)	(AA) Air Defense Command, Stettin (1939)	1/X/40	
v. KOTZE (53)	Luftgaustab z.b.V. 12	1/X/40	

KROCKER, Viktor (52)		1/XII/41	
KÜHNE	C of S, Fifth Air Fleet	1/VI/42	
LANGEMEYER (56)	Staff of Luftflotte 4	1/IV/42	
LECH	(AA)	1/XI/40	
LENTZSCH, Johannes (57)	(AA) (?)	1/III/38	
MACKENZEN v. ASTFELD		1/IV/41	
MAHNCKE, Alfred (53)	A Luftgau	1/XI/40	
Ritter v. MANN, Edler v. TIECHLER, Hermann (52)	(?)	1/XI/40	Bavaria
MOLL (55)		1/IV/42	
MOOYER	Pre-military Training, R.L.M.	1/IV/41	
MÜLLER, Ernst	6 Air Supply Group	1/I/42	
MUSSHOFF		1/XI/40	
NIEHOFF, Heinrich (59)	Oberfeldkdtr, Lille	1/II/38	
PETERSEN (50)	Staff of XI Air Corps	1/IV/42	
PUTZIER (50)	Staff of Second Air Fleet	1/I/41	
v. RENZ (50)	(AA)	1/VIII/41	Baden
RICHTER, Hellmuth (50)	(AA) at R.L.M.	1/VIII/41	
v. RÖMER, Erwin (53)	Zingst Training Area	1/IV/41	Saxony
SATTLER, Otfried (55)	Hamburg Air Defense District	1/I/40	
SCHLEMM	Staff of XI Air Corps	1/VI/42	
SCHMIDT, Kurt (54)		1/I/40	Saxony
SCHUBERT	Staff of Second Air Fleet	1/IV/42	
SCHUBERT (53)	Directorate of Defense Economics, R.L.M.	1/X/40	Saxony
SCHULZ (52)	Insp of Air Force Schools	1/XII/40	Hessen
SCHWUB, Albert (54)	Mechanics' School, Halle	1/X/40	Bavaria
SEIFERT, Johann	10th AA Div	1/VI/42	Austria
SOMMER, Johannes (54)		1/III/40	Württemberg
SPANG, Willibald (54)	Head of Meteorlogical Services, R.L.M.	1/I/42	Württemberg
SPIESS (50)	1st AA Div (?)	1/VIII/41	
STEUDEMANN, Kurt (51)	AA Inspr, R.L,M.	1/I/41	Saxony
v. STUBENRAUCH, Wilhelm	(AA)	1/VI/42	
SUREN (53)	C of S, Fourth Air Fleet	1/IV/41	
WALZ, Franz (56)		1/IV/41	Bavaria
WECKE	Air Defense Zone, Slovakia	1/VIII/40	
Dipl. Volksw. WEIGAND, Wolfgang (56)	Inspector of Armaments, Central Army Group	1/XI/40	
WITTING (51)		1/II/41	
v. WÜHLISCH, Heinz Helmut (50)	Control Commission, Morocco	1/IV/42	
ZOCH, Phillip (50)	Koluft, Sixteenth Army	1/IV/42	

f. Rank: MAJ GENERAL (Generalmajor)

ADAMETZ		1/II/41	
ANGERSTEIN (51)	K.G.1	1/V/42	Alsace
v. AXTHELM, Walter (48)	1 AA Corps	19/IX/40	Bavaria
BAIER, Eberhard		1/IV/42	
BANSE	Air Supply Group, W France	1/IV/42	
BAUR de BETAZ	(Admin)	1/VII/41	
BECKER, Hermann		1/XI/40	
Dipl. Ing. BECKER, Wilhelm		1/VII/41	
BEHRENDT (49)		1/X/41	
BERTHOLD	(Admin)	1/VII/41	
BERTRAM (50)	(AA)	1/VI/39	
Frhr. v. BIEDERMANN (49)		1/IV/41	Saxony
BIWER (48)		1/IX/41	
BOENICKE, Walter	(AA)	1/IX/41	
Frhr. v. BOENIGK, Oskar (48)		1/II/41	Silesia
BOETTGE	GAF Recruit Depot 31	1/X/41	
BONATZ, Ernst (48)	Head of a Section, R.L.M.	1/VIII/41	
BRÄUER, Bruno (49)	1st Parachute Regt	1/IX/41	
BRUNNER, Josef		1/IX/41	Austria
BUCHHOLZ	K.G. z.b.V.3	1/XII/41	
BÜLOWIUS, Alfred (48)	Air C-in-C, Bombers and Dive-Bombers.	1/VI/41	
BUFFA, Ernst (49)	3rd AA Regt	1/VIII/40	
Dipl. Ing. BURCHARD, Heinrich	(AA) Luftgaustab z.b.V. Africa	1/XI/40	
CABANIS, Ernst (51)		1/IV/40	
CARGANICO (55)		1/XII/41	
v. CHAMIER-GLISC-ZINSKI, Wolfgang (47).		1/XI/41	
v. CHAULIN-EGERSBERG	(AA)	1/XII/41	Hessen
Dipl. Ing. CONRAD, Gerhard	Staff of XI Air Corps	1/IV/41	Anhalt
CZECH		1/IV/41	
Dr. DAHLMANN, Hermann		1/XII/41	Hessen
v. DEWALL, Job (61)		1/XI/40	
DÖRFFLER (51)	Air Supply Group, Kiev	1/XI/40	
DRECHSEL, Ernst		1/II/42	Bavaria
DRUM, Karl		1/I/41	Baden
v. EGAN-KRIEGER		1/XI/40	
EIBENSTEIN, Rudolf	12th AA Div	1/VIII/41	Saxony
EXSZ (47)	Armistice Commission, Aix-en-Provence.	1/IV/42	

v. FALKENHAYN, Erich (51)	(Admin)	1/XI/41	
v. FALKOWSKI		1/XI/41	
Dipl. Ing. FINK	Accidents Sections, R.L.M.	1/X/40	Württemberg
FISCHER, Eberhard (47)	An Aerodrome Regional Command	1/VI/42	Silesia
FRANSSEN	Insp of Armaments, Belgium	1/VIII/40	
FRANTZ, Gotthard	C of S, C-in-C, Center	1/IX/41	
FRANTZ, Walther	(AA)	1/VI/41	
Frhr. v. FREYBERG EISENBERG-ALL-MENDINGEN, Egloff.		1/IV/39	
FÜTTERER, Cuno Heribert	Air Attache, Budapest	1/XI/41	
FUNCKE, Heinz		1/X/41	
Frhr. v. GABLENZ	Staff of XI Air Corps	1/X/41	
GANDERT, Hans Eberhard (49)	Head of a Section, R.L.M.	1/XII/39	
GERSTENBERG, Alfred	Air Attache, Bucharest	1/IX/41	
GOLTZ	(?)	1/IV/41	
GROSCH, Walter (51)	R.L.M.	1/VI/41	
v. HACHENBERG (53)	(Admin)	1/XI/40	
HAENSCHKE (48)	C of S, Third Air Fleet	1/II/42	
HANTELMANN (57)	An Aerodrome Regional Comd	1/II/42	
HARTING		1/XI/40	
HARTOG (53)	(Admin)	1/IV/41	Baden
HASSE	(Admin)	1/XI/41	
HERWARTH v. BITTEN-FELD, Eberhard (52)	Aerodrome Regional Comd Warsaw.	1/IV/40	
HESSE, Max	6th AA Regt	1/IV/41	
HEYDENREICH, Leopold	Head of a Section, R.L.M.	1/IV/42	
v. HEYKING, Rüdiger	K.G. z.b.V.1	1/XI/41	
Dipl. Ing. HILGERS (49)		1/IV/41	Hessen
HINKELBEIN	(Admin)	1/IX/41	Württemberg
HOEFERT, Johannes	(Admin)	1/IV/41	Saxony
HOFFMANN (50)	(AA) Liaison with Roumanian Air Force.	1/VI/39	
HOFMANN, Hans	Staff of Fourth Air Fleet	1/VI/41	
HOMBURG, Erich	General Staff	1/XI/40	
HÜCKEL (50)		1/IX/41	
KATHMANN	i.G.	1/IV/42	
KEIPER	Head of Air Mission to Slovakia	1/I/41	
KETTEMBEIL	Air Attache, Lisbon	1/VI/41	
KETTNER (48)		1/IV/42	
Dipl. Ing. KLEIN		1/II/41	
KLEIN, Hans (50)	Air C-in-C, of Fighters	27/VIII/39	

Dr. KNAUSS (51)		1/VIII/40	Württemberg
KÖCHY, Karl (46)		1/XI/41	
KORTEN, Günther	C of S, Fourth Air Fleet	19/VII/40	
KRAHMER, Eckart (49)	Air Attache, Madrid	1/X/41	
KRAPP	(Admin)	1/IV/41	
KRESSMANN, Erich	(AA)	1/II/42	Baden
KRIEGBAUM (49)	An Air Force School	1/XII/39	
KRÜGER, Otto (51)	Koluft, Twelfth Army	1/V/41	
KRUEGER	(Admin)	1/XI/41	
KRUEGER, Ernst	Air Mission to Slovakia	1/VI/41	
KUEN	Luftgau West France	1/IV/42	
Dipl. Ing. KUTTIG, Hans (49)		1/XI/40	
v. KUTZLEBEN (55)		1/I/38	
LACKNER, Walther (50)	Blind-Flying School, Königs-berg	1/XII/40	
LAULE (50)	(Admin)	1/VI/41	Baden
LOHMANN (48)	Koluft, Sixth Army	1/II/42	
LORENZ	Staff of Fifth Air Fleet	1/XI/40	
LUCZNY, Alfons (47)	(AA)	1/II/42	Silesia
MAASS	Air Staff	1/VIII/41	
Dipl. Ing. MÄLZER		1/X/41	Saxony
v. MASSOW, Albrecht (55)	Air Supply Group, Luftgau VIII	1/I/41	
MEINDL, Eugen (49)	In First Air Fleet	1/I/41	
MENSCH (54)	Staff of Fifth Air Fleet	1/XI/40	
MENSCHING (54)		1/XI/40	
MENTZEL		1/VI/41	
MENZEL, George Adolf (55)	Air Defense Command 7	1/X/39	Saxony
METZNER		1/IV/42	
MERTITSCH (49)	Head of a Section, R.L.M.	19/IX/40	
MÜLLER, Gottlob	Aerodrome Regional Com-mand, Sicily.	1/XI/41	Bavaria
MUGGENTHALER, Hermann (53)	(Admin)	1/VII/41	Bavaria
NEUFFER		1/XII/41	Bavaria
NITZSCHE	Staff of Luftgau VII	1/I/41	
NORDT		1/IV/41	
NOWAK		1/IX/41	
NUBER	Staff of Luftgau II	1/VII/41	Württemberg
ODEBRECHT	AA Regt 8	1/VI/39	
OLBRICH		1/IV/42	
ORTNER-WEIGAND, Bruno		1/IX/41	Austria
OSTERKAMP, Theodor (49)		19/VII/40	
PISTORIUS		1/XII/41	

Dipl. Ing. PLOCH, August (47)	C of S, Directorate of Equipment, R.L.M.	1/VIII/40	
POETSCH		1/VIII/41	
PULTAR, Josef		1/VII/40	Austria
Dipl. Ing. RAITHEL, Hans (47)	K.G. 77	1/IV/42	Bavaria
RAMCKE, Hermann Bernhard (53)	1st Assault Regt	1/VIII/41	
v. RANTZAU (48)	III AA Brig	1/IV/42	Bavaria
RAUCH, Hans	Aerodrome Regional Command, Derna.	1/VI/42	
REIMANN (47)	AA	1/IV/41	
RIBENSTEIN		1/VIII/41	
RIEKE, Georg	R.L.M.	1/IX/41	
Dipl. Ing. RIESCH	Aerodrome Regional Command, Werl	1/XI/41	Bavaria
RITTER		1/II/41	
ROESCH (54)		1/XII/41	Württemberg
v. RUDLOFF, Werner		1/VIII/41	
RUDOLF, Viktor	Personnel Branch, R.L.M.		
Frhr. RÜDT v. COLLENBERG, Kurt (59)	Air Staff, Occupied France	1/VIII/40	
RÜTER, Wolfgang (49)	(AA)	1/XII/39	
SATTLER (46)	SigC	1/XII/41	Baden
SCHAUER, Ludwig (53)		1/IV/39	Bavaria
SCHEURLEN		1/XI/40	
SCHILFFARTH, Ludwig (48)	202d AA Regt	1/II/42	Bavaria
Ritter v. SCHLEICH (53)	Air Cmdr, Denmark	1/II/41	Bavaria
SCHÖBEL, Otto		1/X/41	Austria
SCHROEDER, Severin		1/IV/41	
SCHROTH		1/VIII/41	
SCHÜTZE (61)	Insp of Armaments, Prague	1/XI/41	
SCHULTHEISS, Pavel (49)		1/I/41	Württemberg
SCHULTZE		1/IX/41	
SCHULTZE-RHONHOF (51)	C of S, Luftgau XVII	1/IV/41	
SCHWABEDISSEN, Walter	C of S, Holland	1/VIII/40	
SELDNER, Eduard (51)		19/VII/40	Baden
SEYWALD, Heinz	Bomber School, Thorn	1/XI/41	Bavaria
SIESS, Gustav (57)	Head of a Section, R.L.M.	1/XI/40	Austria
SOELDNER		1/IV/41	Bavaria
SONNENBURG (50)		1/VI/41	
SPERLING (49)		1/IV/41	
SPRUNER v. MERTZ, Hermann (58)		1/VIII/40	Bavaria

STARKE		1/VI/41	
STEIN	QMG, Third Air Fleet	1/XI/40	
STEINKOPF		1/XI/40	
STURM, Alfred (53)	2d Parachute Regt	1/VIII/41	
STUTZER (53)		1/XII/40	
TESCHNER		1/XI/40	
THYM, Heinrich		1/XI/40	Austria
v. TIPPELSKIRCH	Air Supply Group, Rostov	1/XI/40	
TRIENDL, Theordor (52)	Air Supply Group, Wiesbaden	1/III/40	Bavaria
TSCHOELTSCH, Ehrenfried (49)		1/XI/41	Saxony
UNGER (51)		1/VI/41	
WAGNER	VI AA Brig	1/XI/40	
WALLAND, Eugen		1/XI/41	Austria
WALLNER, Otto (59)		1/XI/41	Bavaria
Frhr. v. WANGEN-HEIM, Edgar	(?)	1/XI/40	
WEESE		1/XI/40	
WILCK		1/XI/40	
ZECH	GAF Equipment Group, Naples.	1/IV/42	
Dr. ZIEGLER, Günther		1/II/41	

PART F--SEMI-MILITARY ORGANIZATIONS

CONTENTS

PART F

1 INTRODUCTION

1. In this Part a brief survey is given of such semi-military organizations as are likely to be found operating with the German army in the field, although organized, equipped and, if need be, maintained independently; together with lists of senior officers of the SS and police (excluding those whose work lies outside the semi-military sphere), who hold rank only distinguishable from those of military or air force officers by the addition of the qualification der Waffen-SS or der Polizei.

2. The following abbreviations, which will frequently be seen in documents relating to the SS, police and other semi-military organizations, are employed in Sections II to VII below:-

Abbreviation	Meaning	American Equivalent
Abs.	Abschnitt	Defensive sector or SS administrative area
B.d.O.	Befehlshaber der Ordnungspolizei	CG Uniformed Police or Constabulary
B.d.Sipo u.d. SD	Befehlshaber der Sicherheitspolizei und des Sicherheitsdienstes	CG Security Police and SS Security Service
d.G.	der Gendarmerie	Of the Gendarmerie
Gen. Govt.	General Gouvernement	General Government (Poland)
Gestapo	Geheime Staatspolizei	Secret State Police
H.SS Pf.	Höherer SS und Polizeiführer	Higher SS and Police Leader or Commander
I.d.O.	Inspekteur der Ordnungspolizei	Inspector of the Uniformed Police or Constabulary
I.d.Sipo u.d. SD	Inspekteur der Sicherheitspolizei und des Sicherheitsdienstes	Inspector of Security Police and Security Service
K.d.G.	Kommandeur der Gendarmerie	CO Gendarmerie
K.d.O.	Kommandeur der Ordnungspolizei	CO Uniformed Police or Constabulary
K.d.Schupo	Kommandeur der Schutzpolizei	CO Municipal or Local Police
K.d. Sipo u.d. SD	Kommandeur der Sicherheitspolizei und des Sicherheitsdienstes	CO Security Police and Security Service
Kripo	Kriminalpolizei	Criminal Police
N.S.K.K.	National Sozialistisches Kraftfahrkorps	Nazi Party Motor Transport Corps
Oa.	Oberabschnitt	SS Administrative Area (corresponding to former corps area)

Orpo	Ordnungspolizei	Uniformed Police or Constabulary
O.T.	Organisation Todt	Todt Organization
Rf. SS	Reichsführer SS	National SS Leader
Schupo	Schutzpolizei	Municipal or Local Police
SD	Sicherheitsdienst	SS Security Service
SHD	Sicherheits und Hilfsdienst	ARP Emergency Service
Sipo	Sicherheitspolizei	Security Police
SS Pf.	SS und Polizeiführer	Leader of SS and Police
SS Psf.	SS und Polizeistandort-führer	Local Leader of SS and Police
Teno	Technische Nothilfe	Technical Emergency Corps
Vomi	Volksdeutsche Mittel-stelle	Bureau for Repatriation of German ethnic groups
Wkr.	Wehrkreis	Corps area
z.b.V.	zu besonderer Verwendung	For Special Duty or Employment

II THE SS AND POLICE ORGANIZATION- GENERAL

1. The German Police have been transformed by the National Socialist regime from an uncoordinated federal system into a single body, in theory controlled by the Reichs Minister of the Interior but in fact immediately under Heinrich HIMMLER, who since June, 1936, has combined supreme control of the police with the leadership of the SS (Schutzstaffel). The two forces have, since that date, become increasingly intertwined, and many of the senior officers hold ranks in both. HIMMLER's official title is Reichsführer SS und Chef der Deutschen Polizei im Reichsministerium des Innern. The customary abbreviation to Rf.SS emphasizes the dominant position of the SS organization.

III THE SS (Schutzstaffel)

1. The SS is the Corps d'elite of the National Socialist Party. Originally formed as protective squads for political meetings and bodyguards for the leaders of the party, it has been considerably expanded and is now widely employed, both for internal security duties in Germany and German-occupied territories, and in permanent military units.

2. HITLER is the supreme head of the SS. Under him, HIMMLER is the executive chief of the organization, with Hq in Berlin. This Hq is in effect a complete ministry, with branches and departments comparable to most of those maintained by the three service ministries for the recruiting, training, equipment, administration and control of the SS organization.

3. For administrative purposes, much of the work is decentralized to district Hq (SS Oberabschnitte, abbreviated SS Oa.). Geographically, the administrative districts correspond very closely to the Wehrkreise which draft for the army, navy and air force alike, and form the basis of army organization-but they are known by names and not by numbers.

4. The districts (SS Oberabschnitte) are normally subdivided into either two or three areas (Abschnitte), which carry Roman numerals. The following table shows this organization in detail:-

SS District (component areas)	Hq	Corresponding Wehrkreis
Alpenland (XXXV,XXXVI)	Salzburg	XVIII
Danzig-Westpreussen (XXVI, XLI)	Danzig	XX
Donau (VIII,XXXI)	Wien (Vienna)	XVII
Elbe (II, XVIII, XXXVII)	Dresden	IV
Fulda-Werra (XXVII,XXX)	Arolsen	IX
Lothringen-Saarpfalz (--)	Saarbrucken	part XII
Main (IX,XXVIII,XXXVIII)	Nürnberg (Nuremburg)	XIII
Mitte (IV,XVI)	Braunschweig (Brunswick)	XI
Nordost (VII, XXII)	Königsberg	I
Nordsee (XIV,XV,XX)	Hamburg	X
Nordwest, i.e., Holland	The Hague	
Ost (III, XII, XXIII)	Berlin	III
Ostsee (XIII, XXXIII)	Stettin	II
Rhein (XI,XXXIV)	Wiesbaden	part XII
Süd (I,XXXII)	München (Munich)	VII
Südost (VI,XXI, XXIV)	Breslau	VIII
Südwest (X,XIX,XXIX)	Stuttgart	V
Warthe (XL,XLIII)	Posen	XXI
West (V,XVII, XXV)	Düsseldorf	VI

5. Each district is commanded by a senior SS officer, who is also HIMMLER's immediate representative at the Hq of the corresponding Wehrkreis. In the latter capacity he is described as Höherer SS und Polizeiführer (abbreviated H.SSPf., i.e., Senior SS and Police Commander) in the Wehrkreis concerned.

6. In the case of SS and police units stationed in occupied countries, a Senior SS and Police Commander and staff assumes control, cooperating closely with the military administration but closely controlled by the SS Hq in Berlin. Within an occupied country an area may be assigned, if this is thought necessary, to an SS and Police Commander, whose sphere of command corresponds in status to the Abschnitt in Germany.

7. The units of the SS fall into two distinct categories, namely Allgemeine SS (Ordinary SS) and Waffen-SS (Armed SS). The former consists of part time volunteers employed for internal security purposes within Germany, and need

not, therefore, be considered here. The Waffen-SS is described among the semi-military services in section V below.

IV POLICE (Polizei)

1. The Police is divided into two main branches, as follows:-
    Ordnungspolizei, Orpo; uniformed constabulary, including the munici-pal Schutzpolizei (Schupo), rural Gendarmerie, and river, fire-fighting and A.R.P. police (S.H.D.). The barrack police battalions (Section V below) are drawn from this branch, the head of which is Colonel General of Police DALUEGE.

    Sicherheitspolizei, Sipo; security police, comprising the Secret State Police (Geheime Staatspolizei = Gestapo) and the Criminal Investigation Police (Kriminalpolizei = Kripo). The Secret State Police have as their special task the liquidation and prevention of all activity hostile to the regime. This force works in close touch with the Secret Field Police
    , the personnel of which is largely drawn from the Gestapo.

2. The police in general and the security police in particular are closely related to the Security Service of the SS (Sicherheitsdienst des Reichsführers SS, abbreviated S.D. Rf.SS). This was originally the intelligence branch of the SS, but since 1936 it has been directly connected with the security police through the appointment as head of both services (Chef der Sicherheitspolizei und des S.D.) of Reinhard HEYDRICH. (deceased).

3. Police Hq is in Berlin. Within each Wehrkreis there is a unified chain of command subordinate to the Senior SS and Police Commander (¶ 5 Section III), but there is considerable variety in the local administration, which still shows traces of the old federal system. There are still separate police departments for the different Länder into which the Reich is divided.

4. Below the Senior SS and Police Commander, command is exercised by Inspekteure and Befehlshaber (posts which may be held independently or con-currently) -- Inspectors and Commanders-- qualified by d.O. or d.Sipo u.d.S.D., according to their branch of the service.

5. The extent to which German police units operate in occupied countries depends on the extent to which the local national police service is thought strong and reliable enough to maintain law and order and cooperate with the German military authorities. There is a Senior SS and Police Commander in each of the following countries: *the Protectorate, the General Government, Norway, Holland, France, Ostland (Baltic Countries), and the Ukraine.

---

*See Part B, Section XIII, paragraphs 2a, 4, 6, 8, 11, 19a, 19b; the German administrative areas for which these officers are responsible is employed, for convenience, rather than the country in cases such as Poland, U.S.S.R., etc.

6. For service outside Germany, uniformed police are **organized in** battalions described in Section V below. Within an occupied country or a main subdivision of it, the police battalions present may be controlled by a regimental staff (e.g., in the Protectorate there is one such staff for Bohemia and one for Moravia).

V SEMI-MILITARY SERVICES

In the following list brief particulars are given of the principal semi-military services which may be encountered in the combat zone. In each case a note has been added on the uniform and distinguishing badges.

1. Waffen-SS (Armed SS) : This is a fully militarized and permanently organized force, formed into divisions (see **Part C,** Sections IX to XIII inclusive) and a number of independent brigades and regiments. Non-divisional units are normally employed for "mopping-up" purposes along the L of C . They come under the control, in some cases, of the Army Group L of C Commander. They may also be employed on occasions in the front line, subordinated to the nearest convenient Army.

Uniform: Field grey as in the Army, but the national emblem is worn on the upper left sleeve instead of on the right breast. The cap insignia is a skull and crossbones, and the ⚡⚡ sign is worn on the right-hand side of the steel helmet and on the collar.

2. Police battalions. These may be either fully or partly motorized. The battalion is composed of approximately 550 men, organized into a Hq and four companies. It is equipped with rifles, machine guns, antitank guns and armored cars. Police battalions are normally used for internal security or "mopping-up" duties, but they may, if necessary, be employed in the line under Army command. They are numbered in series 1-325 (about a hundred identified).

Uniform : Field grey with dark green collar and cuffs and white metal buttons. The police version of the national emblem -the eagle and swastika enclosed in and resting on a wreath of oak leaves-is worn on the left sleeve and on the cap, or steel helmet.

3. *National Sozialistisches Kraftfahrkorps, N.S.K.K. (Nazi Party MT Corps). The functions of this organization are to assist the police in traffic control duties on the L of C and to provide MT units (Brigaden) to supplement the transport services of the armed forces. Four such brigades exist: -
Heer (Army): To supplement Army transport.

---

*Personnel of these services are equipped, wherever it is thought necessary, with rifles and in some cases with MGs for protective purposes or guard duty.

221

Luftwaffe (Air Force): Assist in the supply of bombs and fuel for the GAF.
    Speer and Todt: Provide transport for the construction organizations, now
under the unified control of Professor **SPEER.**
Within Germany, the N.S.K.K. also trains men in its motor schools and training
units for service with the army's mobile troops. Its basic unit is the motor
battalion (Motorstandarte), which carries a number in the series 1-400.

Uniform: Brown shirt and black breeches. The national emblem is
mounted on a wheel enclosing a swastika, and is worn on the cap or black crash
helmet. White Arabic numerals preceded by the letter "M" on the right-hand
collar patch give the number of the battalion.

4. *Organization Todt, O.T. This was first formed, by the late Dr. TODT,
to assist in the construction of the Autobahn (motor highway) system, and was
subsequently expanded to build the western defenses known in this country as
the Siegfried Line and in Germany as the Westwall. It is now employed to
assist army engineer units in road building, railway repairs, bridge construction,
etc., in the wake of advancing troops, and for longer term work in occupied territory, e.g., restoring communications, preparing sites for aerodromes, building fortifications, clearing harbors of wreckage. It is organized into battalions
with a nucleus of specialist German personnel. It also employs hired foreign
labor on a large scale. Its motor transport is provided mainly by the N.S.K.K.,
but in part by local contractors.

Uniform: In principle, only the German members of the organization
wear uniform-a khaki colored blouse open at the neck, and breeches. On the
left sleeve is a red armband with a black swastika set in a white circle, and immediately above the left cuff is a narrow armband with the inscription "Org.
Todt" in white Gothic letters on a black background. Foreign workers employed
by the organization wear civilian clothing or dungarees and an armband display-
ing the Arabic number of the battalion.

5. *Reichsarbeitsdienst, R.A.D. (National Labor Service): All German men
who are physically fit are normally required to perform six months' service in
the R.A.D. before beginning their military service. They are organized into
companies under a cadre of permanent officers and NCOs, and such companies
are available in considerable numbers for service on the L of C and in occupied
countries, where they provide additional manual labor for the O.T. or the
engineers.

Uniform: Brownish-grey blouse with dark collar and slacks. On the
left sleeve the R.A.D. emblem (a spade-head containing the Arabic number of
the company) and, beneath it, a red armband with a black swastika set in a
white circle.

---
* Personnel of these services are equipped, wherever it is thought necessary,
with rifles and in some cases with MGs, for protective purposes or guard
duty.

6. *Technische Nothilfe, Teno or T.N. (Technical Emergency Corps). Classified as auxiliary police. The Teno is used in the combat zone or in occupied territory for such tasks as the restoration of essential services, the demolition of damaged buildings, the removal of unexploded bombs, or the reconstruction of installations of all kinds. In Germany it plays an important part in A R P work.

Uniform: When serving in the field, field grey, with a narrow armband immediately above the left cuff with the inscription "Technische Nothilfe" in white. Above this is a yellow armband with the inscription "Deutsche Wehrmacht" in black. The national emblem is worn in the upper left sleeve, superimposed on a black triangle. The Teno emblem, a cog-wheel, is worn on the collar patches.

*Personnel of these services are equipped, wherever it is thought necessary, with rifles and in some cases with MG's for protective purposes or guard duty.

VI. SENIOR SS OFFICERS

Name (age)	Appointment

1. Rank: Reichsführer SS.

HIMMLER, Heinrich (41)	Head of the SS and German Police

2. Rank: SS Oberstgruppenführer = Generaloberst

*DALUEGE, Kurt (44)	Chief of Uniformed Police; Acting Protector of Bohemia and Moravia

3. Rank SS Obergruppenführer = General.

*v.d. BACH-ZELEWSKI, Erich (43)	H. SS Pf. Central Sector, Russia.
*BERKELMANN, Theodor (48)	H. SS Pf. Lothringen-Saarpfalz and Chief of SS Oa. Lothringen-Saarpfalz
†DIETRICH, Josef ("Sepp") (50)	Comdr SS Division Adolf Hitler and Chief of SS Oa. Ost
*Frhr. v. EBERSTEIN, Karl (48)	H. SS Pf., Wkr. VII and Wkr. XIII and Chief of SS Oa. Süd
†EICKE, Theodor (49)	Comdr SS Totenkopf Div ; Chief of SS Totenkopf Guards and Concentration Camps
FRANK, Karl Hermann (44)	H.SS Pf. and State Secretary for Bohemia and Moravia
†HAUSSER, Paul (61)	(Former Comdr SS Div Reich)
HEISSMEYER, August (45)	Chief of SS Hq, Berlin
*HILDEBRANDT, Richard (45)	H.SS Pf., Wkr. XX and Chief of SS Oa. Danzig-Westpreussen
*JECKELN, Friedrich (47)	H.SS Pf. Ostland
*KOPPE, Wilhelm (46)	H.SS Pf. Wkr. XXI and Chief of SS Oa. Warthe
*KRÜGER, Friedrich Wilhelm (48)	State Secretary for Security in the Gen. Govt., and H.SS Pf. Krakau
LORENZ, Werner (50)	Chief of Vomi
*MAZUW, Emil (41)	H.SS Pf. Wkr. II and Chief of SS Oa. Ostsee
POHL, Oswald (50)	Chief of SS Administrative Economic Dept
*PRÜTZMANN, Hans (40)	H.SS Pf. Ukraine
*REDIESS, Wilhelm (41)	H.SS Pf. Norway
†SCHARFE, Paul (65)	Chief of SS Legal Dept
*SCHMAUSER, Heinrich (52)	H.SS Pf. Wkr. VIII and Chief of SS Oa. Südost
*Erbprinz v. WALDECK und PYRMONT, Josias (46)	H.SS Pf. Wkr. IX and Chief of SS Oa. Fulda-Werra
*WOLFF Karl (42)	Chief of HIMMLER'S personal staff

Note.— * = also holds police rank.

     † = also holds Waffen—SS rank.

*v. WOYRSCH, Udo (46)	H.SS Pf. Wkr. IV and Chief of SS Oa. Elbe

4. Rank: SS Gruppenführer = Generalleutnant

ALPERS, Friedrich (41)	Staff of Rf. SS
BECKER, Herbert (55)	Staff of SS Oa. Donau
†BERGER, Gottlob (45)	Chief of Waffen—SS Hq, Berlin
BRACHT, Werner (54)	Staff of Rf.SS
†DEMELHUBER, Karl (46)	CO SS Regt Germania
EBRECHT, Georg (46)	Chief of SS Abs. XXVI, Danzig (Wkr. XX)
†GRAWITZ, Ernst Robert (43)	Chief SS and Police Medical Officer
GREIFELT, Ulrich (45)	C of S to Reich Commissioner for Propagation of Germanism (HIMMLER)
HENNICKE, Paul (59)	Police President, Weimar (Wkr. IX) and Chief of SS Abs. XXVII, Weimar
HENZE, Max (42)	Police President, Essen (Wkr. VI)
Dr. HOFMANN, Philipp (39)	Chief of SS Race and Settlement Dept
Frhr. v. HOLZSCHUHER, Wilhelm (48)	Staff of Rf.SS
*JEDICKE, Georg ( )	K.d. Sipo u.d. SD, Ostland
JOHST, Hans (51)	Staff of Rf. SS
†JÜTTNER, Hans (48)	Chief of SS Ops, Hq Berlin
*Dr. KALTENBRUNNER, Ernst (38)	H. SS Pf., Wkr. XVII and Chief of SS Oa. Donau
*KAUL, Curt (51)	H. SS Pf., Wkr. V and Chief of SS Oa. Südwest
†KEPPLER, Georg (48)	Comdr SS Mtn Div Nord
†KNOBLAUCH	Chief of Ops on staff of Rf. SS
†KRÜGER (52)	Comdr SS Div Prinz Eugen (?)
v. MACKENSEN, Hans Georg (59)	Staff of Rf.SS
Dr. MARTIN, Benno (49)	Police President, Nürnberg and Fürth (Wkr. XIII) and Chief of SS Oa. Main
MEINBERG, Wilhelm (44)	Staff of Rf. SS
*PANCKE, Günter (43)	H.SS Pf., Wkr. XI and Chief of SS Oa. Mitte
†PHLEPS	(Waffen-SS)
*QUERNER Rudolf (49)	H.SS Pf., Wkr. X and Chief of SS Oa. Nordsee
RAUTER, Hans (47)	H.SS Pf. Nordwest (i.e., Holland)
*RÖSENER, Erwin (40)	H.SS Pf., Wkr. XII and Chief of SS Oa. Rhein
†SACHS, Ernst (61)	Chief of Communications on Staff of Rf.SS and Chief of German Police
SCHAUB, Julius (43)	Personal Adjutant to HITLER
SCHMITT, Walter (63)	Chief of SS Personnel Dept
†STEINER, Felix (46)	Comdr SS Div Wiking
*STRECKENBACH, Bruno (40)	Security Police Hq, Berlin

Note.— * = also holds police rank.
       † = also holds Waffen-SS rank.

Dr. STUCKART, Wilhelm (39)	Head of Central Bureau for Norway, Ministry of the Interior
TAUBERT, Siegfried (61)	Staff of Rf.SS
*ZENNER, Carl (43)	SS Pf. Minsk

5. Rank: SS Brigadeführer = Generalmajor.

Dr. ALBERT, Wilhelm (43)	Police President, Litzmannstadt (Wkr. XXI)
*v. ALVENSLEBEN, Rudolf (41)	SS Pf. Taurien
*Graf v. BASSEWITZ-BEHR, Georg (42)	SS Pf. Dniepropetrovsk
†v. BEHR, Max (63)	CO Local SS, Vienna (Wkr. XVII)
Dr. BEHRENDS, Hermann (35)	Deputy Chief of Vomi, Berlin
†BITTRICH, Willi (48)	Comdr SS Cavalry Div (?)
BELEK, Andreas (48)	Police President, Magdeburg (Wkr. XI)
BREITHAUPT, Franz (61)	Police President, Breslau (Wkr. VIII)
Dr. DERMIETEL, Friedrich Karl (43)	Staff of SS Hq, Berlin
DIEHM, Christoph (50)	Police President, Saarbrücken and Metz (Wkr. XII)
*DÖRING, Hans (40)	SS Pf. Stalino
†FRANK, August (44)	SS Administrative Hq, Berlin
†Prof. Dr. GEBHARDT, Karl (44)	Chief of SS Medical Corps
†Dr. med. GENZKEN, Karl (57)	Chief of SS Medical Hq, Berlin
*GLOBOCNIK, Odilo (38)	SS Pf. Lublin
†GLÜCKS, Richard (53)	Staff of Chief of SS Totenkopf Guards and Concentrations Camps
*GUTENBERGER	H.SS Pf. Wkr. VI and Chief of SS Oa. West
*HALTERMANN, Hans ( )	SS Pf. Kiev
†HANSEN	Inspector of SS Artillery
†HARTENSTEIN	CO 1 SS Inf Brig
JUNGCLAUS, Richard (37)	Representative of Rf.SS in Flanders
Dr. Ing. KAMMLER	Chief of Section II (Building) of SS Office of Works, Berlin
*KATZMANN, Fritz (36)	SS Pf. Galicia
†KLEINHEISTERKAMP, Matthias (49)	Comdr SS Div Reich
†KLINGEMANN, Gottfried (57)	CO 2d SS Inf Brig
*KORSEMANN	H.SS Pf. z.b.V., Ukraine
KÖRNER, Hellmut (38)	Chief of Food and Agriculture Dept, Ukraine
†LOERNER	Chief of Section I (Maintenance) of SS Office of Works, Berlin
MAACK, Berthold (44)	Chief of SS Abs. XXV, Bochum (Wkr. VI)
Frhr. v. MALSEN-PONICKAU, Erasmus (47)	Police President, Posen (Wkr. XXI)

Note.— * = also holds police rank.
† = also holds Waffen-SS rank.

MÖRSCHEL, Johann (61)	C of S, SS Oa, Nordsee
*OBERG, Karl Albrecht (45)	H.SS Pf. France
PFLOMM, Karl (55)	Police President, Dresden (Wkr. IV)
POPP, Emil (45)	Chief of SS Abs. II, Chemnitz (Wkr. IV) and Governor-President, Chemnitz.
Graf v. PÜCKLER-BURGHAUSS Carlfriedrich ( )	Deputy H.SS Pf. Central Sector, Russia
*v. RADOWITZ, Ernst (73)	Staff of Rf.SS
REINEFARTH, Heinz (38)	Staff of SS Abs. XII, Frankfurt/Oder (Wkr. III)
*Dr. SCHEEL, Gustav Adolf (34)	H.SS Pf., Wkr. XVIII and Chief of SS Oa. Alpenland
	K.d.O. Kiev, Ukraine
*SCHRÖDER	SS Pf. Latvia, Ostland
Dr. SELZNER, Klaus (43)	General- Kommissar, Dniepro-petrovsk, Ukraine
STARCK, Wilhelm (51)	Police President, Augsburg (Wkr. VII)
*WAPPENHAMS, Waldemar (48)	SS Pf. Brest Litovsk, Gen. Govt
*THOMAS	B.d.Sipo u.d. SD, Ukraine
TITTMANN, Fritz (43)	SS Pf. Nikolayev, Ukraine
†von TREUENFELD	CO Waffen SS in the Protectorates
VELLER	Police President, Oberhausen (Wkr. VI)
WÄCHTER	Governor of Galicia, Gen. Govt
Dr. WENDLER, Richard (44)	Governor of Krakau District, Gen. Govt
Dr. WENZEL, Ernst (51)	Staff of SS Hq, Berlin
†*WÜNNENBERG, Alfred (50)	Comd. SS Polizei Division
*WYSOCKI	SS Pf. Lithuania, Ostland
*ZENNER, Carl (43)	SS Pf. Minsk, Ostland

Note.—* = also holds police rank.
  † = also holds Waffen-SS rank.

VII. SENIOR POLICE OFFICERS

| Name (age) | Appointment |

1. Rank: Colonel General (Generaloberst der Polizei)

*DALUEGE, Kurt (44) — Chief of Uniformed Police; Acting Protector of Bohemia and Moravia

2. Rank: General (General der Polizei).

*v. d. BACH-ZELEWSKI, Erich (43) — H.SS Pf. Central Sector, Russia
*BERKELMANN, Theodor (48) — H.SS Pf. Lothringen-Saarpfalz, and Chief of SS Oa. Lothringen-Saarpfalz
*Frhr. v. EBERSTEIN, Karl (48) — H.SS Pf. Wkr. VII and Wkr. XIII
*JECKELN, Friedrich (47) — H.SS Pf. Ostland
*KOPPE, Wilhelm (46) — H.SS Pf. Wkr. XXI and Chief of SS Oa. SS Oa. Warthe
*KRÜGER, Friedrich Wilhelm — State Secretary for Security in the Gen. Govt., and H.SS Pf. Krakau
*MAZUW, Emil (41) — H.SS Pf. Wkr. II and Chief of SS Oa. Ostsee
*PRÜTZMANN, Hans (40) — H.SS Pf. Ukraine
*REDIESS, Wilhelm (41) — H.SS Pf. Norway
*SCHMAUSER, Heinrich (52) — H.SS Pf. Wkr. VIII and Chief of SS Oa Südost
*Erbprinz v. WALDECK und PYRMONT, Josias (46) — H.SS Pf. Wkr. IX and Chief of SS Oa. Fulda-Werra
*v. WOYRSCH, Udo (46) — H.SS Pf. Wkr. IV and Chief of SS Oa. Elbe

3. Rank: Lt General (Generalleutnant der Polizei).

*BECKER — B.d.O. in Wkr. X
*v BOMHARD, Adolf (51) — Police Hq, Berlin
*HILDEBRANDT, Richard (45) — H.SS Pf. Wkr. XX and Chief of SS Oa. Danzig-Westpreussen
*JEDICKE, Georg — K.D. Sipo u.d. SD, Ostland
*KALTENBRUNNER, Dr. Ernst (38) — H.SS Pf. Wkr. XVII and Chief of SS Oa. Donau
*v. KAMPTZ, Jürgen (50) — Inspector General of Gendarmerie and Local Municipal Police
*KAUL, Curt (51) — H.SS Pf. Wkr. V and Chief of SS Oa. Südwest
*MEYSSNER, August (55) — Comdr German Police, Belgrade
*v. OELHAFEN, Otto (56) — B.d.O., Ukraine
PANCKE, Günter (43) — H.SS Pf. Wkr. XI and Chief of SS Oa. Mitte

Note.— * = also holds SS rank
† = also holds Waffen-SS rank.
d.G. = der Gendarmerie (as distinct from der Polizei).

3. Rank: Lt General (Generalleutnant der Polizei)—continued

*QUERNER, Rudolf (49)	H.SS Pf. Wkr. X and Chief of SS Oa. Nordsee
RIEGE, Paul (54)	B.d.O., Bohemia and Moravia
*RÖSENER, Erwin (40)	H.SS Pf. Wkr. XII and Chief of SS Oa. Rhein
*SCHREYER, Georg (57)	Inspector General of Municipal Police
*STRECKENBACH, Bruno (40)	Security Police Hq, Berlin
*WEINREICH, Hans (45)	Chief of the Teno

4. Rank: Maj General (Generalmajor der Polizei).

*v. ALVENSLEBEN, Rudolf (41)	SS Pf. Taurien
*Graf v. BASSEWITZ-BEHR Georg (42)	SS Pf. Dniepropetrovsk, Ukraine
BRENNER	B.d.O., Oberkrain and Südsteiermark, Wkr. XVII
*DÖRING, Hans (40)	SS Pf. Stalino, Ukraine
*GLOBOCNIK, Odilo (38)	SS Pf. Lublin
*GROLMANN, Wilhelm	Police Hq., Berlin
*GUTENBERGER	H.SS Pf. Wkr. VI and Chief of SS Oa. West
*HALTERMANN, Hans	SS Pf. Kiev, Ukraine
*v. HERFF, Maximilian	K.doO., Kharkov, Ukraine
HÖRING, d.G.	B.d.O., Norway
*KATZMANN, Fritz (36)	SS Pf. Galicia, Gen. Govt
KLINGER	K.d. Schupo, Berlin
*KNOFE	B.d.O., Posen (Wkr. XXI)
*KORSEMANN	H.SS Pf. z.b.V., Ukraine
KRUMHAAR	Police President, Kiel (Wkr. X)
*Dr. LANKENAU	B.d.O., Wkr. VI
LIESSEN	K.d. Schupo. Hamburg (Wkr X)
Dr. Ing. MEYER	Inspector General of Fire-fighting Services
*MUELLER	B.d.O., Wkr. I
*OBERG, Karl Albrecht (45)	H.SS Pf., France
*POHLMEYER	K.d. Schupo, Vienna (Wkr. XVII)
RAUNER, Adolf (62)	Bavarian State Ministry of the Interior, Police Dept
Dr. RETZLAFF	I.d.O., Vienna (Wkr. XVII)
*Dr. SCHEEL, Gustav Adolf (34)	H.SS Pf. Wkr. XVIII and Chief of SS Oa. Alpenland
SCHEER	K.d.O., Kiev, Ukraine
*SCHRÖDER	SS Pf. Latvia, Ostland
SCHUMANN	B.d.O., Holland
SIEBERT	Treasurer of the Teno

Note.— * = also holds SS rank.
  † = also holds Waffen-SS rank.
  d.G. = der Gendarmerie (as distinct from der Polizei).

*THOMAS	B.d.Sipo u.d. SD, Ukraine
*WAPPENHANS, Waldemar (48)	SS Pf. Brest Litovsk, Gen. Govt
*Dr. WENDLER, Richard (44)	Governor of Krakau Dirstrict, Gen. Govt
*WINKELMANN, Otto (47)	Police Hq., Berlin
*WINKLER	B.d.O., Krakau, Gen. Govt
†*WÜNNENBERG, Alfred (50)	Comdr Polizei Division
*WYSOCKI	SS Pf. Lithuania, Ostland
*ZENNER, Carl (43)	SS Pf. Minsk, Ostland

Note.—* = also holds SS rank.
     † = also holds Waffen-SS rank.
     d.G. = der Gendarmerie (as distinct from der Polizei)-